Conversations
in the Spirit

Conversations in the Spirit

Lex Hixon's WBAI
"In the Spirit" Interviews

A Chronicle of the Seventies
Spiritual Revolution

Edited by Sheila Hixon

Foreword by Bernie Glassman

Preface by Paul Gorman

Monkfish Book Publishing Company
Rhinebeck, New York

Conversations in the Spirit: Lex Hixon's WBAI "In the Spirit" Interviews: A Chronicle of the Seventies Spiritual Revolution© 2016 Sheila Hixon

Cover design by Kerry Tinger
Book design by Colin Rolfe
Photo editing by Susan Piperato

Printed in the United States of America

Paperback ISBN: 978-1-939681-53-9
eBook ISBN: 978-1-939681-54-6
Library of Congress Cataloging-in-Publication Data

Names: Hixon, Sheila, 1940- editor.
Title: Conversations In the Spirit : Lex Hixon's WBAI "In the Spirit"
    interviews : a chronicle of the seventies spiritual revolution / edited by
    Sheila Hixon ; preface by Paul Gorman ; foreword by Bernie Glassman.
Description: 1st [edition]. | Rhinebeck, New York : Monkfish Book Publishing
    Company, 2016.
Identifiers: LCCN 2016019774 (print) | LCCN 2016034148 (ebook) | ISBN
    9781939681539 (alk. paper) | ISBN 9781939681546 ()
Subjects: LCSH: Spirituality. | Interviews. | Religious leaders--Interviews.
    | Hixon, Lex. | WBAI Radio (New York, N.Y.) | In the Spirit (Radio program)
Classification: LCC BL624 .C6637 2016 (print) | LCC BL624 (ebook) | DDC
    200.92/2--dc23
LC record available at https://lccn.loc.gov/2016019774

Monkfish Book Publishing Company
22 East Market Street
Suite 304
Rhinebeck, New York 12572
USA (845) 876-4861
www.monkfishpublishing.com

Table of Contents

Foreword
by Bernie Glassman

In 1978, I traveled from California to New York to visit the parents of some of our students at the Zen Center of Los Angeles, where I was teaching Zen meditation. We had heard that these parents were worried about their children. They thought that Zen Buddhism was a cult, but they weren't able talk about it in their families because there was a breakdown in communication, so I wanted to meet with them to try to explain what their children were learning with us. The trip was successful and I learned a lot from it.

Lex Hixon was one of the people I called when I got to New York City. He was the host of the radio show "In the Spirit," on which he interviewed spiritual teachers from different traditions and cultures who were coming to America to give teachings. He had a lot of listeners, and I thought that the show would be a good way for me to reach out to people. When I called Lex, he said he had heard of me too, and he invited me to come and be his guest on the program. It aired on Sunday mornings, so he asked me if I would like to come to his house Saturday afternoon and stay over so we could talk and get ready for the show the next day. The rest of his family was away, so he said he would make supper for us. What he made for our supper were peanut-butter-and-jelly sandwiches. I thought to myself that at least he could have taken me out to the local deli!

After supper, we began talking about many things, and planned for the program. We would have many, many more long talks over the years—about our interfaith work, our hopes and worries, our ideas and plans. Some of the best talks we had were in the steam room of the YMCA in Yonkers, New York, not far from Lex's home in the Bronx.

Lex's radio show was making a very important contribution to the spiritual culture of the time. It was one of the only public spaces where people could hear an informed Westerner asking questions of the teachers coming from the East. He was giving those teachers the opportunity to address misunderstandings and describe what their traditions were really all about so that they could become more understood and accepted in our culture. I knew that some people thought Zen was a cult, and I'm sure they thought a lot of other Eastern religions were cults too. Having representatives of those traditions on the show could put many people's minds at rest about their children, friends, or even parents who might be involved in a religion that they had never heard of. People tend to be afraid of ideas they perceive as completely new and unknown. Lex's program was doing exactly what I was trying to do in my conversations with the Zen parents, but on a larger scale.

The morning after our peanut-butter-and-jelly supper, we drove down to the WBAI Studios in Midtown Manhattan. At the time, "In the Spirit" was a two-hour show. We spent an hour doing the interview, and then just before Lex announced that people could call in to ask me questions, he said on the air, "Wouldn't it be nice for Tetsugen Sensei [then my Zen name] to come back to New York City?"

After he asked the audience that question, he shocked me by saying, "Here's my home phone number. If any of you are interested in bringing Sensei back to New York, you can call for directions and come to my house next Saturday. Sensei will give an introduction to Zen, and we'll talk about getting him back to New York." I couldn't believe that he had given his own home phone number out on the air, but when I got to know him better, I found out that it was not unusual. He was an unreasonably generous person when it came to spiritual matters.

I was still in New York City the following week, so we had the meeting at his house. Lex had set up for the meeting in the living room, which overlooked the Hudson River, with meditation cushions on the floor. For me, he had covered his kids' small, round trampoline with a cloth and put a meditation cushion on top of it. That was a little unusual for me, but I thought talking from a trampoline might be quite comfortable and maybe even uplifting. Lex liked to honor teachers, and in Tibetan practice, one of the ways to do that is to put them on a higher seat. It was a good meeting, and afterwards I realized that I had tentatively decided to move back to New York! Before that moment, I'd had no thought of moving anywhere!

I was born and raised in Brooklyn. After I got my engineering degree I went to Los Angeles for work and got married and had a family. That's where I first studied Zen and met my teacher, Maezumi Roshi. I thought I would always practice Zen in Los Angeles with him, and that I would stay at my job in the aerospace industry doing interplanetary work indefinitely.

The Los Angeles Zen Center was growing quickly. I was the first student to be made a teacher, and there were others on their way. I was close with my own teacher and I had said to him, "In my opinion, none of us who have become teachers under you should go out and start centers anywhere else. We should stay here in L.A., and make this a very intense study place, like a pressure cooker." By that time, we had about 200 students living on one block, most of which we owned, in downtown L.A. There was already intense study going on. Genpo Merzel was my dharma brother, and was going to be the next teacher. He wanted to move to Europe, and I told him, "No, no, we shouldn't move away from L.A."

But then I went on "In the Spirit" and had the meeting in Lex's living room and everything changed for me. While I was talking on that radio show, I realized that I was using my own voice. After all, I was from Brooklyn, so being in New York felt natural. Los Angeles was not so natural to me. For 20 years I had been studying in L.A. in a Japanese-style *zendo*, thinking about Japanese Zen. I had even stopped using articles, the way a Japanese person might do when speaking English. (There are no articles in the Japanese language.) That made me sound Japanese, but it wasn't my voice. On that radio show, all of a sudden, I was free to talk like someone from Brooklyn and to share thoughts that might be different from my teacher's. It was very liberating to be among New Yorkers again. It just felt right.

When I went back to Los Angeles, I told Maezumi that my thinking had changed. We discussed everything. He decided that moving to start a new center in New York was a good idea. I told Lex, and he started looking for a place for us to live. He wanted it to be near him, of course. It was through his efforts that we moved to Riverdale to start the Zen Community of New York in an old mansion built during the Civil War, a beautiful place overlooking the Hudson. Lex came on the board of directors and helped me to get the organization started. I still feel a tremendous debt to him for all his support and advice.

I was trained in the Japanese way of leading a community, in which the head teacher is the sole authority making all the decisions, and no one ever disagrees. But now I was going to try a more Brooklyn style, so I chose a board of directors that consisted of many different voices, which made our meetings very lively and unpredictable. Lex was one of the dominant voices. He had his own opinions about how things should happen, and he never hesitated to speak out. He was brilliant, and I liked many of his ideas, so he had a lot of input into how we went forward.

I was always interested in interfaith work, and Lex was a living manifestation of interfaith spirituality. I wanted to create a mystical community like the community of Safed in Israel, where there were Christian mystics and Kabbalists and all kinds of people living together. Lex gave me some special introductions to different spiritual leaders. I took hand [became initiated] in the Turkish Sufi Order of the Helveti-Jerrahi dervishes and took part in their prayers and *dhikr* ceremonies at the small mosque in Soho, in New York City, which Lex oversaw as its sheikh. He also once took me to meet Swami Aseshananda of the Ramakrishna Order in Portland, Oregon, who initiated me and gave me a mantra practice.

Lex was also very interested in the interfaith idea. In fact, shortly before he and his wife Sheila came to tell me that he had been diagnosed with advanced cancer, we were planning to open an interfaith center, the House of One People, and Lex was going to be its first spiritual director. Our shared interest in interfaith work was a theme that lasted from the time I first met him until he passed away.

Lex was the only person I've ever met who entered so deeply into many different belief systems and manifested so completely in that way. The other person that comes to mind—who I've only read about, of course—is Ramakrishna.

Soon after I returned to the East Coast, Lex and I began a mutual study program. While Lex was studying Zen with me, I was studying Tibetan Buddhism with him. Together we studied Tibetan Buddhism's Five Buddha Families, the Five Buddha Energies, and the concept of the mandala—ideas that I used very concretely in setting up the Zen community in New York. Lex finished his Zen studies with me shortly before anyone knew that he was ill. He had been coming to see me every day, early in the morning, for a long time. We did other special trainings over the years, but Koan study was the main element of our work together. Our study focused on the text that traces the enlightenment experiences of the first 52 teachers after Sakyamuni Buddha. That became the subject of the last book that Lex was alive to see published, *Living Buddha Zen*. Lex had a deep appreciation for the feminine aspect in all spiritual traditions, so when we studied the *Denkoroku* text—"The Record of the Transmission of the Light," written in 1300 by Zen Master Keizan Zenji—I asked him to look for that feminine perspective. He was not shy about expressing how important he believed it was to recognize the feminine aspect, even though many cultures that he was working within did not honor it the way he did.

I was in Japan when Lex died, but afterwards, I felt it was very important to give him the title of Zen master. In Japanese, the word for Zen master is *Roshi*, which is the final step in the study of Zen. Lex certainly had manifested that final step, and I wanted to declare to the world that he had been such a person. I gave him that recognition by making his title Jikai Roshi. I know the spiritual scene very well in the United States and Europe, and I can't think of another person who has had the breadth and depth of spiritual practice that Lex had. He is an inspiration for those of us who are continuing the work.

Sometimes, in Zen, we write what we call a "capping verse" to sum up our thoughts. What follows is the capping verse I wrote about Lex. The *hara* in Zen is the spiritual center located in the part of the body that we Westerners identify as the solar plexus.

Capping Verse:
Not standing on his shoulders
But sitting very close on the cushion
Having a hara-to-hara talk!

—Bernie Glassman
Montague, Massachusetts
April 2015

Bernie Glassman (third from left) seated next to Peter Matthiessen (looking down) and Lex Hixon (far right) meeting with other members of the Zen Community of New York

Preface
by Paul Gorman

I've always believed that radio can be an instrument of grace. It has the suddenness and the spontaneity, the magic and the presence, and the vitality of grace. And you can't have grace without its sacred content. It would have been impossible to do "In the Spirit" without Lex to welcome in that grace and to offer our guests and listeners the "tent and the platform" for that grace to appear once again in the world.

When I asked Lex Hixon to be the host of "In the Spirit" in 1971, I had already found him once before, for quite a different reason, in 1962. We were then both at Yale, and he was a year behind me. I was a member of a secret society that had tasked me with finding several new members for the next year. The assignment was to find interesting people who would bring a distinctly unique perspective to the group. Lex had one of the most distinctive files of the many that I was given to look over by Yale's development office. There was his study of Kierkegaard, his flamenco guitar studies, and the summers he spent with the Native American Episcopal priest Vine V. Deloria, Sr. who was his roommate's father. We invited him to join and he did.

When I went looking again for Lex nine years later, it was for WBAI, and my requirements were basically the same: to find someone who would bring a fresh perspective to the radio station. I had started working with WBAI in 1969 when it was still an old-fashioned Pacifica Radio station at perhaps one of its heights of journalistic excellence and activist influence. The most important program we did was "The War Summary," which ran nightly at 10:45pm, providing crucial in-depth news coverage of the Vietnam War using material that was gathered by journalist Paul Fischer, who later worked for Dan Rather. The program's news wasn't the news that was on the networks. The reports came as much as possible directly from Vietnam, not from American sources. The BBC was stationed there, but the French press was the only one with staff in Hanoi, and WBAI was the only news outlet in New York that carried Agence France-Presse's reports. Gradually, at the end of the Sixties, a shriller countercultural voice started to come out of the station. In the Seventies, the counterculture went out into the streets and a lot of divisions developed within the anti-war movement over substance and political sophistication. It wasn't enough to yell "Off the pig!" in the street. There were some people, myself included, who felt that our depth and maturity were in question, and that respect for Pacifica itself was being diminished by the shrill voices.

To balance the extreme voices, the station needed to create programming on a grander scale. We knew that radio could sustain epic cultural events. So, for the 100th anniversary of the publication of Tolstoy's *War and Peace,* we presented a marathon reading of the entire novel from beginning to end. It lasted for four and a half days. The readings were done by 170 assorted people who took turns reading, stopping only for "The War Summary" and regular newsbreaks. The *War and Peace* reading turned out to be the longest continuous broadcast ever aired over radio. There were also marathon readings of Melville's *Moby Dick* and Heinlein's *Stranger in a Strange Land* in subsequent years. It was huge and exciting!

We were trying to figure out who we were, in addition to being counterculture. There's being counter to everything, and we weren't that. But who were we? What was our ethos? What were our standards? How substantive were we? Was the station just for the crazy people who called us up at midnight?

Some people at the station thought seriously about this, in terms of political and cultural analysis. There was a planning group made up of the program director and a drama and literature director, and somebody from the board. They said they wanted trendier programming, and that we needed to pay attention to transformation at the political, economic, and cultural levels, but there were also deeper transformational rivers that were not trends. Was spirituality just going to be covered as a trend-of-the-month? Were we going to ignore the fact that spirituality and religion had been alive before Woodstock? I began to make the case for a program called "In the Spirit" to be part of the deepening content that could be now featured in the folio. Some of the station members were somewhat hostile to this view because, like Hunter College, Pacifica was founded by the secular left or former communists, for whom religion was the opiate of the masses. But, eventually, the station agreed to try out my idea that religious life is not about what we believe, or not even what we do—it's who we are. It's how we engage in everyday issues. It's marriage, it's childrearing, it's work. The way to approach religion and spirituality is through personal and transformative journeys and awakenings.

When I asked Lex whether he would host "In the Spirit," he had some hesitations. We had many conversations about it and some arguments too. He wanted to be the well-prepared person who knows all the questions, and he had an academic model of doing an interview. I told him the power of the interviewer's personality was more important. We needed a reference, a distinctive person whose connection was deep, who wasn't a dilettante, who really knew what this show could mean for everyone.

There wasn't anything that Lex would do without great seriousness and depth. He was somebody who was living a continuous religious and spiritual awakening, with connections to 2,500 years of religious and spiritual awakening. We were talking about the evolution of religious thought, and the crosscurrents of it, and the refinements of it, and everything that thrilled him. I said that if he manifested on the radio how much he was thrilled by this evolution, people would hear that, and they would know that it was alive and contemporary, that the evolution was coming out of the radio at that very moment.

So the challenge was: How do we introduce this to the radio station? Lex still wasn't convinced that such a program would fit the station's audience. We decided we needed to bring in the whole cast of teachers we knew were just starting to show up in great numbers. Our world was getting smaller all the time. When that happens, cultures have to interact, and all of a sudden here is Lord Krishna or the Buddha or Jesus coming up the path to your village, and someone offers them a tent and they start teaching. I thought "In the Spirit" could be like a town square where these teachers, and students too, could show up, and we could offer them a speaking platform and introduce them as visiting troubadours of the spirit.

In the tradition of peregrination, I suggested, "Let's listen to what these teachers have to say, and let's ask them some real questions, and for the stories of their lives." We wouldn't just read the dust jackets of their books; we would try to make connections and friendships. We would try to represent the authentic, democratic voice of our own culture as it awoke to new languages for understanding the universe, and as we learned new ways to live our lives.

There was no reason why those elements couldn't fit in at WBAI. The traditional lineages being introduced were new and interesting, the teachers had personalities and stories, and they could take phone calls. And Lex couldn't help but be an interesting person on the air—in fact, he was a deeper and richer and more interesting person than most. All the things that he liked about the station, he himself could be.

So Lex accepted the role of convener to manifest the richness of the religious and spiritual traditions for WBAI's listeners, and he made it clear that these were big things we were doing. These were big rivers of spirit we wanted to navigate, and he did justice to the amplitude and the orthodoxy and the historical reach of this dimension of human experience.

—*Paul Gorman*
Amherst, Massachusetts
April 2015

Introduction
Radio Days
By Sheila K. Hixon

A great conversation can be revolutionary and it can change people's lives. There are 33 great conversations in this book. They took place in the 1970s and '80s, on WBAI Radio at 99.5 FM, in New York City. Most of them were in the form of interviews discussing the spiritual dimensions of life, with local friends or visiting guests who might have come from distant countries where they were recognized as awakened masters. Very interesting things transpired in these conversations, one particularly revolutionary idea we heard was, that with some considerable effort, we all had the potential for achieving the state of enlightenment. Many such ideas were explored that caused us to re-engage with our own spiritual traditions as well as experience the new ones, and it all contributed to the enrichment of the larger cultural conversation in this country. The conversations certainly changed individual lives, including our own. The many different voices that we heard sometimes sounded familiar, other times they had accents or spoke through translators. Only one voice was constant, that of the bright and earnest young host of this program called "In the Spirit," who was my husband, Lex Hixon.

Lex and I had moved to Greenwich Village in the mid-'60s, where, among other ways of soaking in its vibrant, unconventional atmosphere, we listened to WBAI, the local counterculture Pacifica station. WBAI provided us with a radical alternative education about the Vietnam War, through reporting from the Agence France-Presse on the program "The War Summary." We went on anti-war marches and spent time with artists and friends, including Paul Gorman, Lex's friend from college, who was a speechwriter for Eugene McCarthy's presidential campaign in 1968. In the Village, we were intrigued by posters announcing Swami Satchidananda's first visit to America. We went to see spiritual people like Ram Dass, who talked about his time in India to a packed theater on 14th Street, and Krishnamurti, who spoke at the New School, where we attended classes. Every day Lex practiced flamenco guitar, which he studied with Carlos Montoya, and when the great blues guitarist Muddy Waters came, we saw him in a tiny place on MacDougal Street. Dylan Thomas's poetry was our favorite for reading together, and we ate frequently at the White Horse Tavern, the late poet's favorite New York hangout. When our son was born in 1966, we named him Dylan.

In 1971, Paul Gorman asked Lex to co-produce a weekly ecumenical radio program called "In the Spirit"— its title was taken from the words of St. Paul—on WBAI. Paul had been hosting a daily show there called "Lunch Pail." By then, Lex and I were fully immersed in parenthood, as our two daughters, India and Shanti, had been born in 1968 and 1969, respectively. When Lex began taking graduate classes at Columbia, we moved out of our loft on the corner of Bowery and Bond streets and settled into a house that overlooked the Hudson River in the Riverdale neighborhood of the Bronx.

Paul envisioned "In the Spirit" as having a slow-paced interview format with time for music and readings to introduce the many spiritual teachers who, like Swami Satchidananda, were coming to New York from around the world. New spiritual ideas had been sifting into the American cultural conversation for many years through people like the early Theosophists, Alan Watts, Paramahamsa Yogananda, D.T. Suzuki, and Jack Kerouac. But none of us foresaw that this exotic and fascinating underground movement would actually flood out into the American mainstream consciousness during our lifetime.

By 1971, we had been studying for five years with our first important teacher, Swami Nikhilananda, a monk and scholar from the Ramakrishna Order in India. In 1966, Lex had located the Ramakrishna-Vivekananda Center in New York City, where Swami was then the resident teacher, and we had begun attending lectures and services there as well as special classes taught by Swami. Lex began studying the Advaita Vedanta of Hinduism and entered into a deep spiritual friendship and discipleship with Swami, which lasted until Swami's death seven years later. He took our family under his wing, initiating Lex and me into mantra practices and acting as our children's godfather.

We spent seven summers with Swami at the Ramakrishna-Vivekananda Center's summer location on the St. Lawrence River near the Canadian border. The Center was located in a former Methodist camp where Sri Ramakrishna's disciple Swami Vivekananda had given lectures after his memorable speech at the Parliament of World Religions in Chicago in 1893. We meditated every day in the house where those lectures had been given. When Swami Nikhilananda took his ritual daily swim in the St. Lawrence River, just as if it was the Ganges, Lex accompanied him, and when Swami became ill and stopped speaking, Lex slept outside his room in case he rang for help during the night.

Swami recommended Lex to his professor friends in the Columbia University Department of Philosophy, and he convinced Lex to enter a graduate degree program to "study widely," as he liked to say. He felt that people would be more likely to listen to Lex if he had a doctorate. It took Lex 10 years to complete the degree. He started out studying Ancient Greek, intending to write on Plotinus, but eventually took the degree in Sanskrit and philosophy of religion. His dissertation was on Gaudapada Karika, a seventh-century commentary on the early non-dual Mandukya Upanishad. As part of his thesis, Lex made a complete poetic reworking of the English translation that Swami Nikhilananda had done of this text as a college student in India.

Swami had arrived in New York City from India in 1931 as a young monk with only a few dollars. Over the years, he had established the Ramakrishna-Vivekananda Center on East 94th Street, where he drew a following from among the intellectuals of the time, including mythologist Joseph Campbell, who was to become the president of the center's board. There was also writer J.D. Salinger—or "Jerry," as Swami called him. (There is much evidence to suggest that J.D. Salinger was Swami's friend and a secret student of Vedanta.)

The center's secretary was the niece of photographer Alfred Stieglitz, who made several powerful portraits of the young Swami. Another follower, President Woodrow Wilson's daughter, Margaret Wilson worked with Swami on the work for which he is best known, *The Gospel of Sri Ramakrishna*, a translation into English of Sri Ramakrishna's teachings in 19th-century Calcutta. Sri Ramakrishna taught the men who gathered to hear him (in Hindu culture, men and women were separated) that every religion is true, and he himself observed practices from different traditions.

Lex was immediately drawn to these teachings, and found that, coincidentally, he already had Swami's book in his library. The Advaita Vedantic message of Sri Ramakrishna was a perfect fit to Lex's universal attitude of mind and heart. He took it as a personal philosophical challenge to test and verify the quotation from the Rig Veda that was written on the wall of the Ramakrishna-Vivekananda Center: "Truth is One; sages call it variously."

All of this made Lex an excellent choice to co-host the radio program that Paul Gorman had envisioned. Somewhat hesitantly, he accepted the opportunity, but very soon found that acting as a radio show host came naturally, and he was able to assume the whole responsibility of the program. At the time, we were in the midst of ending a brief involvement with a benignly cultish group that required us to use spiritual names given by the guru Sri Chinmoy in our daily lives. Lex dutifully began his radio journalist career using the unwieldy name of Purushottama to introduce himself, and he continued to do so until we officially left the group in 1972.

The radio show provided Lex with a working laboratory in which to make extended inquiries into many spiritual traditions and to continue immersing himself in those multiple traditions. It also gave him a community with which to share those experiences. Lex enjoyed imagining what he calculated were thousands of listeners within the 60-mile radius reached by WBAI's transmitter signal from atop the Empire State Building. His regular listenership was estimated by a National Public Radio survey to be 25,000 on any given Sunday morning. For some years, "In the Spirit" was listed in the Sunday *New York Times* under "Radio Highlights of the Day."

Lex was an unabashedly sociable person and loved getting feedback. Sometimes, when we were out together as a family, he would embarrass the children and me by asking people at the next table if they were WBAI listeners. If they were, he would engage them in conversation. Often they would turn out to be fans of his program, which pleased him very much.

Lex prepared for each interview by reading the relevant books and going to lectures and initiation ceremonies involving the teacher to be interviewed. Because the questions he posed were always informed and serious, his interview subjects felt his sincere intention and responded accordingly. Once, when Paul Gorman was planning four consecutive shows from midnight to dawn with Ram Dass—including music, phone calls, scripture readings, kirtan dancing, chanting, and a segment called "Ask Dr. Dass"—he asked Lex for some questions. Lex immediately sat down at his old manual typewriter and tapped out six single-spaced, legal-sized pages of 263 questions. Not one of the questions was superficial or clichéd. Lex's energy for generating ideas for questions was seemingly endless. They just poured out of him, including these:

- In this new age will spiritual practice be widespread?
- Can the fascination with another culture wear off?
- Is it better to be critical or liberal assessing a guru?
- Is it harmful for one to accept an imperfect guru?
- Does ego loss impair self-confidence and effectiveness?
- Is there any ego in a realized being?
- Does academic or scientific training hinder spirituality?
- How can we react to conflicting claims of modern gurus?
- Can meditation lead to delusions of grandeur?
- Why do some people have a bitter resistance to spirituality?
- Should one find Divine Love within oneself or interpersonally?
- How concerned with social change should the seeker be?
- Is meditation inherent in human nature?
- Should one engage in small talk?

The movement towards the inner quest during the Seventies was subject to as many aberrations as other social movements of that time. Some of what was foolish or not very useful made its way onto the program, but almost all of what was presented was authentic. Several of the spiritual teachers Lex met through the program became important figures in our own life. For example, after the program with Sheikh Muzaffer Ozak Effendi, Lex joined the Sufi order and Effendi gave him the name "Nur." This began Lex's study and practice of Islam and Sufism, which took him that same year to Istanbul for Ramadan, and a few years later, to make the Hajj with Effendi and his Turkish dervishes.

Eventually, Effendi made Lex a sheikh in the Halveti-Jerrahi Order, and gave him the responsibility of leading a Sufi community in SoHo. This involved learning prayers and Qur'anic verses in Arabic, and leading Dhikr ceremonies every Thursday night. In the 15 years that Lex led the community, our whole family and many of our friends participated in these ceremonies, which often lasted into the early morning hours, giving us an experience of the profound beauty of Islam through Sufism.

Lex's spiritual fieldwork involved not only studying multiple spiritual traditions, but also entering into them on an initiatory level. Sometimes it became almost too much for him logistically and psychologically, but he persevered with the experiment of holding seemingly contradictory positions inside his own person. In his study and meditation over the years, he had attained a level of realization of the innate oneness of reality taught in Vedanta and other mystical traditions. Holding that realization while simultaneously functioning in the world of differences is what leads to enlightened understanding, and this is what allowed him to continue his quest.

Lex always felt a strong attraction to the position of oneness. When he attended the centennial Parliament of World Religion in Chicago, in 1993, he was provided a nametag pre-printed with "Hello My Name Is," which was to be filled in by the participant. He filled in his name on the nametag so that it read "Hello My Name Is...the Open Space Beyond Religion" and boldly wore it as he walked around among the religious leaders of the world who were attending the Parliament. He and an old friend even gave a presentation there with that title.

Remarkably, the deeper Lex's understanding went of the non-dual reality that transcends differences, the more he celebrated and embraced the particularities of the various traditions. By the time his children were grown, the man who called himself "Open Space" wrote them a long, impassioned letter urging them to be baptized into the Russian Orthodox Church in America. He had achieved a brilliant and enlightened sense of balance.

WBAI management ended "In the Spirit" in 1980 after nine years on the air. The station gave Lex another time slot weekdays from 1:00 to 2:00 p.m. for a new program, "Body/Mind/Spirit," billed as "a new integration for the Eighties." Lex continued broadcasting for three years with differing time slots and titles depending on the changing program directors' enthusiasm for the show. By the time it ended, Lex was a published author. His first book, *Coming Home: The Experience of Enlightenment in Sacred Traditions,* was published by Doubleday Anchor in 1978. He was already working on his next books, including one that resulted from his continuing Zen studies with Bernie Glassman, and he was leading several Sufi communities, including one in Mexico City. "In the Spirit" had provided Lex with invaluable lessons and ideas for the next stage of his life.

Very few of the earliest "In the Spirit" shows were taped, but, starting in 1973, Lex gradually began recording more of them on reel-to-reel tapes, and offering cassette copies to listeners. After he died in 1995, our children and I found tapes of his shows packed in open cardboard boxes in the basement. They were beginning to degrade. Over the years, several friends painstakingly transferred the viable tapes from reel-to-reel to digital tape, CDs, and finally, into a digital archive. Over 300 programs have been preserved.

In 2004, Paul Cohen, the founder of Monkfish Book Publishing Company, contacted me, asking if there were any recordings of the radio program, and suggesting that we make a book of them. I was hesitant because I felt that hearing the resonances of the different voices was essential to communicating all that had taken place during these broadcasts. Fortunately, Paul came back 10 years later, by which point we had established a digital archive of the shows. He explained that the book could link readers to the audio of the original programs, allowing them to listen to the full audio version of each show, as well as read a condensed, edited text version of it. Now it made sense to me to make a book.

When I started organizing the 330 programs for the project, I knew that I wanted to use the earliest interviews that we had in order to hear the initial contacts, but it was difficult to decide which shows to choose. I went through all of Lex's papers again, and found the outline for a book that he was already thinking about in 1979. He had chosen the title and 30 programs.

Of course I decided to be guided by the people included in Lex's outline for the book, and Paul Cohen agreed. Fortunately, almost all of the programs in the outline had survived in our basement, which meant that Lex could still be very much involved in the book project. This made the job of organizing the book easier and all we had to do was to include some of the later interviews that were important to the story of that time. It still required taking liberties with the transcribed text, in some cases cutting an 80-page transcript down to 10 pages. As much as possible, I've left the colorful flavor of what was going on in the world around us at that time, and clarified some odd translations. I apologize in advance if I've misinterpreted or misrepresented a favorite teacher in the editing. In any case, the full original audio is available to hear.

Working with the recordings of the programs was a poignant experience for me. Hearing Lex's long-lost but totally familiar young voice made me very happy to recognize what an important contribution he had made, but at the same time I felt very, very sad that he isn't here to see how those early spiritual contacts affected our culture. His voice is immeasurably missed in the ongoing great conversations of today.

—*Sheila K. Hixon*
Riverdale, the Bronx, New York
May 2015

Sri Ramakrishna

Swami Nikhilananda

"May we bow before this wonderful spiritual being,
Sri Ramakrishna Paramahamsa!"

Lex Hixon Talks About Sri Ramakrishna
February 6, 1972

I was turned on to *The Gospel of Sri Ramakrishna* for the second time by a member of the Natural Church and Curandero Center. The members lived on the top floor of the loft building on Bond Street near Bowery, where we lived in the mid-1960s. Their main sacrament was marijuana, which they smoked every day. It made them more "objective," they told me. They used to come downstairs to have coffee with us and talk. One of them saw *The Gospel of Sri Ramakrishna* among my books one day, and said, "Far out, man, that's a far-out book. We're working with the I-Ching now. Next, we're going to work with that one."

After they left, I took the book down and began reading it. I was feeling generally depressed at the time, and I noticed right away that the depression lifted. This experience may have been the key to my desire to enter spiritual life, because I couldn't stand to be subject to these depressions that would come over me. I really don't think it was for any abstract philosophical reason or deep inner calling that I chose the life of a seeker.

I hadn't looked at the book for several years since I had ordered it when I was a senior in college. It was on the recommended reading list for a course that I took in comparative religion, and it was described as a stenographic record of the conversations of a very high saint of late 19th-century India. I was interested in the description and I read a little of it, but all I can remember now was the incense inserted throughout the book and the fragrance. Later, I found out that at the Ramakrishna Center on 94th Street, they stored the books next to the incense, which totally permeates them. I can remember lying in the grass with my face in the book, breathing it in. The fragrance stayed with me, although I put the book down. After I first got the book, I had some hard things to go through. My first wife and I were getting a divorce, and, due to my own mistakes, I had lost my first job out of college as a teacher. It shows that if you're not ready, you just cannot get into these deep matters.

I had to wait for the right time to reencounter the book that would have such a profound effect on my life. It was about three years later, after I had remarried and my wife, Sheila, and I were living in a loft in the East Village, when my stoned upstairs neighbor brought the book back into my awareness.

At the time, I was lifting weights at the Sheridan Square gym and beginning to feel the aesthetic gap between my own feelings and sitting around with my friends at the gym looking at our "cuts" in the mirror, admiring the definition of our muscles. I realized there might be something more in keeping with my hippie-poet lifestyle to get me into physical shape, like yoga.

I decided to go to the address on East 94th Street that was on the back of the book I had started to read again. At that time, we only ventured above 14th Street once a week to the Art Students League on 59th Street, where Sheila was studying. She would paint and draw, and I would sit outside, reading Wittgenstein on a sunny bench. I was working on a Master's degree in philosophy at The New School.

One day I decided to stroll over to Fifth Avenue and take the bus up to 94th Street. The first thing I saw was the elegant Audubon House on the corner of 94th and Fifth Avenue, which gave me a feeling I was in a very different realm than I had imagined. I wandered down the beautiful street, and a few doors in, I saw an imposing gray stone townhouse covered with a huge wisteria vine, which is the Ramakrishna-Vivekananda Center.

I rang the doorbell and a little man who looked like a squirrel fattened for winter came out and told me that there was no yoga, but that the Swami spoke every Tuesday and Friday at

8:00 in the evening and every Sunday at 11:00 in the morning. Sheila and I went to the next talk and I forgot entirely about yoga breathing exercises, the Sheridan Square gym, my philosophy degree, and everything.

After a few months of beginning meditation, I received a spiritual initiation from the Swami. He didn't ask me to cut my hair or beard, but he did ask that I wear a coat and tie to his talks instead of my customary t-shirt. Gradually, he helped me mature, but in such an understated way. He asked us to stop taking part in anti-Vietnam War marches. He thought it was dangerous for us as Sheila was pregnant with our first baby. He also counseled us not to have any alcohol or drugs in our home. We followed his advice and our life became simplified.

It was so difficult to see anything extraordinarily spiritual in him, and yet I felt an inner attraction, the sense of a tremendously balanced, spontaneous, free human being who just happened to wear three-piece suits, had a velvet cape for the opera in his closet, and invited us often to four-o'clock tea that was served out of a proper teapot every afternoon in his study on the third floor of the townhouse.

Before meeting Swami, I had done a few psychedelic trips in the early '60s, but I felt that one should be able to achieve these experiences without drugs. I soon found that the point of meditation wasn't simply to get high by a different method. I never have had many visions or ecstatic experiences in meditation, although I did have one intense experience early on that served to establish my deep connection with Ramakrishna. I was meditating in our loft on the Bowery that had a big storefront window. The sun was floating in. We had been taught to meditate by concentrating on keeping a still flame in our heart. I was deep in concentration when suddenly the perspective changed. I saw that the flame was actually an open portal. I looked through this open portal, and inside I saw Ramakrishna sitting in meditation. His body was golden, the color of the flame. Everything around him was golden too.

I stepped in through this door and when I looked down, I saw my body was also golden. Everything was this golden flame

3

color. I went to Ramakrishna and sat down near him. As I looked around, all I could see was a little black flame in the brightness, which was the way back into the realm of ignorance.

I stayed there as long as I could. It began to fade out, but the bliss that I experienced stayed with me for hours and hours. I wandered around the mid-'60s East Village in a state of inebriation. I tried to order a sandwich at the deli, but I couldn't even speak so I had to leave.

Nothing like this has ever recurred, but at the time I didn't realize how special it was. It was not imagination in any ordinary sense. Since then, I've realized that insight, preparation, and balance are all important in spiritual life. Meditation on Ramakrishna and studying his life has been profoundly purifying, gradually changing our lives.

I went back to graduate school at Swami's request, though I had left the New School, thinking that I was rejecting academic life. Swami regarded study as a suitable austerity for the contemporary environment—more meaningful, in my case, than walking barefoot through India. One day I shaved my beard, just because I didn't want to create any feeling of separation from other people. We moved out of the Bowery. Sheila and I found a quiet place up on the Hudson. We had three babies and I watched them being born. We made a special meditation room in our house. Life became more and more mellow. We spent almost every summer at a retreat with Swami on the St. Lawrence River. Worldly friends wandered away and spiritual friends appeared. Academic life became enriching for me. The insight was deepening. A natural ease was arising. There was a simplifying of speech and thought.

The Sanskrit word for a holy man, "sadhu," ethnologically means "straight," as in straight to the goal. There was an alienation from the hip world, which some of my friends have yet to appreciate. Suddenly, from being a pejorative term, the term "straight" had a new significance.

There is a sense of invisible guidance centered in the figure of Ramakrishna. I am continuing my study and practice of his teachings. He is a truly unique and gifted spiritual being.

Ramakrishna was born in 1836 to orthodox Brahmin parents in a little village far from Calcutta, absolutely untouched by Western civilization. There were signs before his birth and during his childhood that he was a special spiritual manifestation. As a young man with no education, he went to become a temple priest in the Dakshineswar temple garden in Calcutta, worshipping Goddess Kali ritualistically every day.

He fervently longed for a vision of the goddess. It came to him just as he desperately grabbed the sword that hung by her shrine, in order to end his life. He saw an infinite sea of light, which was immensely dynamic, full of waves. The mother's form emerged with four arms, granting boons, fearlessness, smiling, speaking, consoling, instructing. And then he fell into unconsciousness. After this, he had almost unbroken communion with this divine form, and was often heard by his disciples having long conversations with Mother Kali.

Then he began his many other *sadhanas*. All of them rose spontaneously in him. For one, he took the role of Hanuman, the Monkey King, who was the servant of Rama. This is the path that Baba Ram Dass has chosen. The name Ram Dass means "a slave of Rama." And Ram Dass worships the image of Hanuman. But Ramakrishna immersed himself so intensely in Hanuman that he lived naked in the trees, only eating nuts and fruits, and tying a cloth around his waist to make a tail. When he came down from the tree, he would hop instead of walking. This was the intensity of his sadhanas. People understandably took this for insanity.

Finally, Ramakrishna was blessed with a vision of Sita, who is Rama's divine female consort. She bequeathed him her smile. After that, even in deepest states of Samadhi, he always had a bewitching smile across his face.

He used to do Tantric practices that no one directed him to do, but which he simply came upon by himself. He held a rupee in one hand and earth in the other, or feces in one hand and fragrant sandalwood paste in the other. He would practice contemplating the absolute equivalence of these things. At this time, he cleaned the latrines of the poor people with his long hair, practicing radical humility. All this, the advanced spiritual seekers [around him] recognized as divine intoxication.

He consented to be married because his relatives thought it would bring his mind down [to earth]. And a young girl, Sarada Devi, was found in a neighboring village. She somehow understood his spiritual state and they lived separately as celibate partners in the temple garden until his death. Sarada Devi later became a rich dimension of Ramakrishna's manifestation, and after his death in 1886, she carried on his transmission of spirituality into the 1920s.

At this time, Mathur Babu, the head of the Kali Temple, had an interesting vision of Ramakrishna. Mathur Babu was sitting in his office. He was a worldly man, but with an intense, passionate heart. One day he noticed that Ramakrishna was strolling back and forth on the terrace in front of his room at the temple. When Ramakrishna turned to him, he became pale white, covered with ashes, matted hair, holding a trident. He appeared exactly in the form of Shiva. When he turned to walk the other way, his skin became black and he had four arms. He was Mother Kali. Mathur was in an ordinary frame of mind. He rubbed his eyes. He stared and stared, but it persisted. From that time on, he regarded Ramakrishna as a high manifestation, and he protected him.

Finally, after many intense sadhanas, the Vedanta sadhana of the Master unfolded. Vedanta is the path of total non-duality without even a vestige of ritualistic duality. Totapuri was the name of the teacher. All these teachers just happened to come to the temple garden in a very natural way.

That night there was an initiation and Totapuri instructed Ramakrishna to go beyond form. So Ramakrishna concentrated, and immediately the Divine Mother's blissful form appeared between his eyes. He reported this to Totapuri, who said, "You must go beyond form. Try harder." And again, Ramakrishna concentrated, and again, the blissful Mother appeared because his mind was so centered on that divine form.

Totapuri got angry and took up a sharp stone and pressed hard between the Master's eyebrows, saying, "Now concentrate on that pain." And the Master tells us that the pain became a sword of wisdom. When this last and highest form of the Divine

Mother came forward, he obliterated it and his consciousness flowed into the formless. He went into deep Samadhi, and for two days, there was no consciousness or any breath. He was sitting as if he was dead, yet he was certainly not dead. There was a vibrancy and a luminosity about him. Totapuri marveled, "What took me 40 years of intense practice to achieve, this man has achieved in a single night."

This was, in a way, the culmination of Ramakrishna's sadhana, but he had two other sadhanas to accomplish after this. One was the Islamic sadhana. A Sufi master came by the temple garden and Ramakrishna submitted to him as his guru. Ramakrishna took all pictures of Hindu gods and goddesses out of his room and stopped visiting his beloved Kali temple. He repeated instead, incessantly, the name, "Allah, Allah," day and night, feeling immense bliss and had a vision of Muhammad entering his body. Sometime later, the Master practiced Christianity once more, ignoring the Hindu gods and goddesses and temples, listening instead to the Bengali translation of the New Testament and gazing at a picture of Mary and the child Jesus. He finally had an intense vision of Christ entering his body.

And now the Master's great inclusive sadhana was complete. He began to give forth the wisdom and immense spiritual powers he had attained. He maintained his respect for all spiritual figures, including Muhammad, Christ, and the countless Hindu forms of the divine, based on his own experience.

He was a fully-opened, spiritual master, with no sense of the exclusivity of one system of practice; very unique in spiritual history. Powerful young disciples began to come to him, whom he shaped into spiritual geniuses in their own right. Swami Vivekananda is the best known to us. He carried the teachings of his perfected guru to the West for our benefit. May we bow before this wonderful spiritual being, Sri Ramakrishna Paramahamsa!

Alan Watts
November 26, 1972

Alan Watts was born in Kent, England, in 1915. He missed out on a scholarship to Oxford University because his entrance essay wasn't considered serious enough. At 16, he became involved with the Buddhist Lodge in London, where he met Alice Bailey and D.T. Suzuki, and read extensively in philosophy, psychology, history, and Eastern wisdom. In 1938, he married, moved to America, and became an Episcopal priest. When his marriage ended in 1949, he left the priesthood and moved to California. In 1953, he began a weekly program at Pacifica Radio, attracting a loyal following. His first book, *The Way of Zen* (1957), was hugely successful. Watts subsequently lectured at many universities, wrote several more books, and had a major influence on the '50s and '60s intelligentsia, but he remained an outsider to academia. He married twice more, and had seven children. He spent his last years in the San Francisco Bay area between a houseboat in Sausalito and a cabin on Mt. Tamalpais, where he died in 1973. Two of his daughters currently manage his literary estate; a son has archived his talks.

Lex Hixon: Alan, what do you think of your autobiography? It's called *In My Own Way*, just published by Pantheon Books.

Alan Watts: It was very difficult for me to write. I haven't been a man of adventure. I have achieved no great deeds in my life. I have not become extremely wealthy. I have not been an explorer. I have not been a great warrior or an adventurer. I've been rather a sedentary character because I was brought up, really, to be a Brahmin, an intellectual. So I thought, "I can't write a thing like that!" I'm used to writing philosophy, and that's as easy as falling off a log. But writing narrative—I got sucked into it, slowly, slowly, slowly. It was very hard.

Lex Hixon: So you consider yourself an intellectual, and there's nothing terrible about that term in your vocabulary?

Alan Watts: No, no, not at all. In fact, some people think that my position is anti-intellectual; they don't understand that to be effective intellectually, you have to interpose thinking with intervals when you stop thinking altogether. If you don't, you won't have anything to think about except thoughts. So you get unrelated to the real universe.

Lex Hixon: You are an admirer of Krishnamurti. He's one of the people you speak most highly of in your autobiography. He, of course, is an advocate of mental silence, but he also says that one shouldn't cultivate it, that it can't be cultivated.

Alan Watts: First of all, if you try to cultivate it, you will find out that you can't stop the internal turbulence in your mind, no matter what you do. But if you realize that you can't stop it, you get the message, which is that "you" don't exist! That's why you can't stop it! Your ego is nothing more than a concept. It's an abstraction, like the equator. And nobody will trip over the equator. So your ego is your concept of yourself, and that concept cannot stop the babble in the mind. As soon as you realize that, the babble stops itself.

I'm trying to say the same thing as Krishnamurti in a slightly different style. I think he is too serious. He doesn't allow laughter at his lectures. But I love him. I think he's a great man.

I always allow laughter at my lectures. We get into an uproar. There's a great Zen master in this country by the name of Joshu Sasaki. For meditation, he recommends that every morning you stand up, put your hands on your hips and roar with laughter for five minutes. Imagine if Mr. Nixon did that! Imagine if the Queen of England or Mr. Heath did that. Or Mr. Kosygin, or the Emperor of Japan, or Mao Tse Tung. And then, when you think about that, you laugh all over again.

Lex Hixon: Do you still maintain that there's some value in traditional religious forms and practices? Krishnamurti throws them all out. I sense you have some nostalgia.

Alan Watts: Yes. I wouldn't throw them out. I would understand them in a slightly different way, though, from the way in which they are generally understood. In other words, when I go to church, I don't expect by attending Mass that I will get some advantage from the power of God, that he will do something special for me like get me an increase in salary. I don't even listen to the prayers. I listen to the sound of the priest's voice. That's why the Roman Catholic Church made a serious mistake in having the Mass said in the vernacular. They should have kept it in Latin.

Lex Hixon: Why is it that you went into the Church at a certain point in your life, for five years?

Alan Watts: I went as an absolutely knowing subversive. It worked, in a way. But I couldn't sustain the role of a clergyman in those days, I was much too much of a bohemian to wear the Roman collar and the black suit, and come on like I was holier than thou. It just didn't work.

Lex Hixon: In the Zen idea of "nothing special," you mentioned in your book that D.T. Suzuki would sign his letters, "No Special

Person." It seems to be the finest antidote to the holier than thou. Do you feel that way about yourself, that you're nothing special?

Alan Watts: Oh! I do it in a slightly different way than Suzuki. It's a matter of public knowledge that I'm a rascal, that I drink too much, that I sleep with too many women, and that I eat unwisely. Americans don't understand certain things that are understood in Europe and Asia about the joyous life. They are always supposing everything you do must be good for you. Now, life is bad for you. As Jung pointed out—he was joking, of course—"Life is a disease with a very bad prognosis. It lingers on for years and invariably ends with death." And I'm sick of being pursued for my best interests.

Lex Hixon: Have you already gone away? Presumably, if there's no individual ego, and one sees it clearly, one has died.

Alan Watts: If you ask me have I gone away, that's a somewhat paradoxical question. Then I would be claiming credit for being an egoistic non-ego.

Lex Hixon: Presumably, you can carry on a full, articulated life without thinking that it's a "you."

Alan Watts: Yes, of course you can. And it's much more fun than the other kind of life.

Lex Hixon: It's like sitting in on a course, not for credit. I feel very often I'm not taking life for credit.

Alan Watts: That's right. That's a very good comparison.

Lex Hixon: What about this "California dreaming" that you do? In your book, Big Sur and the people there take on almost mythic proportions. It sounds as though you've found something right for yourself, a kind of a final place.

Alan Watts: Yes, although it's an extremely dangerous place to live as a result of the combination of the San Andreas Fault and Governor Reagan. But it is, at the same time, a most beautiful place. It's the American version of the Riviera. So since I can't make a living at my profession in any country except the United States, California is the nearest thing to that sunlit landscape that I sought from boyhood.

Lex Hixon: I'm from California myself, and I feel a sense of nostalgia [for it], but I wonder whether it's just nostalgia, or whether there's something special happening there.

Alan Watts: Oh, there is. It's one of the most stimulating spiritual and intellectual climates that there is.

Lex Hixon: In your book, you said your final feeling about LSD, roughly speaking, is that when you get the message, you hang up the phone. Is that about where you stand?

Alan Watts: Yes. I mean, I would say that, from my own personal point of view, if all the LSD in the world were to vanish tomorrow, I wouldn't regret it, because I think I've learned everything from that kind of experience that it has to teach.

Lex Hixon: Do you think that a whole generation has done the learning for the society? Do you suppose that certain people can completely bypass the LSD experience by building on the experience of others? Or do you think it's good for everyone to get lost in the woods?

Alan Watts: That's a difficult question to answer. I don't really know the answer to that. LSD was a valuable catalyst in showing people that, "There are more things in heaven and earth, Horatio, than are dreamed of in your philosophy," to quote from *Hamlet*. But it is dangerous, and all the more dangerous when suppressed. I can't understand American Prohibitionism because it corrupts the police by asking them to be armed clergymen.

Lex Hixon: But it seems to me that that there are a lot of people in the society today who are deeply exploring consciousness through meditative techniques of one kind or another. It's not outrageous anymore. Do you think there is some New Age of spirit dawning?

Alan Watts: "New Age" may be too pompous a phrase to use. But there most decidedly is a colossal spiritual awakening occurring in this country. It's as alive as all get-out.

Lex Hixon: Do you think it's indigenous? Or is it sustained by people coming from the East and Japan?

Alan Watts: It's both. It's a result of global intercommunication. We're in a situation now where we've got one world and, therefore, all the cultures of the world are merging. And this stimulates every culture. But what we've got going wrong is, we've got a kind of bifurcation. You take your classified telephone directory and open up to "churches," and you will find that it's mostly authoritarian, Bible-banging churches. These people are barbarians who take the written word of the Bible literally, because they have a personal need for something to depend on.

Lex Hixon: What's going to be the outcome of these two different trends in the society?

Alan Watts: Well, the trouble is that the boys who always need papa are violent. They have the guns. They're the types of people who like to be soldiers, policemen, tough guys. Therefore, they have a great deal of power. Although, I must say, recently I had a long talk with a general of the army, who is a Virginian gentleman, who is extremely intelligent. I was quite shocked to find out how wise he was. I've even been invited by the Air Force to lecture at the great Air Force Academy.

Lex Hixon: You mean, there's a Buddha nature in a general?

Alan Watts: Oh, yes. But somehow something's wrong with their strategy. They don't know where they want to go.

Lex Hixon: Suppose you were to say that there is no ego, therefore everything is attained; beatitude is now. I consider these the two foci of your position. Can someone hear that and instantly be enlightened?

Alan Watts: Sometimes, yes. For most people, you see, it needs some explanation. What we call "the ego" is a combination of two factors. On the one hand, it's your image of yourself, your idea of yourself, which has been brainwashed into you since you were a baby. This corresponds, on the other hand, to a certain physical sensation. This sensation is one of chronic muscular strain, which we were taught when, in the beginning, Mama said, "Darling, try to go to sleep," or the teacher said, "Pay attention!" or "Think about this." One does a muscular tension in order to achieve a neurological result. And this tension is useless. It's like when you're taking off on a jet plane, and you think you've gone too far down the runway and the damned thing ought to be up in the air, you start pulling up your seatbelt. Now there's a chronic strain in everybody's muscles. It may be sometimes located between the eyes, sometimes in the heart center, sometimes in the solar plexus, and sometimes in the rectum. It's the feeling of pulling yourself together.

It becomes chronic and associated with the image of yourself, and therefore corresponds to what you mean when you say "I." Whereas, in fact, "I" is like "eye." It's an aperture through which the universe is examining itself. It is always basically unconscious of itself, for the same reason that you can't bite your own teeth or kiss your own lips.

Lex Hixon: So do you feel that silence now?

Alan Watts: Oh, yes, there's a constant undercurrent.

Lex Hixon: Can one have felt the silence and then still have the battle going on? Even if the boiler factory is inside your skull?

Alan Watts: If you can't meditate in a boiler factory, you can't meditate. It's like space behind the stars. You can't have any stars without space. And so, let's suppose I'm absolutely scared stiff and I've got cancer or the great Siberian itch—nevertheless, far, far in the back of my mind, there is an incredible serenity of eternal silence. It isn't negative in the ordinary way Western people think of it. You can't have something without "no thing." Nothing is the mother. It's the womb of the universe and space—as St. Thomas Aquinas put it, "the silent pause which gives sweetness to the chant."

Lex Hixon: Did you achieve that serene space you're in touch with through anything that you've done in your life?

Alan Watts: One doesn't achieve it, you see. That is asking the wrong question. In the same way, one doesn't speak of achieving it, because you have to understand first that there is no separate "you" to achieve it.

Lex Hixon: So it doesn't matter what one does.

Alan Watts: What one does are mostly empty motions. Look, that is the point people need to understand. When you understand it, you can act creatively, because you are acting with the whole energy of the universe behind you.

That energy is Prajna, which means "intuitive wisdom," the fundamental sense of life. We can't talk about it, because it is ineffable. In Greek, that means "what cannot be spoken," in the same way that "mysticism" comes from the Greek verb *mu-een—mu*, which is the finger on the lips—and we say, "Mum's the word." There's something that can't be told, and that's what is important.

Brother David Steindl-Rast
March 18, 1973

David Steindl-Rast was born in Vienna in 1926, and received a Ph.D. from the University of Vienna in anthropology and psychology. He joined the Mount Savior Monastery in Elmira, New York, in 1953, and was a post-doctoral Fellow at Cornell University. In 1967, after 12 years of theological training, and with Vatican approval, he began participating in Buddhist-Christian dialogue, studying with Yasutani Roshi, Soen Roshi, and Suzuki Roshi; he later co-authored *The Ground We Share: Buddhist and Christian Practice* (1994) with Aitken Roshi, and wrote several other books. In 1969, he co-founded the Center for Spiritual Studies, with Hindu, Sufi, Jewish, and Buddhist teachers, for which he received the Martin Buber Award in 1975. In the 1970s, together with Thomas Merton, he provided a renewal of religious orders through the House of Prayer movement, affecting 200,000 members of communities in the U.S. and Canada. He currently runs the online community Network of Grateful Living, does lecture tours, and lives as a hermit.

Lex Hixon: This morning we have a tape of an interview that I did recently with Brother David, a very special man who I feel is carrying on the work of Thomas Merton as a bridge builder between [traditions]. In 1974, Brother David began a special hermitage and training center on Mt. Desert Island in Maine. He has also lived with the Shoshone and Papago Indians, and he is a cofounder of the Center for Spiritual Studies, with Eido Roshi, Swami Satchidananda, and Rabbi Gelberman, in New York City.

Brother David, what do you think about the problem of religions from different cultures in a world which is becoming one? Do you think the religious traditions should maintain separateness?

Brother David: Yes, I think so, but it depends on what you mean by "separateness." Often, it's been interpreted as competition. That's not my understanding, and it is definitely not desirable. What intrigues me is that I know so many people who started out as Christians and who could, psychologically speaking, hardly be expected to really become mature Christians because the tradition had set up a framework that was so uncongenial for them. And then through yoga, or through Zen practice, they come to find again their Christian background.

This happens so often that it really gives one food for thought. And we can't say that they are "coming back" to Christianity because there is no going back on the spiritual path, we can only push through. As long as someone pushes through to the core of the spiritual life, it doesn't matter to me and it doesn't matter to God, and I don't know if it should matter to anybody else, what way they choose to reach the core. This really is my answer to your question. I don't believe in eclecticism, where you pick and choose what you like out of each [religion], nor in confusing everything, and making one big stew out of it all. I believe if you go deeply enough into your own tradition, you will discover that all the others are somehow included in it.

You will find that the paths themselves are very different, but because they are so different, they are mutually inclusive. Our imagery [boundary] breaks down there. But I believe that if you are really a Buddhist to the core, then whether you know it or not, whether you ever heard of Christ or not, you are a Christian in some very deep way.

Lex Hixon: If you are fundamentally convinced that all these are one thing, do you think in the modern scene that people will be called upon to be Buddhists and Christians and Jews and Hindus simultaneously?

Brother David: When I'm in a Zen monastery, for instance, then I'm just really there, and I don't try to carry with me the breviary and fit that in. I spent a long time in Tassajara, and I never had any chance to go on Sunday to Mass.

Lex Hixon: It doesn't have to be that in the morning you go to synagogue and at noon you chant in the Hindu ashram and in the evening go to Mass.

Brother David: I believe what you say is possible, and I'm in favor of it. But it will always remain quite exceptional. Most people will not be able to do justice to even one tradition, so I think it will be very difficult. But it is important that some people do it, and so I'm very grateful that I have this opportunity, and I can, here and there, spend the time in another tradition.

Lex Hixon: When did you first hear of the practice of the Jesus Prayer?

Brother David: Oh, I heard of that when I was a boy. For instance, when we were getting bored, waiting at the dentist or something like that, my mother would say, "Well, why don't you just repeat the name of Jesus?"

Lex Hixon: Was there a particular time in your life when you decided to actually enter this practice in a serious and conscious manner?

Brother David: That started when I came to the monastery. I think most of you are familiar with *The Way of a Pilgrim*. We read that book in the monastery.

Lex Hixon: In your practice in the monastery, did you begin, as the book says, to gradually [reach], say, 6,000 repetitions a day, and then 10,000? Did you count them?

Brother David: I never counted them. But we all do go around with these little *tchotkis*, as we call them, these little prayer beads, and we use them to finger them; many do it, and I personally find it very helpful. It's not a counting device, but as you move the beads with your fingers, it reminds you somehow, again and again, to enter into the repetition of the name. It's partly a toy, and partly...

Lex Hixon: Spiritual doodling.

Brother David: Yes!

Lex Hixon: In *The Way of a Pilgrim*, when the pilgrim's teacher left the body, he appeared in a dream several times to him afterwards at certain crucial moments. Presumably, that inner guidance is the teacher without ever having had any outer embodiment of it.

Brother David: It is really desirable to find the teacher who is really that guru, the spiritual master. It is very, very desirable, I think, in every tradition, but they are just so few and far between that one has to settle for something else. And for us, in the Christian tradition, especially the monastic tradition, this is the community because the Holy Spirit speaks through the community. Wherever there are two or three together, we can really trust that the Holy Spirit is speaking through all our bungling efforts. It isn't a very glorious kind of speaking out, but somehow through our effort to arrive at truth or arrive at the insight, it is really the Spirit of God that is speaking.

Lex Hixon: I also had the good fortune recently of spending the day with Brother David. We drove up to Yale University where he was to give a seminar at the Divinity School. Before he became a monk, Brother David received a Ph.D. degree in experimental psychology from the University of Vienna and he begins this seminar on the note of the psychological realm and the spiritual realm.

Brother David: I started out in the psychological field and eventually came to see that I wouldn't find the spiritual there. It didn't seem to be an element of the psychological study.

Somehow, in the course of [those] years of studying psychology in Austria, I came to see there were certain areas that made human beings human, which we didn't get into in depth at all because we never asked the questions that belong to that. As a student of psychology, I came to see that you don't find the spirit in psychology unless you ask spiritual questions. If you ask psychological questions, you will always get psychological answers.

Also, there must be openness to the questioning. You will not find the spirit as an element, as something discrete. The best expression that I have come across so far is "the human being's openness toward the divine." I think this has much to do with what we call "the heart." I think for most of us it suggests the bottomlessness of human existence.

What we really mean when we say that something speaks to our heart is that we give ourselves to it and that it goes to our very being. We are not using the term "heart" in the emotional sense, but in the biblical sense, in which it means the whole person. It means the taproot of the whole person before we are spread out into intellect, will, and emotions. It means all our emotions. It also means all our intellect and all our willpower, the whole human person, and somehow that whole human person at the point at which we are open in freedom.

I cannot leave out the concept of freedom when I speak about the spirit and that is exactly the point at which psychology stops, because as far as psychology is concerned, everything is determined. But on the level of the heart, somehow you find that freedom. It is not tangible; you can never say, "That's why I know," or "This was a perfectly free choice, you could have done this or that." It is more like an intuition.

What I am really looking for is gratefulness. I think you can detect a grateful heart. It is a phenomenon; you can somehow grasp it phenomenologically. It is somehow entering into the realm of psychology, sociology, in every respect, but it is a phenomenon of the spirit. It transcends sociology and psychology. That's what I look for.

Lex Hixon: I consider the matter of monastic or household life merely a question of lifestyle because it seems to me that the real practice of the spirit—for instance, the Prayer of the Heart, which is a real Christian practice of meditation—is something open in every time to every person and it is the core of experiencing the spirit. It is the practice of the divine presence in the heart. You talked about the heart in the beginning, and I wondered if you could say something more about the heart, more specifically about a technique for getting into the heart.

Brother David: I'm glad that you point out the Prayer of the Heart, the Jesus Prayer, in this connection. There are certain practices that really bridge the gap completely and they are as open to the householder as they are open to the monk. The Prayer of the Heart is one of these. It's the repetition of the name of Jesus, which has been practiced by monks and laypeople throughout the centuries.

Most people know about it from *Franny and Zooey* by J.D. Salinger, or from *The Way of the Pilgrim*. It really consists in bringing your mind into your heart and repeating the name of Jesus there.

Lex Hixon: How do you come to your heart?

Brother David: This is a very difficult thing to tell anybody else. I can only say, when you take something to heart—and we have all used the expression—well, you took it somewhere, and it is a conviction of mine that anything you take to heart turns into prayer, because the heart is the realm of prayer. The Litany of the Sacred Heart was very popular in the Catholic Church when I was a little boy. The Sacred Heart is described in one passage as "a burning furnace of love." That is a tremendous image. When we come to our heart, each one of us is reaching a point in an inner realm that is not only most intimately ourselves, but most intimately united with all other human beings because, ultimately, we have only one heart. We are one heart—anything that you throw into that fire turns into fire, and that is prayer. So anything that we take to heart we are turning into prayer because it is burned up in the one heart that is the heart of creation.

It would take a tremendous mastery of the Prayer of the Heart to really combine it with the Zen approach. But I do believe that it is possible, because "the Word" always leads us into the silence if we only give ourselves, and that "just" of Zen, of course belongs to that realm of silence. If you really practice the Prayer of the Heart, it will lead you into that silence. It is possible.

And now let us close with a prayer:

Since we are truly one in the spirit, we ought to be able to find a common expression of the spirit that moves us at this moment. But our languages tend to separate us. However, where the language of words fails us, the silent language of gestures helps us to express our unity. I invite you to rise and stand and let's really, truly make this now a common gesture of the heart. Let our standing be a gesture of mindfulness of the ground on which we are standing, that this poor mistreated earth belongs to all of us together.

As we stand, then, like plants on a good plot of ground, let our roots go down deeply into our hidden unity. Let's stand in awe before all those thousands and thousands known and unknown, who have laid down their lives for the common cause of our human family, and let's bow our heads to them. We share the glory of the human greatness and the shame of human failure.

Standing firm then, in this oneness, let us close our eyes. Let's close our eyes to bring home to ourselves our blindness as we face the future. Let us close our eyes to focus our minds on the inner light, our one common light in whose brightness we shall be able to walk together even in the dark. And let us close our eyes in the gesture of trust in the guidance of the one spirit that will move us if we open our hearts. The human heart is unfathomable. Into this depth let us silently sink our roots, for there lies the only source of peace. In a moment, when I will invite you to open your eyes, I will invite you also to turn, in this spirit, to the person next to you with a greeting of peace, and let our celebration culminate and conclude in this gesture by which we will send one another forth as messengers of peace. Let us do this now.

Peace be with all of you!

Guru Bawa Muhaiyaddeen
June 17, 1973

Bawa Muhaiyaddeen was a Sri Lankan Sufi mystic who taught Hindu, Muslim, and Christian students. In the 1940s, some pilgrims encountered him as an old man in a forest and invited him to their village, where he began attracting students. Later, he met a Westerner who brought him to Philadelphia in 1971. In 1973, a group of Guru Bawa's Philadelphia students formed the Bawa Muhaiyaddeen Fellowship; the mosque they built together has operated since 1984, and fellowship groups were also established in Sri Lanka, Australia, Canada, and the United Kingdom. Guru Bawa wrote 25 books and recorded 10,000 hours of video and audio. Although very little is known about his background, it is believed that he was well over 100 years old when he died in 1986.

Guru Bawa: To my most loving children, to my most loved children, I express my heartfelt love and greetings. In this world, among all of the creations, among all of the different beings, I am indeed most lowly. There are not many things that I know about the various explanations of the world.

All of the creations of God seem to me to be greater in wisdom than myself. So, like an ant or like a fiber, I am very small and a slave of God. With compassion, I am a slave to living beings. I'm not educated. I have not been to school. I have no titles. I am not a swami. I am not a guru. I am not a great person. I am very small, and very least in wisdom. Since these children requested me to come here, and it is not possible to disappoint them, I have come.

But since I'm not imbued with a great amount of education or a great amount of wisdom, there is a certain amount of tiredness and a lack of courage that is felt. So if there are any mistakes in what is being said, I seek your pardon for them.

Lex Hixon: This morning we have an unusual situation. We're in Studio C with about 100 people, and we have Guru Bawa with us, who is a teacher from Ceylon who has been visiting Philadelphia. Mohammed Mauroof will be translating because Guru Bawa speaks in Tamil.

Good morning, Guru Bawa! In our culture, today is Father's Day, and we wish you, with all our hearts, a happy Father's Day.

Guru Bawa: We are all here, and God is our father. For all creation, for all beings, God is the father. He has many names, and there are many ways of describing him. But he is the one father for all beings. So it is He who conducts creation, sustenance, and protection. Even if our parents forget us, He always protects us. In this world, among different forms of life, we find all different beings performing their duties as fathers and mothers. But they are all in one family. And the father of that family is our God.

So, all of us, the creations, are a funny family of God—a funny and interesting family. And let us, altogether in this funny family, pay our respects and obeisance to our father today.

Lex Hixon: Guru Bawa, your children spontaneously call you "Father." What is the relationship between you as father and God as father?

Guru Bawa: It is like the relationship between the earth and the sun. In that same way, there is this relationship between the children and Him. So it is He who is the father, not we.

Everything that disappears, which can be destroyed, is not our father. But that which does not disappear, which is always present—that is our father. There is within us, to a certain extent, His treasure and His wisdom. So there is a duty to bestow that wealth and wisdom to others—that is what we are accepting.

Lex Hixon: Guru Bawa, when we look at you, we see an ordinary human being, but within you, is there anything except the qualities of God?

Guru Bawa: No. For us, as well as for the children, there is this aspect of the body, the physical element—the earth, the fire, the water, the air and ether. This is something that everybody can see. But within this, there is a mystery. That mystery is something that cannot be discovered by anything, not even by the power of the atom. It is not something that can be discovered by science. It is a power, which is without any form or any image. It has no color. It has no hues. It is not in the races; it is not in a religion. It does not recognize differences. It is that type of power. It is within human beings. One who has seen that power will only keep that power within himself, nothing else. That is the one secret. That is what he has.

Lex Hixon: Guru Bawa, can you tell us a brief account of your personal history, or is personal history not important to you?

Guru Bawa: What person of history can we talk about, what can we say? This is a school. It is like a university. There are, in this world, so many creations, so many beings of God, from whom we can learn. Whatever it is that we see, from all those things we can learn. From the ants that crawl, to the sun and the moon and all of those things beyond, in everything, there are things to learn from for a student. Everything is a wonder! There are so many examples in things, so many different kinds of lights and colors and different states of wisdom and knowledge that are to be gained from all of these things.

So when there are all these wonders to learn from, and when the student is learning about all of these wonders, should we be concerned about his history? It is the history of the one who created all these wonders that we should be concerned about.

Lex Hixon: Guru Bawa, are you going to be reborn again into this school, or have you graduated from this school?

Guru Bawa: There is no question of being reborn, and I'm not going to say that I have graduated either.

Lex Hixon: I think that someone from the audience may want to ask a question of Guru Bawa, so raise your hand if you have a question.

Audience member: Which is more important: faith or meditation?

Guru Bawa: Without a fire, you cannot cook anything. Like that, what a human being needs first of all is a strong faith. That is the first requirement. Secondly, what human beings need are the qualities of God, such as love. The third requirement for a human being is the divine conscience. The human being has to realize that his life is equal to the life of others. Fourthly, even if he still sees differences, he requires the patience to tolerate them. So, having received the beauty of that patience, fifthly, he has to receive wisdom, the wisdom of God. And then he has to utilize it. But as a first requirement, it is absolutely necessary to have faith, conviction and certitude.

Without the qualities of God, without having the divine qualities of patience, tolerance and peacefulness, how can we worship or meditate upon God? It will then be like trying to take water from a pond without a vessel to take it in. It will be like looking for light in a room where there is no light. That's the way it will be.

Audience member: Do you feel that a life in the material world can go hand in hand with a serious spiritual life in a place like New York City?

Guru Bawa: There is no place, no city anywhere where there is no materialism, where there is no illusion. There is no place anywhere in this world where there are no demons, where there is no Satan, where there are no evil spirits, where there is no magic, and so forth. In fact, the beings of 18,000 universes exist within your body formlessly, in an essence.

All of it is within this body. The demons, the spirits, the lions, the tigers, the peacock, and the birds, and all of these things are in here. So, if we have all of these things within us, what would we go to another city or another place for? That is not the way. It is not possible to migrate to another place to achieve spiritual satisfaction. It is here that we have to destroy this forest. We have to distill the ocean of illusion. We have to grab hold of this monkey mind and chain him. There are 70 battalions of monkeys. And there is a huge dog here—the dog of desire.

But, my children, do not worship, asking for heaven. And do not cry, asking that you be saved from hell. If you reflect and think, and if you look in yourself, you can see that wherever your mind, your intelligence, your wisdom, and your senses, reside, that is where your world is.

There is a power within your eye. You can discriminate and if you look with that light that is within you will know the truth of the creation of God. There is a microphone within, which is capable of receiving the sound that emanates from Him, from God. It is able to receive the sounds that come from the heavens, from the fairies, from the angels and other divine beings. It is possible to receive divine words and divine music with the antenna of wisdom.

And if you begin to inhale with that divine luminous wisdom capacity of smelling, then you are bringing in all the fragrances of the qualities of God and you can lose yourself in ecstasy in that experience. With wisdom, you can extract the taste and the pleasure of the divine within us, if that transmission can take place, then he would indeed become a God.

Lex Hixon: Guru Bawa, what about the five elements? If God alone exists, He must have also projected those five elements. And they cannot be anything else but Him.

Guru Bawa: That is true, but it is not a projection, it is a creation. It's His creation. There is the soul. There is His light and a power from there. It is something that cannot be consumed by fire, or by anything else. It is His power. It is indestructible. It is everlasting. This earth, and all of these other things, are His creations, and therefore are subject to change and transformation. Gravity pulls toward earth, but that power is capable of pulling toward Him.

It is shadowless. God is without shadow. There is no form and there is no shadow. These things, however, have shadow. If you light a lamp, that has a shadow. Look at an ant. That has a shadow. Whatever you make in science—those things have shadows also. So all these things that have shadows are subject to transformation, to change. They come and they go.

Lex Hixon: But in your consciousness of God, there's no shadow. Perhaps there are no shadows. Perhaps the shadows are illusory.

Guru Bawa: What has a shadow is destructible, will be destroyed. Everything that has a shadow will be destroyed; it will change, to come in different forms. Now, we call this, the city of New York now, once upon a time, this was underwater. It was ocean. And some other time, it may have been a mountain. At some time, this may have been full of forest and jungles. Now this is a town. We call it New York. Like that, this is something that changes. That is unchangeable. We don't change.

Lex Hixon: When one is conscious of this unchanging thing, can you see the changes at the same time?

Guru Bawa: Before that can be known, before the unchangeable can be known, the changing thing has to be understood. You have to know it thoroughly. Without knowing this, that cannot be known.

Lex Hixon: But assuming you've known it, Guru Bawa, can you see the unchanging and the change simultaneously?

Guru Bawa: I don't know that. I'm still learning. I have a lot of work, a lot of learning to do.

Lex Hixon: Guru, if children came to you, would you accept them as your special children? Would you guide them as their own personal father?

Guru Bawa: My work is the work of a slave. I perform the services of a servant to my children. The work that has been assigned, we do. And the work that I have learned, I train others to do. And what I know of, I teach others about. This is the work of a slave.

Robert Thurman
July 28, 1974

Born in New York City in 1941, Robert Thurman received a doctorate in Buddhist studies from Harvard in 1972. This came after marriage as an undergraduate, the birth of a daughter, the loss of an eye, a divorce, and a pilgrimage to India in 1962. He was the first American to take Tibetan Buddhist monk vows in 1964. In 1966, he renounced his vows, remarried, and returned to Harvard for PhD studies. After graduation, Thurman taught at Amherst College, where he founded the American Institute of Buddhist Studies, until 1988 when he joined Columbia University's religion department. He remains there as the Jey Tsong Kapa Professor of Indo-Tibetan Buddhist Studies. At the request of the Dalai Lama, his close friend, Thurman co-founded Tibet House to preserve Tibetan culture in exile, in 1987, and the Menla Mountain Retreat and Conference Center, a Tibetan healing arts facility, in 2001. He has written many books on Tibetan Buddhism and has been named as one of the 25 most influential Americans by *Time* magazine. He and his second wife, Nena von Schlebrügge, live in New York, where they raised four children, including actress Uma Thurman.

Lex Hixon: Robert Thurman teaches at the Amherst College and Harvard, and he has had an interesting pilgrimage. To give you an idea of him as a person, we'll talk about how he got involved in the kind of engaged scholarship that he is doing.

Bob, where would you start?

Robert Thurman: I would start with when I dropped out of school in the early Sixties. I was at Harvard and was not really very engaged by my work in the English department. I felt that Western civilization was crumbling and didn't look very promising. Somehow the kind of learning that one had in school in those days seemed to me very empty and just merely intellectual, leaving out some of the more fundamental issues in life.

Through reading Gurdjieff and different Sufis and psychologies, I finally encountered Buddhism. I was encountering these things, but I wasn't necessarily giving over my energy to them, because I was still living a thoughtlessly happy American consumer life. I was still not quite connecting to my guts with these ideas.

Then I had an accident and lost one eye. I would say the beginning of my deeper interest in those things came from that accident, which was a tremendous trauma, and it made me realize the impermanence of life, that death was very nearby, that pain was very real. Subsequently, it was one of the great good fortunes of my life that it happened to me. One of my teachers later told me, "You should always say, when you think of it, 'Well, I lost one eye to gain a thousand.'" I do like to think of it in that way.

So I went to India. The Tibetans had just been kicked out by the Chinese around 1959 and '60; they were just settling down in India, looking for friends and help, and I started to get involved in helping them. Then my father died. I came back here, and then met Geshe Wangyal. That had a funny aspect, too: Having pilgrimaged all the way to India, and traveled all around looking for various teachers, I found the teacher who would give me major assistance for my main study in a man who had lived about one and a half hours by bus from where I was born in New York City. He'd been there since 1955. I'd never, of course, met him.

Then, after that, I went into the Buddhist trip and I became a *bikkshu*, shaved my head, was ordained in India, meditated a lot, and lived according to some of the ascetic precepts—you know, not eating any food after noon, staying up late meditating, and reading and studying a lot of books in Tibetan and Sanskrit. I was really off toward that sort of religious life until the mid-Sixties, when a monk in Vietnam gave me a second big shock in the opposite direction— Thich Quang Duc, I think his name was. We all can remember, I am sure, that image of him smilingly sitting there while blazing himself with gasoline to show the world in some undeniable, non-polemical, totally visual way how things were going on in that country that were intolerable, that even he, a man of great peace and tranquility and detachment, could not tolerate. In spite of the precept in Buddhism against mortification of the flesh, being old and being soon to die anyway, he decided he would use his death as a teaching to many people, that they should really rise up and put a stop to the daily burning of infants and women and children through napalming and so on, by burning himself.

That image really shook me at the time, and I felt, "Who am I here, enjoying my life as a monk?" It was a very peaceful life. I was reading a lot of things, enjoying having great pleasures of the mind and visionary meditation and study. I thought, "Who am I to sit here enjoying this while the world is burning like that? Isn't the Mahayana something that means universal vehicle, including all of the community? So maybe I should get involved more."

And I did. I finally ended up going back to Harvard for graduate school and getting a Ph.D. in Buddhist studies and trying to affect the world more actively as an educator, and yet also maintain my own study of and interest in Buddhism.

That's sort of the circuit by which I come to be here now. My sort of work now is to teach at Amherst College, and I'm moonlighting at Harvard sometimes. We have an organization called the American Institute of Buddhist Studies, which is working to create an institutional vehicle for enlightenment teachings to be carried on within the province of academia—to precisely reconcile the dichotomy that drove me in leaving academia and going out and then coming back and reintegrating over a 10-year cycle, to perhaps make it a little more effective for younger persons in future generations to become educated and liberate their consciousness simultaneously, and be supported by the culture in doing that. Also, to learn at the same time how to contribute creatively to the growth and development and practical aspects of the culture—hopefully, looking forward to a time when our leaders and responsible persons in various positions in society are also enlightened, ideally by having enlightenment education and liberal education aligned as indeed perhaps they really truly should be.

Lex Hixon: Staying on the level of your own personal development, I know that you're not too anxious to talk about some of these transitional phases, but people who are listening could find that intensely meaningful.

Robert Thurman: Right.

Lex Hixon: Could you say something first of all, about the difficulties you may have experienced in making the transition from an ordinary American life to a traditional monastic life? And then some of the problems you had in re-acculturating—leaving that monastic life and feeling comfortable again at Harvard?

Robert Thurman: Those kinds of things still go on. After the culturally dreary period of the late Fifties, when the U.S. was still Eurocentric, in the early Sixties there was a sense of wanting to blast out of that and to get into a more planetary civilization. We were the war babies. We were born after World War II, and so on. We wanted to find new perspectives through which to view things. There was not a large number of spiritual teachers and gurus running around at that time. It was kind of an esoteric thing. Of course there was mescaline, psilocybin; LSD was beginning to be around in those days. Actually, trips were kind of good, because it was professionally-made stuff and it was not illegal. There was no huge paranoia about it and not a lot of people were doing it.

So that was also very helpful, in a sense, as Aldous Huxley wrote in his book at the time, to "open the doors of perception" of a certain group of Western people—in a sense, temporarily canceling the conditioning patterns of their own upbringing and their own cultural outlook, and throwing them into this sort of maelstrom of an unconstructed perceptual reality, which then helped them to take much more seriously the various codes by which one does structure it, which then relate to, for example, different religions.

Now, I consider myself lucky, in the sense that I never did fall into the thinking that just psychedelics in themselves were good enough, and all you had to do was sort of blow out your mind, and that was enlightenment in itself.

I took the lesson that I think many of the people who have benefited most from that movement did, which was: "Wow, there's a lot more to the world and life; and your preconceptions determine how you perceive it and experience it. Therefore, let's look at these ancient disciplines of different religions, which teach one how to change one's given, culturally-induced concepts about how one sees reality, and modify them and improve them and come to a deeper and more true perception of life."

So I had that background both because of the physical accident that happened to me and being involved in the psychedelic scene. The rigors of the homeless mendicant's life were not that great for me, because I was very determined to attain some sort of higher awareness, changing my perception to a higher perception: a permanent one, not a temporary sort of artificially-induced one. I was outside the home of my original attitudes and looking for another home, and so I took to that very, very organically.

Coming the other way was almost as difficult, in a way—back out of that Tibetan culture and into Western culture. Having been for four or five years a mendicant, a *bikkshu*, and living in a culture where they were very much respected, and having some knowledge about those matters, and learning the languages and so on, I was used to a certain kind of consideration on the part of others as some sort of religious person. When you come back to America, into the world, you're just *you*, you know.

Lex Hixon: Well, *you* don't have to be just you. I admire you for being just you. You could have come back with your robes on and done a whole number like that.

Robert Thurman: Well, that was a temptation and some people thought it might be a good idea; in fact, they considered I was just copping out by trying to cultivate what I subsequently came later to call the "yoga of normalcy." The yoga of reconciliation of dichotomies that we see in the *Vimalakirti Sutra*, for example, where he talks about being homelessly at home in society, and not giving up your detachment and not giving up your inner renunciation, and applying that detachment to crunches and hassles and times when your emotions might get involved negatively, and yet be totally normal and don't hold yourself out by any ritual or symbolic badges of shaved heads or robes or whatever.

I got into that as a kind of yoga, but it was a rocky road, and I was unused to crossing the street. My driver's licenses had expired.

My Sanskrit teacher used to tease me. My pride used to get wounded, daily. This was very healthy, though. It helped me come to a better understanding. And I certainly would not say that I just went back to get a Ph.D. at the second round, just for the credentials. Not at all. I learned something from those people. They're very disciplined men. They're great scholars. Now I also have, luckily, my students to teach me. I'm learning in the context of having to explain things to them and deal with their questions.

When I was back at Harvard, it was possible for me not to fall into the trap that I had originally fallen into there because, in my preconception, this was just all words and all intellect, you know? It was not really going to change my life and change my experience. I was originally there as a goof-off undergraduate. I thought, "This is all meaningless," and so on. Whereas later, I could say, "Well, all this may be drudgery to learn Sanskrit grammar thoroughly and memorize all these paradigms and memorize all these Chinese characters and all this, but in all these things is the enlightenment. This is the jewel of the dharma: these words, this grammar, this grammatical structure. This is the gift of

Manjusri to human beings. It's Manjusri's sword of wisdom to cut away ignorance, and so forth. It comes through these letters and syllables and words—they're all mantras, in a way. I could keep myself from freaking out and goofing off, and I really studied, and I really learned them well. I kept a kind of non-duality to it, and it was through the Tibetan non-dual idea, in that context, that I was able to do that.

Lex Hixon: And possibly some of the discipline of the life of a bikkshu gave you a strong sense of inner discipline that could be applied to academic studies and concentration of mind.

Robert Thurman: But the level of hectic energy in the bikkshu framework is not as much, and you tend to relax, and you don't overstress yourself to learn. Sometimes academic learning patterns are too intense and your mind, your brain goes cranking on. The monastic form of learning is usually a little more relaxed and balanced.

Lex Hixon: The American Institute of Buddhist Studies is integrating [Buddhism] into Western patterns of academic studies, but how much are these other things available? For instance, the quieter learning pace of the monastic life, and the practice of Tantric visualizations and meditations? Are those things available?

Robert Thurman: Yes. We're not trying to preempt the rule of the monastic institutions or the meditation centers. The retreat centers still would be required, always. But the point is that there should not be such a tremendous dichotomy. The time that one puts into integrating what one understands and learns, for example, through a retreat, more quiet digesting of what one has learned, should be respected and considered part of one's education.

If meditation is over-simplistically understood as mere quietist mental tranquilization or mere one-pointedness, not focused on anything, mind-emptying, then the benefit can be somewhat limited, and one does not find ways of transforming one's brain patterns. One simply temporarily suppresses the manifestations of those patterns. Then, when one goes back out of the meditation session or the retreat session, one is involved right away again in the confusions of the world, with no better insight or leverage over the actual structured matter of the world. Traditionally, in Buddhist teaching, they talk of *shamatha* as that one-pointed type of meditation and *vipassana* as the analytic, conceptual, critical, liberating of the conceptual mind. Those two must go together.

We're hoping to accelerate, catalyze this integration process between the two types of institutions. We don't really want to replace either. Both are good. We'd just like to develop their coordination better.

Lex Hixon: You said that you were motivated to enter this rigorous, traditional spiritual life in order to reach a spiritual level of perception, quite apart from [the use of] psychedelic substances and all that. To what extent did you achieve that in the course of your rather brief traditional monastic career of four or five years? Do you feel that when you came back you had been given the gift of the tradition, of the real spiritual perception, which was qualitatively different from your previous way of seeing the world?

Robert Thurman: Yeah, I think so. I don't claim enlightenment by any means or any final stage of it. There are stages of enlightenment that are accessible to all of us. That is one of the nice things about the Buddhist tradition: It is very universalistic, Mahayana in particular, and it is anti-authoritarian.

There is a notion that the student should actually know it for him- or herself, and a teacher is therefore not implanting some knowledge in there. The teacher is not sort of lending a little share of his own great knowledge. In the authoritarian mode, you have the idea that things are degenerating, and the teacher is so great, and the student can maybe catch a tiny reflection. Whereas in the Buddhist context, especially the Mahayana, there is the idea that the teacher is a *Kalyana Mitra*, a spiritual friend. The word used is "*mitra*," meaning friend, not guru. In Mahayana, the main mode of relationship is that of a friend who inspires you to develop in your own real inner wisdom.

I remember Geshe Wangyal was very much like that. He always used to say, "Oh, I know nothing. I'm just an ignorant old man. I've read all these different books though, and I think I've had some experience in life, and perhaps if you learn them and I can help you learn them, then you'll get a better idea, probably much better than me."

I would come back from meditating or thinking on something he taught me, I'd be all sort of vibrating with it and feeling thrilled about it, and think that it was the greatest, and I would say, "Oh, you are a great guru." And he would say, "What, are you putting me on? Who are you? What are you telling me? Guru? You know, I'm just an old man who likes these books. If you get something out of it, that's great, but don't give me this stuff about being a guru. As much as I may be nice to you, then I've been a guru. As much as you behave in your life and you help other people, then maybe I have taught you something. So don't make me into a big guru and be devotional to me."

He would never let me do it. And at the time, I used to be frustrated, because I was young and [looking for a] father figure, mother figure, authority figure I wanted to fasten upon him. He pulled that rug out from me. He said, "Oh, I'm just your friend, just an old man who has something to show you."

So you're forced to somehow take the responsibility of representing the tradition yourself. And you can't just think, "Well, I have a badge now, I have a robe, and this or that person I officially studied with, and that's it." But rather, inasmuch as I control my anger in this situation, I'm a little better in that situation, or I do something useful to someone in another situation, then I am representing the tradition of love and compassion, and that's showing some wisdom. So I try to do that. I don't make any claim to having any exalted state, but rather at least I do, however, avow my intent to attempt to keep integrating these things and keep trying to grow.

The nice thing about being a teacher in the Western academic tradition is that you can continue your own study as you teach. In the process of teaching, you learn a great deal more by having to explain things to younger minds and answer their questions.

Lex Hixon: I had a good experience teaching at the New School, where the classes would consist not only of undergraduates, but people of all ages. Do you have that at Amherst?

Robert Thurman: Absolutely. We are small but we do feel that part of American education in general, irrespective of the enlightenment issue, [is] making liberal education into a lifelong process. But the problem is that in most academic administrations, the bureaucrats who run those things haven't quite overcome this kind of ivory-tower notion {[or] gotten into the idea of doing a public service for the community.

And yet the public really needs this. One of the reasons for some of the more authoritarian groups that can allow something like the terrible Jonestown happening and other things of that kind is that people need a sense of growth and a sense that they are cultivating themselves and developing later in life, which, if not fulfilled by the responsible institutions of the society, will be exploited by irresponsible persons.

We want to bring enlightenment studies into the mainstream of the culture by mounting them, as it were, in the educational institutions under controls of liberal education. Our curriculum in general is structured on three lines: Asian studies, then Buddhist studies, and then what we call "enlightenment studies." Now, the middle one, Buddhist studies, involves translating the Tibetan canons, and all of the magnificent psychological and philosophical and technical works that exist in all those languages, of which only two percent has been translated into English. But we are more than happy to sponsor and organize the teaching of Asian histories, world history, other religious traditions, their different theistic beliefs, devotional cults, their monastic organizations. We'd like to become an umbrella of all the different religious teachings, to be taught in that liberal context.

Lex Hixon: And when spirituality is integrated well with an educational movement, it will penetrate the culture in a healthy, organic way that individual movements and cults just never will be able to achieve.

Robert Thurman: We feel that the founding fathers of this country were *bodhisattvas* with this kind of insight that we try to embody. By making the separation of church and state, having experienced the domination of different orthodoxies in Europe, which then persecuted people of other faiths and persuasions, the founding fathers realized that the main thing was to allow all religions to flourish, but not to allow any one of them to dominate the political life of the country, because then there would inevitably be this orthodox imposition and then some sort of inquisition.

I think if we stick to that guideline, we can very clearly keep this whole cult phenomenon sorted out in the sense that we have to tolerate and support the freedom to practice whatever kind of practices people want to practice. But we should draw the line when they try to assume political power, I think.

Lex Hixon: Our wanting to be free from that kind of persecution and, as you say the founding fathers' wanting to have a kind of religious freedom here, makes American society open to become a Buddhist culture, a Hindu culture, a Jewish culture, as well as a Christian culture. For instance, why is New York City perhaps the largest Jewish community in the world? Why do some of these great lamas and other teachers choose the United States to come to? It's not simply because of the affluence. It's deeper than that. It's precisely this spiritual openness that is not just an attitude of mind, but is actually written into law and is part of the structure of our culture.

Robert Thurman: It's a very, very precious thing, really, as we see in those nations where there is no religious freedom.

Lex Hixon: So there's a great possibility here in the United States, and we have to struggle very fiercely to maintain the freedoms that are guaranteed here.

Robert Thurman: Absolutely.

Lex Hixon: But I think it's a rich ground for a Buddha field here.

Robert Thurman: It definitely is. It's a tremendous challenge too, as Ben Franklin said outside Independence Hall. The crowd was waiting when he came out after the Constitutional Assembly, and they said, "How did it go? What's the news?" And he said, "Well, we've developed a system here which guarantees your liberty. Now let's see how long you can keep it." So I feel we're still trying to answer that challenge—we should never rest complacent.

Swami Muktananda
November 3, 1974

Swami Muktananda was born Krishna Rau in 1908 in Karnataka State, India. At age 15, he met Bhagavan Nityananda. He traveled through India on foot and studied for 20 years before meeting Nityananda again and receiving *shaktipat* initiation from him. In 1956 Nityananda gave him land near Mumbai, where Swami Muktananda built an ashram. He led the first Shaktipat Intensive in 1974 in Aspen, Colorado, founded the Siddha Yoga Ashram in Oakland, California in 1975, and the Shree Muktananda Ashram (originally named Shree Nityananda Ashram) in upstate New York in 1979. He traveled extensively and wrote many books, including his spiritual autobiography, *Play of Consciousness* (1978). He died in 1982, having established hundreds of ashrams and meditation centers around the world.

Lex Hixon: Swami Muktananda was written about in *Time* magazine with a certain amount of respect and interest. He probably is one of the most important Eastern teachers around today. I did this interview through a translator a week or two ago up in the Catskills in South Fallsburg, where Swami Mutkananda has been presiding for the summer; he has very, very graciously been inviting everyone to come visit, and sharing his energy with everyone.

Perhaps the people in South Fallsburg are listening now, and perhaps Baba himself is listening. It's a very special day today in Hindu tradition, Devali, the day of Lakshmi, the goddess of fortune and abundance and we pray to her for spiritual abundance. Last night was Kali Puja, and I was up all night making offerings to the Divine Mother in her blissful form as Goddess Kali. So it's a very potent time.

Do call your friends now who may be interested in Muktananda and who may be interested in the direct transmission of spirituality. As you know, this radio program is a sort of empirical experiment on how spiritual energy itself can be transmitted over the airwaves. Sometimes we have guests who are very highly advanced spiritually and have a great gift of transmitting spiritual energy, and Muktananda is definitely one of these people. So I wouldn't be at all surprised if many of you receive a direct transmission of spiritual energy through hearing his voice. His voice is a very intimate part of his being, so it carries a great deal of Shakti or divine energy. So it's not really necessary to see him—just to hear him. In this particular interview, he was definitely transmitting. Something opened up between him and me, and there was a wonderful transmission that occurred. So the next words you hear will be those of Swami Muktananda.

Baba, we're reminded again and again that life is impermanent, and I want to know what people should do when eventually you leave your body.

Swami Muktananda: It's not that life is completely impermanent. We can make it permanent because life itself is so beautiful. It can be permanent, bewitching; it can be anything that we want it to be. God gave birth to this creation from his own being. He gave birth to this creation as he was, not different from himself. God is very disciplined, he is very regular, not for one second does he change, he makes every second come at the right time. So how come we're not like that? Therefore, we should think about that very deeply.

Lex Hixon: When a person dies, the impermanent parts of their being must disappear, leaving something permanent. What is it that really remains after physical death?

Swami Muktananda: That is the truth, that is the self, that is God, that is consciousness or *Shakti*, energy. Through that, we're able to perform all actions. The supreme truth never changes. It always remains the same. It is not dimmed by impurity or purity or anything else. And through that consciousness, we are able to perform actions. We always say "I, I, I," but we're not aware of that "I." When we say "I," we don't know what that "I" is. Do we call some parts of the body "I"? The *prana* helps the body to function. Do we call that prana "I"? The self of the universe, God, exists inside this body. He makes this universe work, so do we call that "I"? Are we aware of which "I" is I?

Lex Hixon: So that "I" is not really a personal being. That I is not either Lex or Baba Muktananda.

Swami Muktananda: That "I" is the supreme truth. Neither is that "I" Muktananda or President Carter or the Pope. That "I" is the supreme truth, consciousness, and that "I" is, in fact, everything. From this "I," many worlds arise and subside. From one seed, many trees; from many trees, many seeds. And even if the trees no longer exist, the seed is still there. From that seed, many more trees. So the seed is the "I." It is the supreme truth, consciousness. It is the same for everybody, it exists for everybody, it belongs to everybody. That consciousness exists within itself in the same way, in the same measure. Also, it exists in everybody, in Nityananda, my guru, and also in Jesus.

Lex Hixon: So when this form of Muktananda passes away, that same supreme "I" will remain exactly as it is now?

Swami Muktananda: Yes, it will remain the same even if the body leaves. The Supreme "I" does not leave. The body leaves and comes, but that is always there. I can explain this to you in very simple words. For example, the inner space of this room is there. Now, whether the walls are there or not, the space will always be there. That is permanent, so that is the truth. People call the same thing God. You call it God, we call it Rama, somebody else calls it Allah—it's the same thing.

Lex Hixon: But there seems to be a special manifestation, for instance, through Baba. The supreme "I" is not as clearly manifested through other people. What is that particular stream of manifestation that we call Baba Muktananda?

Swami Muktananda: It's not like that. The inner truth that's inside me also exists inside you and everybody else. There isn't the slightest difference. The only difference is that I have turned within and I have perceived it, I have made that reveal itself to me. However, you don't turn within and you don't see it because you always want to be outside. If you turn within yourself, then the stream will flow out of your body too, just as it does with me. Truly speaking, in God's creation there is no disparity, there is only one quality. For example, from one factory, the same objects are manufactured. They're all the same. In the same way, everything is the same in God's factory, in the Lord's factory.

Lex Hixon: But still there appears to be some difference because people find their spiritual consciousness awakened being in the presence of Baba, and not being in the presence of even some other spiritual teachers.

Swami Muktananda: There may be such difference as of now. However, if everybody were to become like me, then the difference would vanish.

Lex Hixon: What would be left?

Swami Muktananda: Only the supreme truth.

Lex Hixon: Still manifested as the world or formless?

Swami Muktananda: Even in the form of the world, the truth exists. The world is not different from the truth. From water [comes] ice, and the ice becomes water again. In the same way, the world comes out of the supreme truth and it exists in the world, so the world belongs to the supreme truth. So this world comes out of the supreme truth. For this reason, Shaivism says the world is the play of consciousness. The first aphorism in Shaivism is also the very statement of the Lord: "The self is consciousness, the world is consciousness."

Lex Hixon: Baba, you have opened the door to pure consciousness for those who love you. Will that door stay open through you for the next 100, 200 years?

Swami Muktananda: It will always remain open because this lineage will never be broken. For example, Baba Nityananda, my guru, gave me his work to do. So when I leave this world, I will have to make somebody else responsible for this. When Nixon left, Ford came in. When Ford left, Carter came in.

Lex Hixon: Have you anyone in mind for this heavy burden?

Swami Muktananda: Somebody will pop up from somewhere.

Lex Hixon: Do you think it will be focused on one person or will it be several people?

Swami Muktananda: One. However, he will need many other people's help. Look at me, I do a lot of work. However, I have so many people with me to help me. Does President Carter do all the work himself? No, he has a lot of people's aid. However, the president is one.

Lex Hixon: It seems that people who have been close to you have received your grace to the point where they can transmit it to some extent to other people, and I wanted to say we're grateful for that. Thousands upon thousands of these people have popped up in this country.

Swami Muktananda: Yes, many people are working in the same line and the power is working in everybody. And many in the future will also do the work, so this mission will continue to increase. Many will do the work.

Lex Hixon: In your autobiography, we read your marvelous experiences, where you feel that your true being is permeating everything on all planes, and so I assume that someday when this form of Baba Muktananda disappears, your special presence will always be felt on all planes of being.

Swami Muktananda: Yes, that will remain on all planes. That will continue to do the work. My Baba, my guru, is still doing the work. Even if you put his photo somewhere, his photo also works. And people should not feel awkward about this. What place exists without consciousness? That consciousness is in the photo, too.

Lex Hixon: When you say your guru, Baba Nityananda, you don't mean anything other than the supreme "I," or is there something particular about him?

Swami Muktananda: The same thing, the supreme truth, Nityananda. In Nityananda, too, the same supreme truth existed and the same supreme truth became Nityananda.

Lex Hixon: Can we say the same thing about Jesus, Rama, and other great teachers, great beings—that they really are nothing more than supreme truth, or are there different lineages extending from these different teachers?

Swami Muktananda: The self is the same in all of them. However, their mission may be different. For example, Krishna. The people who lived in his time said that he was the incarnation of the supreme truth. He was never defeated by the wicked people or the terrible people. So a great being or the supreme truth is that which is never defeated by anybody and which never fails. So from the point of view of the self, everyone is the same.

Lex Hixon: You spoke about the fact that different teachers could have different missions. Baba, can you say something about what your mission is in this life?

Swami Muktananda: My mission is not any particular religion. This is the spiritual revolution. My teaching is: Look within, understand yourself, perceive yourself, attain your own self. In my teaching, to learn this, you don't have to depend on external things. I don't say that somebody is up there living and that one day He will come down to help you. However, I don't say deny the existence of somebody up there. But I say He is inside you too in the same measure, so look within and attain Him right inside yourself. I don't give much importance to any class or caste or any particular religion or anything else like that. It doesn't matter if you're black, white, yellow, or red because all colors and all classes have come from God, and for this reason I don't like to make any distinction. But my purpose is to say the supreme truth exists inside everybody, so look within and perceive that and attain that.

Lex Hixon: But just by looking within, no one will achieve anything if they don't have your grace.

Swami Muktananda: It's true that you need grace also. When I tell you, "Look within, enter inside," that means that grace follows with these words.

Lex Hixon: So it's not like the ordinary words, "Look within," but somehow when Baba says, "Look within," it contains the actual Shakti or energy that makes it possible.

Swami Muktananda: You're absolutely right, both the grace and Shakti follow those words. The Shakti, the energy of the self is so great.

Lex Hixon: Well, [there] may be thousands of people listening to this broadcast—Baba, please tell them to look within and transmit that Shakti right now to them.

Swami Muktananda: Not only to the thousands, but I want to tell the entire world to give up your notions of different castes, different classes, different sects, different religions, stop living only outside. Enter within, look within, and see what you perceive inside.

The reason you perceive differences from one society to another, from one caste to another, from one country to another is because you only look outside. However, if you turn within, and attain the inner self, then you'll see the same inner self in all countries, in all individuals, and in all places, and … you will experience the same divine bliss in all of these.

If everyone were to look within and perceive the inner self, then nobody would have to make weapons. For example, the countries wouldn't have to make weapons; they wouldn't have to have hatred, hostility towards one another. They wouldn't have to plant different things in the air and just wander and wander, trying to get to this country and that country. God has created this world for his own pleasure, and he created this wealth for his own joy. We use this wealth to make poisonous ammunitions. We don't use that wealth for our own good and for our own pleasure.

Lex Hixon: This "looking outside"—even the ignorance of human beings must be part of God's play, too?

Swami Muktananda: It's not God's play. It's the result of forgetting God.

Lex Hixon: But if everything is the play of consciousness, how can one forget? How can consciousness forget itself?

Swami Muktananda: It's not that consciousness has forgotten itself. However, we have made it so that we have kept [our] consciousness [on] other than ourselves. For example, a king was asleep, dreaming that he has become a beggar, and weeps and wails. We are in the same predicament.

Lex Hixon: There are no tendencies or *samskaras* [habitual patternings] in pure consciousness, so how can consciousness have this dream of being limited persons?

Swami Muktananda: There is no limitation in consciousness. It's our own samskaras from the past that make us feel that we are contracted. Through these samskaras we become contracted and once we have the right understanding, once again we expand. Therefore, a person should expand himself.

Lex Hixon: Doesn't some of the highest Vedantic teaching imply that there is ultimately no expansion or contraction?

Swami Muktananda: It is very true. Once you attain that ultimate understanding then you know that everything is expansion and the pervasion of consciousness. Therefore, Shaivism says, "The world is the sport of consciousness."

Lex Hixon: So when you, Baba, look at the seekers of truth who come here and see them expanding and contracting in their own eyes, you really ultimately don't see anything but the play of consciousness. No expansion, no contraction.

Swami Muktananda: From my point of view, from my vision, they have no contractions, but they think that they're contracting. For example, take an ornament to a jeweler, a goldsmith. He looks only at the gold. He does not look at the ornament's different shape and size. However, if a customer goes there, he looks at the ornament; he does not look only at the gold.

Lex Hixon: Baba, thank you for sharing our limited nightmares and dreams with us even though you remain beyond the dream state.

Swami Muktananda: It isn't like that for me because, from your viewpoint, you're dreaming, but from my viewpoint, you're not. You are the truth. You watch your own dream, but I don't watch your dream. I see you as my own self.

Lex Hixon: So from Baba's point of view, there really are no dreams. There are no limitations, no individuals apart from pure consciousness.

Swami Muktananda: Only the play of consciousness. Only the drama, only the dance of consciousness. For example, an ordinary drama. How does a producer look at the drama—isn't it a mere play for him? I am very pleased with your interview because you asked the exact questions that should have been asked in an exact interview. Many reporters have come to me, many television interviewers and radio interviewers, and they all bring a big list of questions. Only you ask questions without papers. I really want to thank you with all my heart. You have asked questions without papers so you are the right person to interview anybody and everybody. Even if they have to ask very few questions the journalists bring so many papers, and even if they have to give a small lecture, a small talk, they have pen and paper.

Lex Hixon: Baba, the questions come from you as well as the answers.

Swami Muktananda: That must be right. They must come from the same place. In my entire tour, you are the only one who has come to me and asked questions without the papers. And you ask the right questions. Otherwise, people ask questions about politics, Jim Jones, and robbing the bank. They don't ask questions of the people they should; [instead] they come and ask them of a *sadhu*, a holy man. Otherwise, they forget about their own poverty and they think about the poverty of other countries.

Lex Hixon: You always mention the play, the dance of consciousness. Why does it play, why doesn't it stay still?

Swami Muktananda: Even when it is playing, its stillness is not disturbed. In the ocean so many waves leap up and down, up and down. Although that happens, the profundity is not disturbed. The ocean remains as profound as it ever was.

Lex Hixon: So Shakti is the playful aspect and Shiva is the still aspect?

Swami Muktananda: Yes, Supreme Shiva always remains supremely serene, quiet and still, and Shakti that vibrates from him does all the play.

Lex Hixon: The communion of Shiva and Shakti. Does that mean what you indicated before—that the play and stillness exist exactly at the same time and are actually synonymous?

Swami Muktananda: Even though the play takes place, the stillness is not disturbed. For example, I'm sitting here very quietly without moving. I move my hands, making gestures, but the stillness is not disturbed, it is still there. In the same way, while the play goes on, the stillness of the supreme truth is not disturbed. It's the stillness of understanding.

Lex Hixon: Are some people more drawn to the supreme stillness and others drawn to the play?

Swami Muktananda: Most of the people are drawn to the play, and the reason for this is that they don't have the understanding of the truth.

Lex Hixon: Baba, please bless us that we can be drawn to the stillness and receive *Shivapat* [Shiva energy], not only *Shaktipat* [Shakti energy].

Swami Muktananda: From all the questions that you have asked, I understand that you have the understanding and belief of Shiva to an extent.

Lex Hixon: Please bless us that it may increase and deepen.

Swami Muktananda: It will keep increasing and increasing and increasing. It will keep increasing until the state of Shiva, and once you reach that state, it will stop there. If people were to hear this much, it would be enough. I give this message to everybody, not to a particular society or caste. My message is:

Meditate on your own self, understand your own self, attain your own self. The supreme truth dwells within you as you. In infinite forms, he pervades everywhere. However, he's the one, no division in him. However, we categorize him, so we should stop categorizing him and we should see him as one.

Whatever role you have taken upon yourself to play, play it with great responsibility and very well. Take care of your family life with great respect and with love. Take care of your children. No matter what work you're doing, have the moral standard before you all the time and have God before you. Don't think that you are different, your reaction is different, and God is different from you. Therefore, see the entire universe. Although it is infinite and manifold, it is one. Attain this awareness. With great respect and love, I welcome you all with my heart. The same supreme truth dwells in everybody.

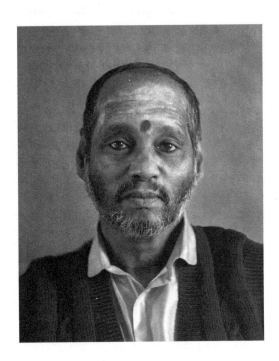

Swami Satchidananda
March 16, 1975

Swami Satchidananda was born as Ramaswamy in 1914 in India. As a child, he denounced the caste system and showed spiritual tendencies. He studied agriculture at the agricultural college in Coimbatore. After losing his wife, he immersed himself in spiritual practices with Sri Ramana Maharishi, among other luminaries. In Rishikesh, he met his guru, Sri Swami Sivananda, who later sent him to serve in Sri Lanka, where filmmaker Conrad Rooks met him and invited him to the West. Pop artist Peter Max hosted Swami Satchidananda in New York in 1966, and helped convince him to stay in the United States. In 1969, after founding the first Integral Yoga center in New York, and as Integral Yoga centers were being established globally, Swami Satchidinanda opened the Woodstock music festival with a talk followed by meditative chanting. In 1979, he founded Integral Yoga's headquarters at Satchidananda Ashram –Yogaville in Virginia; he built the Light Of Truth Universal Shrine (LOTUS) to world peace there in 1986. As a humanitarian and pioneer of interfaith dialogue, Swami Satchidananda received many honors and awards, including the Juliet Hollister Award, the U Thant Peace Award and, posthumously, the James Parks Morton Interfaith Award. He died in 2002.

Swami Satchidananda: Don't forsake your peace, even for the sake of the whole world. Peace is very important. If you lose your peace, even if you are going to get the whole world for yourself, you are not going to enjoy it. It's something like a man wanting to buy a painting and the price he paid is his own eyes. He paid his eyes as the price, and he bought the painting—how is he going to appreciate it?

Likewise, you pay your peace as a price and you get the whole world. What are you going to do with that? Don't pawn your peace for anything. If you are contented, if you are peaceful, everybody will recognize that peace in you. And they will love to be with you. Name, fame, success, friends—everything will come to you.

So practice what is the God in us. Peace in us is the God in us. Seek ye that kingdom first. And everything else will be added unto it. It is exactly the same saying that you see in the Bible that is given in the form of a proverb. Just be contented! Don't run after things!

Lex Hixon: Thank you, Swami. There is something that I am curious about, Swami, Could you tell us, what is "Satchidananda"?

Swami Satchidananda: That's a very good question! Because many people think that there is a person by the name Satchidananda, about five feet, 11 inches tall, long beard, and this and that. No! What you see is a composition of the elements. You don't see the *satchidananda*. But you can experience it. It's a combination of three words: *sat*, *chit*, and *ananda*. *Sat* means existence, or the truth, the one that always is. *Chit* is the expression of that existence. And *ananda* is the bliss that you get out of it. So existence, knowledge, and bliss is what we mean by satchidananda. It could be compared with the Holy Trinity. The father exists always and he expresses himself as the son. So through the son, you know the father. If he doesn't express himself, you can't know the father.

So, satchidananda—when you know [your life as] that, you get the bliss of it. It is everywhere, in everything. That is the common name for everything. See, we are all common in satchidananda.

I'm not talking about only human beings. Everything, even dust is satchidananda. There it is, it expresses as dust and it brings some kind of joy. So everything is satchidananda. If you see everything as satchidananda, you have the vision of spirit. But on the worldly level, we are [still] the name and form.

If somebody asked you, who are you, you just don't say, "I am satchidananada." The answer is, "Oh, I am Jacob. I am a boy." See? So you have a name and a form, a masculine form, and a name, Jacob. But, unfortunately, the masculine form and the name will go away again. But satchidananda will remain, even when you get into powder form.

So the name and form change constantly. When you were born, you were called a baby. Then you grow into a young boy, then a teenager, then a student. Then probably later on, you become a boyfriend. And then after some time you become a hubby. You get all the different names. And after hubby, you become a father, then a grandpa and a great-grandpa, and an old, old man, and, ultimately, you become a dead body.

The common element [in all these changes] is satchidananda, but it expresses itself on the worldly level with different names and forms. That is what you see. So, if you have the proper eyes, you use the name and form for your convenience, but you will also go deep into the satchidananda and see the oneness in everybody.

Lex Hixon: Why does the satchidananda express itself in name and form?

Swami Satchidananda: Well, if everything is going to be just satchidananda, without a name and form, don't you think the whole world will be boring? We are all the same. You just take a big piece of wood, maybe you even chip it into small pieces. But there's no fun, there's no game. Only when you carve it into a king, a queen, a pawn, a knight, a castle, and a bishop, then you have a nice game of chess.

Lex Hixon: But why would satchidananda want to play games?

Swami Satchidananda: Satchidananda must have been simply satchidananda for a long time and got bored, and he just wanted to play a game, so he multiplied himself. That's why, even the Bible said, "In the beginning there was only God, nothing but God." Probably God got bored, so he said, "Come on, let me multiply myself. Let me separate myself into different names and forms, and let's just have fun." So it's the Lord's play. It's fun.

Lex Hixon: Do you think you'll ever get sick of this game?

Swami Satchidananda: Well, probably. Sometimes we get tired of it if we don't play the game well. If we make a serious thing of defeat, then we get tired of it. Otherwise, we always enjoy the game. See, we do! People play different games. There's no winner or loser. At the end of the game, they shake hands with each other, and they go have coffee together. But in the worldly game, we don't play that well. We take it seriously, and we fight. An enemy remains an enemy, an opponent remains an opponent.

Lex Hixon: Is there any reason to wish to be liberated from this game?

Swami Satchidananda: The only time will be when you get tired of it. When you really feel caught in it, then you sit back and think, "Why did I get caught? Ah, I forgot. That is all just for our enjoyment. And ultimately we are all one. We just took different names and forms to play the game. I forgot the common spirit behind everything. I gave too much importance to the differences, which is the name and form, so now I am in a terrible state. So let me go down to the deep root of it."

That is when you become a religious person. Because, what is religion? You are trying to bind yourself back to the original. The word "religion" [comes from the Latin verb *ligare*, which] means "to go back" or "to bind back." Just for the sake of fun, you had some names and forms, but you forgot the satchidananda because it is not always there visibly. So you just catch the superficial things. Then when you are tired of it, when you try to go back, you are called a religious person. You are going back. You are trying to get reunion with your original self.

Lex Hixon: You mentioned that satchidananda is sort of like the Christian Trinity. But Christians regard the Trinity as having a personhood apart from the world. Is there anything personal about satchidananda?

Swami Satchidananda: God is not personal. God is unlimited. He is infinite. Everything that is infinite cannot be a person. Then you limit it. You just name it, you give a form to it, and then you miss the spirit of it. In Hinduism, it clearly says, "He is nameless and formless." Because we are limited, our thinking is finite. We cannot understand something infinite. So for our convenience's sake, we bring that infinite one to the finite state.

What if you wanted to bring a little sea to your house? How will you bring it? The sea is infinite. If you want to bring it to your home, you will have to just bring it in a bucket. So the bucket limits the sea and you say, "Hey, I have a bucketful of sea." Your sea becomes a bucket full of sea. It's a bucket of sea; it's no more the real sea. You have limited it.

So due to our own limitations, we limit. Each mind has its own capacity and limitation. According to each mind, you perceive God in your own way. As there are so many minds, you see so many perceptions of God. But when we forget that originally God is nameless and formless, and because of our limitations, we limit it, we forget the truth and then we fight. We say, "My God is the real God." Then you say the same thing to me. And for God's sake, there is no ending to the quarrel. That is why even in the name of God, we see so many fights, because we lost the original truth.

Lex Hixon: Talking about going to the sea with buckets, is there any way to bring the sea back to your house without using a bucket?

Swami Satchidananda: You cannot bring the sea into the house. You can get into the sea and become the sea. Then you are in the sea, not as a separate you, but as the sea.

I get lost in the sea. I am no more separate. It is something like a drop [of water] wanting to know the depth of the sea. As long as it's outside the sea as a drop it can never fathom the sea. And if it jumps into the sea to see the depth it loses itself as a drop. It's no more a drop, but it has understood the depth of the sea by becoming the sea. We cannot understand something by staying outside as a different entity. The real way to know something is to become it.

That's why there is a very simple proverb in India, a Tamil proverb. The meaning of it is, "A snake will know the snake's leg." That means, only a snake will know how the other snake crawls. We cannot. We can theorize. But if you want to really know how a snake could crawl, you have to become a snake.

That's why God knows God. A guru knows a guru. A thief knows a thief. It takes a thief to catch a thief; in the same way, it takes a God to catch a God. If you are something different, there is no real understanding possible. You can get an idea. And that is the reason why the Bible says, "Who can see God? Blessed are the pure in heart. They shall see God." Because God is pure, only when you become that purity will you know God. So to know God is to become God.

Lex Hixon: But even if one has the best intentions and wakes up in the morning and says, "I'm going to know God today," one finds it very difficult.

Swami Satchidananda: That's it. You are trying to know [the unlimited] with your limited mind. See? It's not within the grasp of the mind. You have to understand it, know it without the help of the mind. Mind has its limitations. I must rise above my mind. Or at least I must use a clean and pure mind, which is almost similar to the God in you.

And you should also listen with the same clarity. Then we understand each other. So the best way to know ourselves is to keep our mind clean and crystal clear. That's the only way. We don't need to worry about God at all. God is there always within, without, everywhere. It will just shine by itself, if we could clean the mind. Something like, if you keep cleaning the surface of a wall—polish it—all of a sudden you get the reflection.

Lex Hixon: Are there techniques to polish the mind? Or is it just by this kind of thinking itself that the mind polishes itself?

Swami Satchidananda: The direct way is just to analyze. But not everyone is clever in doing that, so they have to slowly remove themselves from the binding definitions to other definitions, which will not ultimately bind them.

So, instead of doing the wrong, undesirable thing, you do something right. You do some holy practices like your mantra, your *japa*, your prayers. But the truth is truth. You cannot even depend on your mantra and prayer. Then you are still not independent. You are not free. If you want to be free, you have to one day completely free yourself from the gurus, from yoga practices, from everything. Just be alone. Be free. The scriptures talk about it clearly. By renouncing everything you are going to achieve God or the immortal principle in you.

Everything includes all your practices. But until we come to that level we still have to have some hold somewhere. That's the reason why you do something useful for people. So from bad to good, from good to something neutral—that's the process. Because, ultimately, God is neutral.

What is the core of God? The very central part of the word God, G-O-D? The center of God is O. What does O stand for? It could be a completeness, or it could be a zero. So God is a zero. God, have mercy on me. Sometimes I feel that I am insulting Him or something. He knows I am telling the truth because He is neutral to everything. God is that big O. O is either full or empty or both extremes. He is complete—He is nothing.

Lex Hixon: What if someone heard your talk and was so impressed by this that they decided that they wouldn't engage in any spiritual practices at all, but they would just go right to the zero?

Swami Satchidananda: Fine, if they can do that, fine. If they can go right to the zero, they are immediately enlightened. I hope there will be a thousand people, at least, like that. If they become zero, what happens? They become completely neutral and it's the neutral people that are going to be very useful for everybody because they are not taking sides.

Take, for example, a judge. He should be completely neutral. A politician should be completely neutral. Anybody who wants to serve the world should be completely neutral. He cannot be prejudiced by anything. He cannot have anything as his own because if I say, "My country is India," then I look at America as something different. I'm limited to my country, and I see that's your country, that's my country.

If I am neutral, everything is mine and nothing is mine. Then I serve everybody equally. I'm not prejudiced. I don't see one man as different from the other man. I don't have a friend or a foe. God is like that. God never distinguishes between people. He serves. He blesses both the thief and the policeman. Otherwise, why should the God allow the thief to get away with that thing? But the time will come when the policeman will catch the thief. God remains neutral. He blesses everybody. He hates nobody. That kind of neutrality is very, very important. To judge people, to weigh people, and to serve them equally, like a judge. Where do you have justice? In the balance, is it not? The symbol of justice is a scale. In very many courts we see that. What is it? He is a balanced man. He never swings to the defendant's side or the offender's side. He is neutral, impartial. God is like that.

Lex Hixon: We've been talking on a high plane. Can you give us a sense of some of the practices that one might adopt in this spirit?

Swami Satchidananda: We should know first what ultimately is going to happen. We have to renounce everything and be completely neutral. But when we cannot do it right away, then what is the next alternative? That means we will have some practices. And that is where there are many names with the same aim; names such as prayer, meditation, mantra, japa, chanting, and doing everything as service to humanity, which we call karma yoga.

Karma yoga is just serving humanity, serving everybody— the path of service. And Bhakti yoga is the devotional path. You use your devotional aspect and perform services, puja or worship, pray, repeat holy names, praise God. This is very good.

Lex Hixon: Thank you, Swami, for taking us to a high plane and then delivering us safely back to earth with the reminder of the spiritual value of service to our fellow beings and praising God.

Swami Satchidananda in Paris, 1966.

Tarthang Tulku
September 21, 1975

Tarthang Tulku, a Tibetan lama in the Nyingma tradition, was born in eastern Tibet in 1935. As a young man, he received extensive formal Dharma training from many important teachers, including his root guru Jamyang Khyentse Chokyi Lodro. He left Tibet in 1958 and taught for several years at Sanskrit University in Varanasi, India, where he started a Tibetan printing press. In 1969, he relocated to Berkeley, California, with his wife, the poet Nazli Nour, and established the Tibetan Nyingma Meditation Center, Dharma Publishing, the Tibetan Nyingma Institute, and the Tibetan Aid Project. Today the center includes over 20 nonprofit organizations worldwide, and there are Tibetan Nyingma Institute satellite branches in the Netherlands, Germany, and Brazil. In 1989, Tarthang Tulku founded the World Peace Ceremony in India, where, over the last 27 years, he has distributed more than 4 million Dharma books, free of charge, to the Tibetan diaspora. He has also restored monasteries and holy places in Tibet and India, and created the Odiyan Retreat Center in Northern California, a temple complex on more than 1,000 acres. He has written and edited over 100 books for Westerners, including *Gesture of Balance, Knowledge of Freedom,* and *Revelations of Mind.*

Lex Hixon: We're here with Tarthang Tulku Rinpoche, who has his main center in Berkeley, California. Rinpoche is in the city for a couple of weeks and is holding seminars and meeting with people, possibly with the idea of starting a Nyingma center here in New York.

Rinpoche, I notice here in the bulletin for the Nyingma Institute that there are three meditation courses that are taught by you. Could you talk a little bit about each one? The first is the introduction to Nyingma meditation. Can you give us some samples of the type of thing you would do in that course?

Tarthang Tulku: Yes. First of all, a few words about Nyingma: The word *nyingma* literally means "the ancient one." Before the eighth century there wasn't any formally established Buddhism in Tibet. [With] the arrival of Padmasambhava, followed by many great scholars, the entire Buddhist canon, about 108 volumes of the Buddha's doctrine, was translated. This coming together began to be called Nyingma.

But Nyingma, if you examine it carefully, is not necessarily a sect or school. It is the original *sangha* groups who hold and continue the teachings of Lord Buddha and Padmasambhava. That is the background of Nyingma. I may say it this way: Nyingma is not really sectarian. Nyingma wasn't politically involved through the whole history of Tibet. There were not big, huge thousands of monasteries, but still there were always small groups available.

Lex Hixon: Rinpoche, you are married and you belong to that tradition of married lamas, which is particularly prevalent in the Nyingma lineage.

Tarthang Tulku: That's right. Today you can find that is the case in half of the monasteries. According to the Nyingma tradition, married lamas are very acceptable. Other schools today are very much influenced by the Theravada Vinaya system. It is very important that first you be celibate; otherwise, you have no chance to become enlightened. But the Nyingmas can accept life as a married householder or as a celibate. If you practice or study, your chance to reach enlightenment is equal. There are no differences.

Lex Hixon: This idea seems to be particularly suitable for America. Certainly, there will be people who want to lead the celibate life, the monastic life, but I don't think they should be considered more advanced or more privileged.

Tarthang Tulku: That's very true.

Lex Hixon: Rinpoche, what sort of a person was Guru Padmasambhava?

Tarthang Tulku: Padmasambhava [was] the great master of the esoteric Buddhist Tantrism, who is said to [have been] born in a lotus. Lord Buddha, after going into *parinirvana* [nirvana after death], mentioned that the second teacher will come. Buddha explained that Padmasambhava could teach more direct esoteric teachings than himself because he would be a Nirmanakaya form. Buddha said that he could only teach certain teachings externally, but that Padmasambhava would teach the esoteric path. So Buddha said to follow him. And several *sutras* predict this. Padmasambhava [came] many years after and he learned all aspects of the Buddhist teachings. After that he left [India] for Tibet. He taught there for many years. Some [historical accounts] say he lived in Tibet for 112 years. It is clearly known that he lived there many years. Eventually, Santarakshita, King Trisong Detsen, and Padmasambhava—those three very great, important masters—transmitted the entire Hinayana or Mahayana Vajrayana Buddhist teachings to Tibet.

Lex Hixon: To return to the meditation course that you teach, could you give an indication of what a beginning visualization might be?

Tarthang Tulku: You may sometimes feel that meditation is foreign. But meditation, the way I understand it, is dealing with your own mind, working with your own mind, working on your feeling, working on your own awareness. In this beginning introduction, what I'm asking is: Do your mind and body work in an integrated way? Especially in this very educated, intellectualized country, most of the knowledge is on the intellectual level. When people live on the intellectual level, they are not living in the heart, so it is very unique to begin to be very calm and relaxed. After this relaxation comes, then you can gradually develop awareness. As soon as this awareness is increasing, you can focus on your own awareness, not just on an intellectual concept, but on awareness itself. Once you establish this, then you can do visualization exercises, such as Padmasambhava or Avalokitesvara or Buddha. I give all this at the introductory level. That's about it.

Lex Hixon: Rinpoche, could you possibly tell a little bit of what a visualization of Padmasambhava might be?

Tarthang Tulku: If you [would] like to visualize Padmasambhava, beautiful in the lotus, upon your crown, see him as the same size as an eight-year-old boy, beautiful, transparent, with all kinds of light emanating from his body, and he is radiating all kinds of beautiful color. All his robes are beautifully designed, and are translucent. Once you have a vague image there, then increase your concentration, and then you will have more clarity. Light and energy come from his body and merge into your heart and you feel oneness.

Sometimes the visualization does not come exactly. But in the beginning, you can imagine, or look at some of the pictures. Gradually, it becomes three-dimensional. A more beautiful or wonderful image you have never, ever seen. The parts of his body have become wisdom or knowingness, radiating powerfully to you and all your friends. You all become one with him. At the end of that, you meditate and there isn't anything other than Padmasambhava. The sound has become Padmasambhava's teaching or mantra. The form has become Padmasambhava's image. The mind, the thinking, the concept itself has become

Padmasambhava's heart. So it is an experience of becoming oneness. That is part of the sadhana or visualization.

Lex Hixon: And is the mantra *Om Ah Hung Vajra Guru Padma Siddhi Hung*?

Tarthang Tulku: That is correct, and there is no mistake you can make. You can chant it in any way, morning and evening, whenever you like to chant; especially in this dark age, Padmasambhava shall help you directly.

So the mantra is *Om Ah Hung Vajra Guru Padma Siddhi Hung*. The Om represents all Buddhas. The *Ah* represents all Dharmas. The *Hung* symbolizes all the teachings, the enlightened state. *Vajra* means your own indestructible nature. *Guru* means the supreme knowledge, which we have and which is within our own mind. The *Padma* is the pure form and symbolizes purity and action. *Padma Siddhi* means the absoluteness, the truth, which is what Padmasambhava attained. *Hung* means that you and Padmasambhava have become inseparable in form, become oneness.

He says that his teaching will be more effective the more the Kaliyuga progresses—the more dangerous, the more difficult, and dark the time.

Lex Hixon: Can you give some concrete description of one of the [Kum Nye] exercises?

Tarthang Tulku: There are several levels of the Kum Nye exercises. Once your body is completely still, you need to breathe very slowly, shallowly. Inhale, exhale, and once you have done that, the whole body has become totally tranquilized by slowing down your breath. This is very simple. You can get it by yourself. If you [would] like to, you can open your eyes, or you can close your eyes. Let's close your eyes in the beginning. Gradually, it is recommended to have open eyes. It becomes a much more effective meditation to open your eyes than to shut them down.

Then, as much as you can, relax your alertness. You need to develop intrinsic alertness. Be completely alert: bodily, breath-wise, and mentally. Once you understand that, you don't need to try to force yourself to relax. That makes you more agitated. So if you really want to develop relaxation, let everything go. Let it be itself. Just be still without any forcing.

It is a complete-openness situation. This is the way meditation increases. This is part of the Kum Nye technique. The source of the total body energy is within that breath. If you know how to use the breath properly, there is a great help to your own life. It makes you relax, enjoy, be very cheerful.

There are times we have negativity—negative feelings and emotions—and become very depressed. If we know how to take a breath by ourselves, there is much that we can learn. The first step is to very shallowly take a breath and be aware of your breath. And the second part is to take time to concentrate or pay attention. This way, your whole body system will become completely refreshed and alive. This is part of the Kum Nye.

Lex Hixon: The other course that you offer at the Nyingma Institute is called Shin Jong.

Tarthang Tulku: Most of the meditations are done like this: always focusing on something. The meditation, the awareness is always aware of something. It's like being aware of something is some kind of grasping, a subtle grasping, because you are aware of something. But in the Nyingma techniques and meditations, some of the scriptures advise you ... to [not] always focus on a particular position. No matter wherever you are, hanging onto something, it is a part of bondage. It's making you limited. So you need freedom, or liberation. If you want, that means you are not necessarily aware of something. You need to give up everything to experience [complete] openness. There is not necessarily any particular observing or concentrating form. So you are totally open. Once that happens, this is the beginning.

Then there is a higher awareness, intrinsic awareness, which is part of the luminosity, or your own intrinsic response itself. Let it come, not necessarily preparing anything. Once you are more open this way and this situation continues, in the ordinary level of daily life, [then] when you are working at something, and at your psychic level or spiritual level you're working on a meditative stage, they are both working and can function simultaneously. Otherwise, in most meditators, one side can function while the other side may be collapsed. Therefore, the important thing is that the higher awareness together [with total openness] can cope in daily life; although they are living meditative states, they can work [in the world]. They can survive. They are not collapsed, in a state where they cannot function physically or mentally.

Lex Hixon: Is this a feeling or an insight?

Tarthang Tulku: It is a very high, subtle feeling. It is beyond feeling. But as soon as you look at your own mind directly, at present— everyone, whoever is listening—as soon as you look at the surface, there is something. But if you look behind there, it is nothing.

Lex Hixon: There's an article in here by someone who has attended some of [your] seminars in California. The article is about dream, in general and ... about the perspective of Tibetan Buddhism on the dream world and the waking world and their relationship. Not only is this a philosophical position, but also is a basis for possible practices that are called Dream Yoga. Rinpoche, can you expand on this idea of the waking state as dream and the possible implications for spiritual practice?

Tarthang Tulku: This is not my idea, it's [from] the Buddha. A lot of the sutras talk about it. Like dream, like mirage, like echo, like *maya*, like this, like that. Everything is the same. Finally, they describe each other. The daytime and the nighttime—there is not that much difference between the two aspects [of] experiences because the two are actually [only] consciousness [experiencing itself]. The consciousness experience, once we are in the awakened state, [has] specific characteristics which are a solidity, always stable, always available, always permanent, always reliable. The same thing I can receive, on and on. I feel it because I am [in an] awakened state, [that's] the experience.

Lex Hixon: But isn't a characteristic of insanity or psychosis the inability to distinguish between one's dream projections and what's really required of one, what's really there? It seems that one might become mad if one couldn't distinguish between one's dreams and the traffic.

Tarthang Tulku: No, the fear is our fear of a fear, because as soon as I have fear and ego position and mind, then I have these problems. But if I can allow myself to relax, and if I don't have positions, I can lose it, actually. Exactly, I can lose it. Conceptually, yes, I believe there is seriously something you have to tie down, hold [yourself] to, but actually you can't lose it. Not many people think about what you are actually losing. There's nothing to be lost. The fear comes because I may lose something. I'm afraid of losing something. But what can we lose?

Lex Hixon: So, in other words, you can't really look upon the waking state and dream state as the same until you have no more fear of anything to lose.

Tarthang Tulku: Right. And I will interpret it this way: The more [you] discover what is ultimately real in this whole thing, the more you realize it is like a dream and you can take advantage of this. You can enjoy. You can make your mind lighter. You don't necessarily have to be serious.

The fear comes from fixed seriousness. Then you are caught and stuck there. You have no freedom. As soon as you [find the relief] that you have no need to have bondages, you yourself make [yourself] free. And there is a sort of fun and beauty or truth—a lighter sense. And you also gain the cheerfulness that you are not a prisoner. You are not necessarily concerned if somebody says something wrong, or society believes something, or about the habit patterns you may have. These are all flexible because you have the inner ability of interpretation. You understand your own wisdom. You can interpret it yourself. You are [no longer] depending on something.

Lex Hixon: How can you feel compassion for beings if you think it is simply a dream?

Tarthang Tulku: That is the best way you can understand. So [for example], if [a] person is dreaming [that her] child is born and becomes sick, then she is upset and she can't cure the child. The baby is dying and she is extremely upset and possibly she becomes insane. But I am the outside observer, and I know exactly her feelings and visions and problems and sufferings. Yet at the same time, I know also that it isn't true. It's in a dream. So you have understanding about it and it makes you compassionate—more compassionate because unnecessarily, unrealistically they are doing this. It's not because they are knowingly doing it. They are enduring torture, they are suffering. But the double compassion comes because of the lack of awareness.

Reb Zalman Schachter-Shalomi
November 23, 1975

Born in Poland in 1924 and raised in Vienna, Austria, Reb Zalman spent three years as a teenager running from the Nazis across Europe before landing in New York, where he entered the Lubavitch Yeshiva. He was ordained in 1947, and became one of the first Chabad outreach emissaries. He later received a doctorate in Hebrew Letters and taught in Canada and the U.S. He also studied with transpersonal psychologists and did LSD for the first time in 1962 after meeting Timothy Leary. His friends included Thomas Merton, the Dalai Lama, and Ken Wilber. He was also a friend of Pir Vilayat Inayat Khan, who made him a sheikh in the Inayati Order, and he was likewise initiated by Sheikh Muzaffer Ozak of the Halveti-Jerrahi Order. He opened the rabbinate to women, was active in inter-religious dialogue, and founded the Spiritual Eldering movement and ALEPH: Alliance for Jewish Renewal. His many books include *A Heart Afire: Stories and Teachings of the Early Hasidic Masters* and *From Age-Ing to Sage-Ing: A Revolutionary Approach to Growing Older*. In 1995, Schachter-Shalomi moved to Boulder, Colorado, with his wife, Eve Ilsen, to take the World Wisdom Chair at Naropa University, where he taught until 2004. He died in 2014.

Zalman Schacter (singing): "*Rebbe Nachman of Bratslav used to say,/Friends do not despair/For a difficult time has come upon us,/Joy must fill the air./We must not lose our faith in living,/We must not despair./For a difficult time is upon us,/Joy must fill the air.*"

So, you think you know about joy? Once, they knew how to rejoice!

Lex Hixon: Hello! We have Reb Zalman Schachter-Shalomi [Reb Zalman] in the studio today. That was from a record he made, *The Seven Beggars of Reb Nachman and the Torah of the Void.* He also recently wrote a book, *Fragments of a Future Scroll*, that's published by Leaves of Grass Press in Germantown, Pennsylvania.

I want to start at the top and work down. In the book, it says that a certain rebbe said that every human being ought to pretend for at least half an hour, once in a while, that he is a perfect *tzaddik* [a holy person]. I'm sure people listening know that tzaddik is like Roshi, or high lama or God-realized yogi. Presumably, since you wrote this in your book, you've practiced it. Can you give us your impression of the perfect tzaddik?

Zalman Schacter: Let's start out with the fragmented person first, so we can build from that. Most of the time, we are in a place paying attention to what we are doing, whatever the job is. And then, on top of that, we run another track of whatever we are preoccupied with. And on top of that, we might run yet another track, checking the two tracks. Most of the time, that is where it stays. There are four or five main tracks in a person's life. The one is very much a "down" scene: what's here, his time, his space, the job that he is on. The other track that we run has to do with energy. Do I have enough energy? Does it feel good? Then there is another track that has to do with: "How do I stand in relation to the other people around me?" And then there is another track that has to do with: "Does it make sense? Is it consonant with where my life is going?" There is still a further track, which has to do with the basic essence: "Is that what God wanted the world for?"

Now, if you can run all those tracks together in harmony, can you imagine how much energy there is in that? So that the divine purpose, my life, my feeling and harmony with the people around me, my access to the energies at my fingertips, and the space and the time in which I find myself are all in consonance to wanting it to be perfect for the way in which God had hoped it would be.

Lex Hixon: There's a little passage in the book that gave me a glimpse of what this might be. It's in the conclusion, when you write about the patriarchs. You say: "It is written that the patriarchs kept the Torah before it was given. Their illumination was so great, as were their bodily purifications, and the limbs and organs of their spiritual bodies were so attuned to the divine that they saw and heard only Torah, divine will, and wisdom. In that sense are we to understand that spiritual seekers and divine wisdom are one."

I really feel that expresses for me that feeling of being the perfect tzaddik, the feeling of God-realization that seekers, spiritual seekers, and divine wisdom are one. There's really no place to go beyond.

Zalman Schacter: I like seekers sometimes better than finders. There's always a question, "Why do you call them seekers? All their lives they are looking around. Don't they ever find?" I get the sense that a seeker is better than a finder because the finder has already set his contours, whereas the seeker is keeping his contours soft, to make him conform to the will of God. Maybe that *is* the will of God. So he is constantly searching for that which will conform to the will of God.

Lex Hixon: There is a problem in seeking that all spiritual masters have pointed out. The soul masters of Jewish tradition are no different. In fact, Rebbe Nachman talks about it in a certain place, and, again, this is from the book. Those of you who are interested really should get this book, *Fragments of a Future Scroll*. It's very rich, and very special. It is subtitled "Hasidism for the Aquarian Age." Rebbe Zalman is a rebel as well as a rebbe.

Zalman Schacter: *Midrash*! You are right indeed. You are right in the tradition that loves words and plays with words, because it doesn't take the words more seriously than the content.

Lex Hixon: There are a couple of passages that I want to read from Rebbe Nachman about this business of [being] a seeker. In a certain sense, there are certain teachings, deep meditation teachings that say that you are already there. It is an incorrect attitude to seek. You can only put more distance between yourself and that feeling of being the tzaddik by seeking.

Rebbe Nachman says, "There is no counsel for anyone who desires to fall asleep, except to cease to desire it. The more one will tense oneself to sleep, the greater will be the resistance. He who pursues sleep will find sleep fleeing. This holds true in anything else. Everything flees us upon our pursuit."

So how would you respond to that? How can we be seekers in that sense?

Zalman Schacter: The Jewish trip is very strong on longing. We don't quite believe that the world we're finding right now is easy. It's a heavy world. And so we speak of the divine presence being in exile. It's a heavy thing for God to be in exile in this world. So it's not such a perfect world yet that we can talk so much about finding and saying, "Be here now."

I get to where Victor Frankl once put it. He says, "Can you imagine someone as well adjusted in a concentration camp?" Sick, terribly sick, right? And there's enough stuff in this world that, to be well adjusted, and to be here now, and to say this is all there is, is so foreign from where we are with that.

We thrive on longing. That's kept us from a triumphalism about our religion, about our claiming finding, because we get to where the divine can now be found most is in the seeking.

Lex Hixon: It's a kind of sleeplessness then, rather than falling asleep. And maybe people had better stop practicing meditation if they think it's falling asleep. Maybe they ought to be sleepless in that way.

Nachman also says [something] in this connection, which puts it in a very interesting way: "There is one thing that requires great mercy from Him, or immense effort, or even both, and that is to reach the point where the fermenting sediment clouding one's consciousness settles down and the mind is at rest and at a standstill, so that one ceases to desire anything in the world in order that everything may be equally unaffecting."

Here it says, "ceases to desire anything in the world," but doesn't that mean that you are not desiring God? There's a sense of a purely transcendent longing with the mind being still.

Zalman Schacter: I read something yesterday by the Hasidic master who is interpreting the sentence that goes, "O God, all my longing is against you." The usual translation means "all my longing is for you," right? It's in front of you. It faces you. He kept on saying, though, "all my longing is against you." Which is like saying, "I'm even willing to give you not only the physical longings, I'm willing to give away my spiritual longings." That is like saying, "I love you so much that I'm willing to give you all my expectations, all my attainments, and so on."

But what Nachman is saying here about the sediment of the mind settling down, he is not talking about longing in the sense of, "I want this." Somebody says, "Do you really know what you want?" [And you say,] "Well, I don't know, maybe I want it and maybe I don't want it. If the sediment is still there, then I don't know whether I really want it. Maybe I want this, maybe I want that." But when the sediment has settled, then [you] say, "I don't want your world to come. I don't want your paradise. I only want you."

So he isn't looking for light, he isn't looking for graces, he isn't looking for any of the shiny things that they tossed down from heaven in order to get you deflected away from grabbing for the heart of God. So I don't see a contradiction.

Lex Hixon: I know a lot of us for a long time have been looking for people to bring to life again the wisdom teachings of Kabbalah and Hasidic traditions. Rebbe Zalman is now living in Philadelphia, and is available to people in New York. He would never say this about himself, but he is a real soul master. He is a spiritual guide. I'll read these words that he writes in his book, *The Fragments of a Future Scroll*, describing the relationship between the rebbe and the Hasid, or the guru and disciple, if you want to put it that way. You can tell that the person who wrote this passage knows what he is speaking about:

"The Rebbe does not so much intermediate between the Hasid and God as merge himself and the Hasid in the infinite one. The Hasid makes the momentous decisions for himself. He becomes aware of the network of relationships and responsibilities of his present life. The Rebbe helps the Hasid to bear the shock of sharing the experience of cosmic consciousness, of experiencing the complete and yet dynamic oneness of the all.

"The Hasid knows the function of being helped while the function of the Lord is to be the unmoved source of the energies. The function of the Rebbe is to be the one who remembers, who so polarizes the random divine energies that they will be at the service of the Hasid, and who so polarizes the Hasid that he will be at the service of God."

This is the kind of thing that maybe people have been seeking from gurus who represent the Eastern traditions, but we tend to forget this possibility exists, at least in our so-called Western traditions. It's just a matter of having the people who will bring it alive.

In *Fragments of a Future Scroll*, Reb Zalman defines Kabbalah in a very, very disarming way. He says, "Even when we've just realized that there are different mental and spiritual spaces, we are already engaged in some form of the Kabbalah. When we find ways to describe how to get in touch with these spaces in us and in the cosmos, and in actuality bring about contact with them, effecting changes in our lives, we are involved in the practical aspect of the Kabbalah."

By that definition, Kabbalah is something very living, something that people are engaged in all the time if they are on that plane. It is not something that is hard to reach. Now, Reb Zalman talks about three kinds of Kabbalists. I'll just describe them briefly. The first one is the fundamentalist Kabbalist. What makes us seem so distant from Kabbalah is the point of view of this person. [Reb Zalman writes]: "*The fundamentalist Kabbalist speaks with a stern, authoritative voice. He has fulfilled the orthodox, legal requirements of filling his belly with Talmud and codes. He is over 40 years old, meticulous in his observance of the most specific details of the law, and of exemplary virtue, having completed all the penances for the sins of his youth.*

"*The very idea of the fundamentalist Kabbalist seems to us to be a contradiction in terms. Kabbalah, which seeks to free itself from the fetters of constrictive, mundane denotative thinking, does not lend itself to fundamentalism. Furthermore, the fundamentalist Kabbalist who cuts himself off by choice and peer pressure from contemporary thought and experience cannot be in touch with what the Holy Spirit reveals in this generation. He also finds himself in a conflict he cannot easily remove.*

"*The same forces which cut him off from contemporary thought and experience also sever him from the acceptance of other religions as vehicles for the transmission of divine life and light. Reb Nachman of Bratslav dared to profess that, 'The Holy Spirit showers forth even from the tails of the gentiles.' Characteristically, the fundamentalist Kabbalist is heavy. He enters into his consciousness as if it were the only one describing this and other realities. It is largely static. His words do not dance freely. He would be disturbed to think of his involvement in the mysteries as a cosmic game or dance.*

"*Involved in a cosmic battle between the forces of holiness and sheol, the forces of evil, he is solemn and serious and not much in touch with his own body. Only the complete tzaddik can afford to do that. For the tzaddik, every carnal thought leads to God. But most fundamentalist Kabbalists are warned to refrain from such risky attempts and are bidden to suppress such thoughts. For them, the time has not yet arrived prior to the Messiah when the Torah is engraved in their own limbs. Yet the great tzaddikim, like the Balshem Tov, are in touch not only with heaven but also grounded in their bodies, and are even known to understand body language and the language of plants and animals. Because the fundamentalist Kabbalist is so wary of carnality, he can only trust the guidelines of the law in its strictest observance.*"

Zalman continues to indicate another possibility, which he calls the "behaviorist historian" of Kabbalistic studies. Now, this is the process, the dialectic, the secularization you could say, in contemporary civilization, which frees you from the heaviness and the constraints of a tradition. The tradition lives, undoubtedly, but it's like a stream that's cutting deep but is not broad. Zalman writes:

"The well-informed student of Kabbalah, who is in the position of the behaviorist historian, may very well be able to teach us a great deal of the Kabbalah and its history. He might delineate for us the development of concepts to the point that we would understand them even better than if we were to study at the feet of a fundamentalist Kabbalist. He could be a more effective teacher than the fundamentalist because he would organize the material, concepts and content in the same coherent manner that would more closely correspond to the way in which our minds have been regimented from our first year in school. While the behaviorist teaches in a familiar western way, the fundamentalist teaches from a dense, closed web of interlacing Torah homilies, which seem to have no clear beginning and no end."

This is kind of the thesis and the antithesis. The synthesis comes in the form of what Zalman calls the humanistic transcendentalism of the Kabbalah. I was strongly moved by this thinking because this not only applies to Kabbalah, it also applies to various mysticisms, various esoteric teachings of all the traditions. They simply are not acceptable in their deep, dense traditional forms. It's very, very hard to make them live. You can live in them, but somehow then you become cut off from the world. Zalman writes: *"What remains essential for the Aquarian seeker is to find in this jungle-like garden of exotic [prescriptions] a healing for his own yearning and disease. He will not be helped by either the traditional fundamentalist Kabbalist or the behavioristic historian of Kabbalah studies. The first does not recognize the Aquarian's condition as valid. His advice to that seeker would be to become an anachronism, to close himself off from the universal stream of global communication or a major part of it, and from the spirit of the times. In fact, many who have for a time taken up residence in the camp of fundamentalist type of Kabbalist have had to leave that nostalgic place when they felt that their specific needs had not been met.*

"And so many people have had this experience of leaving that nostalgic place. It could be in Hasidic circles, it could be in Buddhist

or Hindu circles. It is not probable that the behaviorist historian of the Kabbalah can help him either. For his approach lacks access to the transcendental realm in the here and now which many of us so urgently desire.

"In other words, these things really work. The plane of being we can see with our senses is just a tiny little part of the entire spectrum. No secular thinker really knows that or thinks that, so the fundamentalist is right on in that sense, because he is not a little child who just thinks that what is before him in his playpen is all that there is. Lacking models in the past, the New Age seeker must forge his own [way] through the process. He rediscovers the Kabbalah and learns to use it to help him on his path."

I think that's really an accurate description, not only of Jewish spiritual seekers, but of all spiritual seekers. Zalman, maybe you can say something about this process. Is it different or the same as that carried on by people who are involved in the dharma? You say that the Torah and the dharma are two possible ways of structuring one's path.

Zalman Schacter: The sense is that time is texture, and to be in touch with the texture of time is like someone who carves wood. If he carves against the grain, he isn't going to do it right. The spiritual masters, when they carve the shape of the way in which one conforms best with the best thing for souls at this particular time [are the most helpful].

Like, there is a soul vintage of 1975. We remember very strongly the soul vintages of the late Sixties, right? There were good, good—if you need to get spirits from that time, they really had good ones. There are some times that are so, and some times that are different. There is a statement that goes like this: "Why is it that people pray and aren't being answered?"

According to the statement, it's because they don't pray to the right name, because the divine name keeps on changing every year. Every time it keeps on changing—every month, every day—there is a different way in which a divine name comes up. If I am in touch with where the divine name is now—what am I saying, "divine name"? I mean the interface between the infinite and the finite. That is the "name." If I am in touch with that place, then that's where the spirit flows, that is where the flow is both ways, where we offer to God our experiences, our lives, our being here now, and that's where we pull it down, and so we connect and we make a union.

Now, when people come and bring along a lot of stuff that does not fit into the mesh of time, they bring keys. They've gotten the keys from way back, but the locks have been changed and the combinations aren't the same anymore. They're trying those keys and they don't work. So they run into real trouble. Some people, because of the honor and the dignity they give to the material that they receive, teacher to disciple and on down the line, feel that the material that comes down to them is infallible.

And so it is infallible for that particular moment in time when it was first revealed. It turns out that, at other times, new stuff is coming in! New sparks of holiness are being released, and new tasks are given to mankind each time. Say, someone is going to come and say, "Do it the way in which they used to do it in the past, that's the only authentic way. I want some of this old-time religion. It was good enough for my father, it's good enough for me."

But Papa doesn't live where I live, and I don't live where Papa lives, and so there are changes. So the basic question you have to keep asking of every guru is, "On what basis do you really have it clear and on what basis do you make a decision as to what of the past to carry on and what to drop of the past?"

And I've had the sense that—whether they're more on the radical side or less on the radical side, more traditional—even if I think of the gurus that are around today, even Prabhupada and the Krishna Consciousness people are cutting corners as far as the Vedas are concerned, you know? But [the guru] doesn't let that on. It comes on as if, no, no, he is presenting the authentic. The authentic wasn't printed in such books; it wasn't used by such methods. Other times and places he utilizes them, so it must be then that every teacher who teaches, and teaches the live stuff knows how to filter out the stuff of the past. Yet some people, for the sake of strategy with their disciples, keep saying, "My stuff is authentically old-time vintage." If it were, they couldn't even connect with their disciples today. So there is this kind of conundrum. Put it this way: Why is it then, in all the things of Torah, we have a whole book of the Talmud? You want to know how to celebrate Sabbath? There's a whole book of the Talmud on Sabbath. Want to know marriage laws? There's a whole book on marriage laws. Why is there not a book in the Talmud on how to love God, and how to be in awe of Him? Because He can't write it in the book! It's impossible to write it in the books. So God in His grace sends down teachers in every age so they should *be* the living book of those duties of the heart, which you can't write in any book. I guess this is what's happening all around, that's why so many of the teachers are coming here, because this is where the energy now is.

Lex Hixon: What do you think about people who had the good karma, as Shlomo Carlebach would put it, to be born Jews, to be born open to this particular revelatory path? Working in terms of Buddhism and Hinduism and that kind of thing—what's your attitude about it?

Zalman Schacter: Let me tell you something: This is a real concern of mine. We had a whole day devoted in Berkeley to the question of Torah and Dharma, because, as the Swami once told me, "You Jews are very spiritual people." And I said, "Why do you say that?" And he said, "The Vedanta Society, Baha'i are all full of Jews. Very spiritual people." On the one hand, I was happy because it's true, and on the other hand, I was sad because it's true. How come people have to go to another place and can't come home? So Shlomo came up with an interpretation that he sent to us that day on tape and it bears repeating: "Concerning the priest, it is written that a priest is the one from whom you should seek the teaching. Further, it is also written that a priest must not defile himself to the dead. Why not? Because no one can see a corpse and not be angry at God."

It is in the nature of confronting death that we all meet our finiteness, and we see in a sense we have been cheated. Nobody makes it into this world in such a way that he doesn't have to die. Everybody has to die. So getting in touch with the raw fact of death, you get—for a moment—angry. Then you can't teach. You can't teach the good teaching when you are angry at God. When it came to this time, and Jews were so angry with God, there weren't any teachers around who could say the good word about God without some kind of anger, having looked into the face of that destruction from 1939 to 1944. So God in His grace had to send us teachers from other places who, at that moment, didn't have any particular reason to be so angry with God as we had. But then comes the point where a person has to sort of go home. And at first people don't want to hear that. It comes on like, "Yeah, I'm sitting, doing my zazen, and all of a sudden I see my grandfather in front of my eyes and I get into all kinds of Jewish stuff. I don't want chicken soup. I want to get away from it."

And it keeps on coming all the time. So as you sit in zazen, you do "mind burping," right? And a lot of stuff starts coming up. And you say, "I only want the dharma. I only want Mu. I only want the void. I only want the answer to my koan. Shunyata is what I want. I don't want chicken soup!" But the same place from which the shunyata comes, on top of that there is a layer of chicken soup.

Lex Hixon: Maybe they are the same thing! Maybe that's the answer to the koan.

Zalman Schacter: You know what? That's true. Guru Maharaj-ji used to speak of the nectar, you know? And Jews always refer to the nectar as *schmaltz*. So when it comes from Hinduism, they call it the nectar. When it comes from Judaism, they call it schmaltz. Isn't it strange?

Lex Hixon: Yeah.

Zalman Schacter: It really may be the same thing.

Lex Hixon: What do you think about the possibility of Hasidic and Kabbalistic tradition and teachers becoming open-cultural? For instance, the Hindu swamis were used to being very tight. For them, it was to lose caste even to come across the ocean. And

Vivekananda was one of the first ones who came over here, and many of his contemporaries thought he was polluted because he came to the West. So that's an indication of a very tight cultural tradition, Hinduism, where you really had to be a twice-born, where you had to be into it in order to [be accepted]. Now that tradition has somehow found its own spiritual core and comes out and finds it is able to teach to other cultures, and no Hindu swami says that you have to have been born a Hindu to do this meditation.

I don't see Hasidic and Kabbalistic masters doing that. Very few of us see them anyway. Even in the Jewish context, you know, really living. Now they are beginning to reemerge. But do you think there will be a possibility that the Kabbalah and the Hasidic tradition can somehow revision itself so it isn't primarily directed towards people who happen to be born Jewish?

Zalman Schacter: Let's go over that for a bit. You are right. Vivekananda came like a lion. He knew that he had to be the lion because he felt the call, he was given a thing to do, and when he came to the Columbian Exposition he didn't want to translate everything. He said, "Karma." So people asked him, "Why don't you say cause and effect?'" He said, "[If] I'm going to say 'cause and effect,' you people are going to make mistakes. You will think you understand what I am saying. So I want to use a word so that you hear it time and time again in different contexts, and then you'll understand it."

Now the people who spoke for us, the spokesmen for Judaism, were by and large people who came from Reform Judaism. They were the ones who spoke in English and felt it was important— the mission to the gentiles. So they were the ones who sort of took the lead. But they spoke out of the 19th-century rationalism place and they were embarrassed by the dark things that were benighted and superstitious that came from Kabbalah, right? They thought of merely dirty people writing amulets, you know? And people hanging them up and not taking good care of sanitation, so they were terribly embarrassed to own up all that stuff.

When you asked a Reform rabbi of those days, "What is the belief in the afterlife?" they would say, "One life at a time. We don't talk much about it." But there is a whole literature. There is a Jewish book of the dead, very much like the *Bardo Thodol*, called *The Mahavarya Book*. It talks about how to be with a dying person and help them across the thing. It's in Hebrew and hasn't been translated yet. They didn't own any of these things up. Little by little, Hasidism is making its way, again with an inner dialectic operating. The word was America, *emicra*, the depth of evil. "Don't go to America." Same thing about losing caste.

Then came the Second World War, and there was no other choice. They felt badly about having to come to America because when the Torah was given at Mount Sinai, so they argued, it was light there, but it was dark here. This continent, this half-hemisphere didn't have it. But this hemisphere had holy sparks that needed redeeming, so they were pushed as it were by destiny to come over here.

Now they were beginning to use media, they were beginning to utilize all this stuff that's already here in this society. Tonight, for instance, at 770 Eastern Parkway in Brooklyn, the Lubavitcher will celebrate the release from prison of his ancestor [Schneur] Zalman, the first founder of the Chabad movement. And there will be people plugged into some radio stations to hear what he has to say. And there will be telephone linkups to many cities on this continent, and even to the Holy Land, where people will tune in to what the Rebbe has to say.

That's a new kind of thing, yeah? Now that raises a question: Where do *goyim* [non-Jews] fit in? What do you do with goyim here? On the one hand, I deeply sympathize with the issue: "Take care of your own first." If Christianity had followed that pathway back, instead of sending people to China, to Africa, and cleaned up its own house, it wouldn't have had to have any inquisitions or any wars. They didn't do that. So by sending missionaries, as it were, to Jews first....

Lex Hixon: But a footnote has to be made there. For instance, St. Paul—so-called St. Paul, Saul, if you want to call him by his Jewish name—it was his insight that this Hasidism, this Essene teaching that's coming through this rebbe from Nazareth, Rebbe Jesus of

Nazareth, you know, should go to everybody, not just Jews. So it wasn't a matter of missionaries to Africa at that point. This was something very much at the roots, the beginning of the movement. There was a decision made there that it wasn't just going to go to Jews. Peter thought people should be circumcised first before they were baptized because, after all, this was a Jewish trip.

Zalman Schacter: Right. In that space you get where Paul says [that] you send missionaries to the ends of the earth, right? And then you don't take care of them. So apparently the scene hasn't changed from before to now. But what I want to get to is the essential. I just don't want us, and the listeners, to get confused about the basic issue as to why you set your own house into order. Most religious teachers teach you the "ought," and then they say, "My ought is better than yours." You know? I don't like that. But if we could have a model and say, "This community lives God's life in a deliberate way," and then, "Come and see how this works," then we aren't just preaching with words, we're preaching by example. That's another kind of trip. That's the reason why I want to push. The energy first has to go to get that trip together so that you have a model that you can show, not merely words. The good news is when you can see it in front of your eyes.

Lex Hixon: But the trouble is, if you get a model going of, say, Hasidic and Kabbalistic work that is just Jews doing it, then how are you ever going to break out of that model and open it up to other people? Now I think it's good to speak the language. Like, if we can learn karma and Nirvikalpa Samadhi, then we can learn all sorts of terms in the Kabbalah too. But this is like some Buddhist community saying, "First we're going to get a bunch of Buddhist monks over here. They're going to be Tibetans by birth and we're going to get it together. And then, slowly we're going to let people come in from the outside." But aren't those people going to feel like outsiders?

Zalman Schacter: Look at the way in which Geshe Wangyal did it, right? He just did exactly what you described. And now I can see a Buddhist community in operation, a bunch of nice New York Jews coming to Boulder, Colorado. Instead of running their Papa's business, they run Rinpoche's business. There is something to be said for that, but I don't want to spend energy on that. I want to go to the other place.

The other place has something to do with—and here I'm going to get in hot water—the other side. What is it that we can share with the non-Jew? First of all, we have to share the basic humanity and divinity thing. So people used to call it the fatherhood of God and the brotherhood of man. It was a very nice slogan. I think the best thing we can do in this situation is to open up first with everybody [who] has a lot of grief [and] to the people on the outside of the thing, to be able to start talking and say, "You know, you let me down. You really let me down. That last United Nations resolution—you really let me down!" You know? And to be able to say that, as I feel it, to people, and to know I am being heard, is then a way of inviting: "Let's now share and see what can we do for the people who have been wronged in Israel." Then we can start talking about the refugees.

So I'm moving from the high plane to this plane. But I'm saying there's so much garbage in the way that needs cleaning up before we can do heart-to-heart and mind-to-mind and look at each other in the third eye and zap each other with Kabbalah and Dharma.

Lex Hixon: Let me throw something in here. Of course, a reincarnation is an esoteric teaching and esoteric Jewish teaching has that too. Now, this is the way that Hindu and Buddhist people deal with this. When you say, "Talk about your own house first," they come over here and they feel that the people who are drawn to them, maybe in past lives they were Hindus or Buddhists. What if you had introduced this into your situation? Wouldn't that blow the roof off it? What if I was a Jew in my last life?

Zalman Schacter: If you say it with that intonation, Shalom Aleichem, Lex! Sure. You see, now we are not talking, but watch this, this is important. Now we are not talking about abstract principles. There was the Jewish in you coming out and meeting the Jewish in me before, when we were talking about other things, there was the – I'm sure that somewhere along the line I had a Hindu life. I know it is not the proper teaching, but I know also that I was at one place a Hindu. I was at one place along the path a Catholic. I was all kinds of beings because I feel the affinities within me really alive. So now what you are saying is, did the Kabbalah of the past teach that? No.

Lex Hixon: No, I am not asking that. I'm saying can the Kabbalah of the present teach that?

Zalman Schacter: It hasn't got a choice. You see, when I started asking the question, "Who are the people who are so spiritually active all over?" Sufi Sam had a way of saying, "Just check the birthdates and see when they were born." Between '39 and '43, the people born during those years—quick reincarnation—made it out of the death camp, come down, take another body and this time find the situation in which they can make it and not have to come back ever again because Auschwitz was a giant step toward realization of what the whole kit and caboodle was all about.

So then this time they made it, and they come back as Sufis and as swamis, and make their way back to a connection of Judaism this way so they can work out that particular deposit in their lives.

This is hot stuff. As we talk about it, I feel in touch with a lot of energy, a lot of buttons, a lot of stuff where the sediment of the mind hasn't settled. In a sense, I'm anticipating when the phone calls will start coming in and we'll have to deal with some of that hot stuff. More heat than light stuff.

Lex Hixon: I'm just so grateful to Zalman for coming. Zalman, can you come sit down again and maybe give some sort of a prayer or invocation or something like that that will keep us way up there?

Reb Zalman: The Irish used to have this nice [saying]: "May you be in heaven half an hour before the devil knows [that you arrived]." And I would like to say: May you be in heaven half an hour before you know that there is a devil!

Mother Serena
December 21, 1974

Mother Serena, who was born Gladys Miller in New York in 1894, was an astrologer and healer. For over 60 years, at the chapel she created in her Upper West Side brownstone in New York City, she gave a noontime healing service every day but Sunday for the peace and wellbeing of the world, and requested help for a long list of people. Her husband, George Winslow Plummer, headed Societas Rosecruciana, a branch of Rosicrucians that opened to women members in 1916. Dr. Plummer affiliated the group with an esoteric branch of the Orthodox Church and became a bishop in the church. The couple traveled extensively, filling their house with water and earth samples from holy places. After Dr. Plummer died in 1944, Mother Serena married the next head of the church, Stanislaus deWitow; when he died, she became the church's leader. She corresponded with students from around the world on astrological and spiritual matters. In 1980, she was consecrated as a bishop. Mother Serena died in 1989.

Lex Hixon: Several evenings ago, I went to Mother Serena's small house and chapel on the Upper West Side, where she's been engaged in esoteric studies and healing work for over 50 years. She is a grandmotherly figure. Her deep insight is expressed in sweetness, and with a simplicity which should not distract us from her intense clarity. She is a deeply qualified spiritual guide; but as with many such genuine saints, she is veiled in ordinariness, radiant in obscurity. I've meditated quite often in her daily healing service over the last two years, but not until now have both of us felt comfortable about bringing her quiet work into this large radio community.

I want very much to present accurately the intense intimacy and quiet dedication of Mother Serena's work. She is an 82-year-old woman who is truly serene and yet sparkling with energy. Her dedication to others, her joy and clarity, are what await the genuine spiritual seeker after his or her long road. Mystical experiences are just an adjunct. At the end of our conversation, Mother Serena performs her healing service, so we will all taste of the extremely pure light and love that she is able to focus in this ceremony, which she has performed every day for over 50 years, becoming fused with its prayers for the peace and health of the whole world, as she says, in body, in mind, and in soul.

Mother Serena: We do not claim to do any healing ourselves. We act as channels of the healing grace of God and of Christ to flow through us, to whoever has asked for healing. We also believe that there are two healing angels at every consecrated altar in the world, not just ours, that are broadcasting healing light and love to the world 24 hours a day. The people that stand before the altar don't realize it. But if they did, they would open themselves up to these tremendous vibrations of healing and love that are being broadcasted, and be helped, no matter which church theirs would be.

In our own church, we have painted behind our altar two healing angels to remind us of that fact—that there are two healing angels broadcasting divine light and love. If we but realized it, there are divine hierarchies, the angels and archangels and thrones and dominions and principalities. These divine beings have grades of spiritual development and they have very definite functions to perform in helping God in his creative plan. And we as mortals are being trained to become helpers of God, too, eventually, when we are ready. That's why we have to come again and again into incarnation to perfect ourselves more and more in different phases of life so that we can become instruments of constructive good in God's creative plan.

And now our healing service is conducted daily from Monday to Saturday at noon and anyone who wishes to come to this service is welcome to do so. Be careful that you don't pass by without realizing it's there, for it is in a little brownstone house where we have been located for the past 52 years.

Lex Hixon: Do you notice a difference in your life after performing a service like this for 52 years, do you notice a deepening of experience?

Mother Serena: Oh, definitely, and a deeper feeling of faith. Being there all the time, I don't realize how strong the vibrations are in the chapel, but when I go out into the outer world and then come back, oh, I'm so grateful for this place!

I have been a member of the Society of Rosicrucians for 60 years. It is a very ancient institution, but in its present phase, it is only since 1909 because before that, our particular branch of the Society was confined to Masons. Dr. Plummer, who became its head in 1909, said: "This is incredible that we should deny ourselves in one incarnation what we've attained in a previous one. That means that women are not allowed, and that restriction has to be removed. Hereafter, as long as I'm the head of this Society, everyone is going to be welcome who can qualify, whether they're Masons [or men] or not."

Since then, we have been opening our doors to all seekers of truth, and being a member of the Society does not mean that you have to leave your church. It should make your church more meaningful because our teachings are actual esoteric Christianity. [Editor's note: Most churches today are exoteric.] It's the mystical side of Christianity. We believe in reincarnation and in Karma, we believe in the angelic kingdom.

We believe that man is a threefold being: he has a threefold body, a threefold soul, and a threefold spirit. When we make the Sign of the Cross in our church, we make it the Eastern Orthodox way. Instead of touching the left shoulder first and then the right, we do it the reverse—we touch the forehead, where the divine spark of man is, and then the heart, where the Christ center is, and then the right shoulder and the left shoulder. That horizontal line represents the Holy Spirit or the vitalizing forces in the universe and in man. We're all one. During the whole healing service, whenever we mention the Trinity, we always make the Sign of the Cross to remind ourselves that we have the Trinity actually within ourselves and we don't know it; we are trying to activate our consciousness of it through the making of that Sign of the Cross.

Lex Hixon: You mentioned that in the forehead center there's a white light. Is that the same white light that is the healing light?

Mother Serena: That is the same light. What is light? It's the radiance of God. The word "glory" means light, too. The Bible is just full of glory, full of light. Both light and love are emanations from God. They're the most healing emanations of all. In our service, when we have it in full form, we sing a song that goes, "From love to light." You've got to have love before you have the light. Sometimes people think that if they have the light, they'll get the love, but it seems to work the other way. That is why the one commandment that Christ gave above all was to love thy neighbor as thyself. Why do we have to love ourselves, by the way? That would seem selfish, wouldn't it? What is yourself? It's not the body; it's the divine in you! When you are loving the divine in yourself, you're loving God. When you love God, you're gonna love your neighbor. It's as simple as all that. Isn't that beautiful? If we but realize it, we have all the tools in our hands to build a wonderful life, no matter what our station is in life, because all lives are beautiful and wonderful, whether we're scrubbing a floor or we're the president of the United States. We're all doing constructive work if we allow the divine in us to come through and guide us. Someday—I'm afraid I'm not going to be alive when it happens—humanity is going to realize that, and when that happens, there won't be any more wars because love will be the ruler of the world.

Lex Hixon: In the healing service, is there a sense of projecting love as well as light?

Mother Serena: Yes, definitely. Now, in the healing service, we always instruct those who are here for the first time that when we mention [someone's] name for healing, to visualize the figure as surrounded with divine healing light and love and to try to project that light and love to that individual. If that were done correctly, in every single church in the world, the light that would be emanating from this world would be just astonishing.

Lex Hixon: What's the problem? Why are these things obscured?

Mother Serena: Because man doesn't believe it. I explain this as carefully as I can; I say, "Are there any questions?" and "Do you accept this?" and people say, "Oh, yes, I accept it completely!" And then the next thing that they say or do proves that they didn't accept a single word I said.

Lex Hixon: Could this healing service also help psychological or emotional problems?

Mother Serena: Oh, definitely! Most of our illnesses are caused by our way of thinking. Definitely! Our thoughts create these circumstances in our lives. Dr. Plummer wrote a book called *Consciously Creating Circumstances*, and that title in itself tells us a story—that we unconsciously create our circumstances through the type of thinking we do. If you go out, for instance, in the world looking for a job, and think, "I know I'm not going to get any job today," you don't! You're just radiating negativity and people sense that negativity. When you come in full of good will and good cheer, they say, "Oh my, wouldn't it be wonderful to have this person around here all the time." You get a job! It's as simple as that.

Now ... we feel that healing is one of the most important acts of the Christian church. If you remember, Christ, during the three years of His ministry, when the Christ-spirit took full possession of Him, He healed. But remember one statement: "According to thy faith, be it unto thee." He, the Christ-spirit, said, "Thy faith has made thee whole." He Himself never claimed to heal a soul. "Thy faith has made thee whole." And He stressed faith at every point. And what is faith? A soul that has been very helpful in our work on the other side of life, defined faith as "the power of the spirit." It's as simple as that.

Lex Hixon: So faith is not some sort of belief of any kind.

Mother Serena: No, He claimed that faith is the power of the spirit. As your spirit grows in power, your faith grows. That's His definition anyway, and it was very helpful to me in helping others. Now, our healing work is one of the most important works in our society. It's the number one [priority] in our principles and practice for the students to pray for others. It is so important that if we removed the healing from our society, it would have really almost no purpose for existing, because healing is done in a very strange way. People think, "Oh, healing is only on the physical plane in the sense of healing the body," but we go further—healing people's thinking, healing people's emotions, healing people's spirit—so that it's a healing process on every level of consciousness.

We believe and teach that man is being trained to become a helper in God's kingdom, in the spiritual realms beyond. When you stop to think of the fact that there are billions of galaxies in the universe, can you imagine why God needs helpers? It is such an immense creation, and we are so conceited that we think that this tiny little speck in the cosmos is the only inhabited planet in all the universe.

By the way, our healing is all gratis. For anyone who asks to be put on our healing list, there's only one requirement: that they believe and join with us, no matter where they are, in prayer, and if they can, possibly attend one of our healing sessions so that they know what's going on and can visualize it when they're away from it. But they should never think of themselves as sick; if they are the one asking for healing, but as already healed. Because by taking that constructive attitude, they're already opening the doors for the healing grace of God to come and help them. Immediately, a veil is lifted from the different vehicles and the divine healing light can pour in and do its work. So we ourselves stand in our own way through our disbelief.

Lex Hixon: And the belief is simply that we are already whole, we are expressions of divine light?

Mother Serena: Exactly. We say this in our healing service. We quote from St. Paul to the Corinthians: "Know ye not that ye are the temple of the indwelling spirit of God, and that God dwells in you." That's the whole answer.

Lex Hixon: Why did you suddenly believe these things? As a young woman, when you first joined the Society, were there times of unbelief for you, or did you just automatically believe?

Mother Serena: I had a very fine grandmother. She was a Theosophist who believed in reincarnation, so I've believed in reincarnation all my life, from childhood up, and I have been receptive, as a result, to all these teachings. I've probably been exposed to them before, so it was just picking up from where I left off. Egypt has a marvelous fascination for me. So has ancient Greece and, strangely enough, England. As a child, when I was going to Europe on a ship I wanted to throw myself overboard to swim to England because some people were getting off the boat, but we were going on to France! I was only 11 years of age at the time.

Lex Hixon: What's the esoteric significance of Glastonbury in England?

Mother Serena: Joseph of Arimathea, who was an uncle of Jesus, was in the tin business, and England was the place where there was tin in those days. Joseph periodically made a long trip from Jerusalem to England, to where the tin was, in Glastonbury, and the people there got so fond of this gentleman that they gave him this small acreage. The next time he came to England, he brought a staff with him from Jerusalem to use to climb up the hill where his place was, and he put the staff in the ground, saying, "This ground is ours." He left the staff there, and on his next trip, to his amazement, he found that it had grown roots and budded! It became known as the Glastonbury Thorn, and there was quite a legend about it. It grew and grew, and only flowered around Christmas. By the way, two little branches were sent to us from Glastonbury when they found out that our church was named St. Joseph of Glastonbury, and we have a little wooden bowl that's made out of a branch of one of the children of that original thorn, and there's a grandchild of that thorn in the Bronx Botanical Gardens.

St. Joseph decided to build a little chapel of willow branches on his land. He called it the Wattle Chapel. He discovered a well there, and the water from that well was very clear and pure. Tradition says St. Joseph hid the chalice of the Last Supper in that well, and the water became healing water. People began to come from all over England to drink water out of that well, to be healed. Time went on, and, of course, St. Joseph died. They built a little monastery there, and then they built this huge abbey, and it was very, very influential, so much so that the king became jealous of the influence of this abbey and it was burned. It stood there in ashes for years and years.

Lex Hixon: Do you feel that your chapel has any etheric or subtle qualities of Glastonbury?

Mother Serena: We have a stone, part of Glastonbury Abbey, under the throne of our bishop, and we have some of the ashes from the Wattle Church, and I feel that there's something here from Glastonbury, definitely.

Lex Hixon: I feel that the strength and tremendous spiritual power that you yourself feel in the chapel is a direct emanation from that tradition.

Mother Serena: Yes, I feel that. Whenever anyone suggests that we move, I feel, oh, dear, it's taken us 52 years to create an atmosphere here through all the prayers and all the things that have occurred here.

Lex Hixon: Now we're going to hear the healing service that you do every day and have done for 50 years here. How could people best open to this service?

Mother Serena: They should try to keep every other thought out of their mind while they are listening to the prayers that are being said. It's not going to be easy for those who haven't been trained, but the idea is to concentrate on what is being said so that they can feel something, because if they'll do it wholeheartedly, they will be uplifted. Every word in this service means something. It's not there by chance.

Lex Hixon: Because you've said it for so many years and it's become so much a part of your being, I feel that it means more coming from you than if one were just to happen to stumble across the service in written form.

Mother Serena: That could be. When you get so used to something, you don't realize what it actually is doing or anything; it's just part of you, you know?

Lex Hixon: Will this service, as it's broadcast on the radio, be an actual healing service itself?

Mother Serena: It all depends on the recipient, on how they feel, whether anything is going to happen or not to them. God is everywhere; He's not just in our chapel. Take someone that's bedridden and can't come here. If they hear this service and they feel and listen to every word—and believe—there's no reason why they shouldn't experience a healing.

Lex Hixon: When you say "believe," what do you mean?

Mother Serena: Do you believe there is such a thing as God? Do you believe that God dwells in you?

Lex Hixon: What would God be?

Mother Serena: A divine creating spirit.

Lex Hixon: Who has created this universe in order to—?

Mother Serena: Who has created *everything that exists*! Everything! That's the thing that we find so hard to understand.

Lex Hixon: Why? I mean, from our limited human understanding?

Mother Serena: Why did He create it? If I were God, I would be able to say why. But being that I'm not God, I can't. I don't know why He did—I often wonder! But the thing is, He wants to create. Take us humans—we want to create all the time and make things if we're creative people, and we're not happy unless we're creating something. I think that it is the divine in us that's urging us to be creative. God is the most creative spirit in all the universe, and is constantly creating, and has never stopped creating, and is still creating, making new worlds all the time. As fast as He is constructing and building, we are trying desperately to destroy, yet nothing is going to be completely lost and wasted. Every atom is going to be accounted for. It's going to change form and usefulness, but it's not going to be wasted. God has a tremendous recycling process that we're going to have to learn to emulate.

Lex Hixon: So belief then simply means belief in this divine creative spirit that's flowing as a kind of light or love?

Mother Serena: Yes. We have a concept of the Christ-spirit that I should explain a little. The divine spirit of Christ, which is called in church circles the Son of God—we're all sons of God, for that matter—was preparing for many, many, many, many, many millions of years for the job of becoming the indwelling spirit of this planet and assuming the karmic responsibility of every soul on earth, regardless of their religion or race. The soul of Jesus had been prepared for many, many incarnations to become an instrument for the Christ-spirit. The Christ-spirit took possession of Jesus's body and He became Jesus the Christ. He only was able to house the spirit of Christ for three years—had it been a longer period, it probably would have burned him up, because this divine spirit of Christ was so tremendous. At the Crucifixion, the divine spirit of Christ, through the shedding of blood—which is the river of life, and it's a very mysterious river—entered the earth. There was an earthquake and everything shook and the Christ-spirit was able to take possession of this earth just as He had taken possession of Jesus's body. We have progressed more rapidly since the Crucifixion than we did in all the millions of years before. Our progress may seem to be going backward, but it's only a seeming thing. We are going forward, we are growing, and we're going to speed up more and more. Believe me, we're going to go places. This world is going to become a veritable paradise because everyone's going to be busy wanting to help everybody.

Lex Hixon: We've been having this conversation with Mother Serena in her study, surrounded by ancient artifacts and esoteric texts, and large piles of letters—her correspondence with truth-seekers all over the world. We now move to her chapel, where the concentration of spiritual energy is immense, but not heavy.

Mother Serena: Right after I light the red candle on the altar, I say this prayer:

"O holy Father, may this tiny physical light, symbolical of Thy divine living healing light so abundantly present in this Thy holy altar, shine forth into the four quarters of this city and land, and the world

at large, and bring Thy light and Thy peace wherever there's darkness and strife. Amen. In the name of the Father, and of the Son, and of the Holy Spirit. Amen.

"Blessed is our God always, now and ever, and unto the ages of ages. Amen. O heavenly King, the Paraclete, Spirit of Truth, who art in all places and fillest all things, come and take Thine abode in us and cleanse us from every stain, O Holy One. Amen.

"O Holy God, Holy and Mighty, Holy and Immortal One, have mercy upon us. O Holy God, Holy and Mighty, Holy and Immortal One, have mercy upon us. O Holy God, Holy and Mighty, Holy and Immortal One, have mercy upon us. Glory be to the Father, and to the Son, and to the Holy Spirit, always now and ever and unto the ages of ages. Amen.

"O Holy Trinity, have mercy upon us. O Lord, wash away our sins. O Master, pardon our transgressions. O Holy One, visit and heal our infirmities for Thy Name's sake. Lord have mercy. Lord have mercy. Lord have mercy."

Mother Serena stands before the altar in her home on the Upper West Side of Manhattan in the 1970s

Mary Bailey
January 12, 1975

Mary Bailey was the second wife of Foster Bailey, a Theosophist and 32nd-degree Freemason who founded the Arcane School in London with his first wife, Alice Bailey, in 1923. Alice received telepathic teachings from an entity she called "the Tibetan" which were published in 24 volumes by the Lucis Trust. Alice died in 1949; in 1951, Foster married Mary Bailey, an Arcane School student, who worked with him until his death in 1977. She was the president of Lucis Trust, and head of the Arcane School for 33 years. Her book, *A Learning Experience* (1990), recounts the Arcane School's international growth. The Arcane School now has branches in New York City, Geneva, and London. Mary Bailey died in 2007.

Lex Hixon: From 1919 to 1949, there was a very important esoteric teacher in this country named Alice Bailey, who received transmissions from a discarnate Tibetan master. For those 30 years, the master's words were channeled through her own conscious mind. She received a tremendous amount of material, which has been published in 24 volumes. She and her husband, Foster Bailey, called the work the Arcane School, and it has been a profound influence in a quiet way on New Age thinking. For instance, much of the theoretical base of the Findhorn community in Scotland is based on Alice Bailey's work. This morning we're going to be hearing about the spiritual groups that the Tibetan master organized as an experiment for his students to implement his teachings.

Mary Bailey is here today to lead us through this discussion. She is the second wife of Foster Bailey, and generously took up the forwarding of the work of her predecessor, Alice Bailey.

Mary Bailey: The teaching that Alice received has one main objective, and that is to help individuals who accept it to be able to apply the teaching to their own developing forms of service. The teaching only has value to the extent that it is applied to the conditions in the world now and into the future. Alice and the Tibetan emphasized this over and over again. In fact, all the teachings that he gave through Alice were given in that context.

The Tibetan related the whole of his work and the formation of these groups to world affairs and the necessity to train disciples for world service. I want to quote just a few bits from his introduction given in 1933. He said:

"This is the arc of humanity's greatest opportunity. And if men can pass triumphantly through this, and by the strength of their own souls, surmount this very present evil; then the evolution of humanity will be hastened beyond all that was believed possible.

"What I and all who are affiliated with the hierarchy seek to do at this time of desperate crisis is to find those who are dependable points of living energy, and through them pour out the love, the strength and the light which the world needs and must have, if this dawn is to be weathered.

"That which appears is not always that which truly is. That which rends and disrupts the personality life is frequently the agent of release, if rightly apprehended. That which will emerge when the forces of light have penetrated the world darkness will demonstrate the nature of the undying human spirit."

The Tibetan emphasized the need for individuals to transcend their separateness and to learn and to function as a part of a group.

Lex Hixon: As I understand the groups, there is no emphasis at all placed on physically meeting or even knowing the other members of the group. It's more of a simultaneous spiritual practice.

Mary Bailey: Yes, the whole direction of the teaching he gave is to encourage individuals to recognize their inner relationships. When one has been able to establish soul contact, which is the center of discipleship, one comes into contact with other souls and minds that are functioning on the same wavelength. The subjective grouping is essential and of first importance, but from that, outer forms of service groups should begin to emerge and focus on specific work to be done. This is already happening in many parts of the world.

Lex Hixon: Can you give us some idea of the categories that the Tibetan saw?

Mary Bailey: The experiment was to try to form an outer branch of the inner ashram. He intended to have this outer group, which he was in contact with through Alice, form into nine different groups, according to a specific form of activity.

The first three groups were almost entirely subjective. The first group was the telepathic communicators. Now, the telepathic communicators implied a group that was becoming receptive to impression, not necessarily capable of sending and receiving messages, one to the other, but were becoming, through a developed sensitivity, receptive to impression from the master.

Lex Hixon: You said that in the Arcane School, that's beginning to be experienced, that various members of the group are simultaneously awakening to certain higher teachings.

Mary Bailey: Yes, we do have students in practically every country of the world, even one in Russia. China, I think, is the big exception at present. The Arcane School group has integrated to the point where different members in different parts of the world are beginning to pick up the same impressions, the same ideas simultaneously. We hear that the plan, which is impressed from a higher source, is being picked up and acted upon in different parts of the world, which is the important thing.

According to the Tibetan, this group of telepathic communicators would also work with the facilitation of communication between individuals, so that rules and the methods whereby speech can be transcended, may become known, and the new way of communication be brought about. So this type of telepathy will become more prevalent as we move on into the New Age—an ability to project a thought from mind to mind.

Lex Hixon: But I understood it was not so much from mind to mind as from super-mind to mind.

Mary Bailey: Yes, that's perfectly true, but as a result of that, the more individual type of communication should develop along sound lines, because of the inner point of synthesis from which it emerged.

The second group, the trained observers, was to be trained to see clearly by means of the intuition. Intuitive understanding and intuitive perception is another very essential development because this would help to dissipate glamor and bring in illumination. At some point, the Tibetan remarks on the fantastic effect there will be when humanity has become, as he puts it, "disillusioned and de-glamored."

The third group is the magnetic healers. Here, the Tibetan isn't talking so much about physical healing, but about the psychological healing of mind and spirit. Emotional healing should also eventually emerge as healing on the physical level.

Lex Hixon: Did the Tibetan choose the members of the nine groups according to their different temperaments?

Mary Bailey: No, it was very much a matter of ray equipment, or the energies that control their different vehicles.

Lex Hixon: So temperament is really a psychological term, whereas when you say "ray equipment," you mean something on the psychic level?

Mary Bailey: No, it is something much more profound than that. We're all governed by [cosmic] energies of different kinds. There is one type of energy that controls us as a soul, another as a personality; another controls the mind, another the emotional body, and another the physical manifestation. Depending on the [cosmic] ray [influences]of the different disciples, he would select the group most appropriate for them.

Lex Hixon: So one might not at first respond from a personality level, saying, "This is the right thing for me."

Mary Bailey: No, it would not be intended that way. He would probably select a soul ray as the dominating influence in determining the group.

Lex Hixon: So one might feel resistance at first.

Mary Bailey: Oh, they did. There's no question about it. This was one reason why eventually he had to disband the groups.

Let me just give you very quickly the names of the other groups. The fourth group was the educators of the New Age, working along the line of culture and bringing in new types of education. The fifth [group] was political organizers concerned with political factors in every nation and dealing with problems of civilization and international relationships. You see how practical they are. And the sixth was workers in the field of religion, formulating the universal platform of a new world religion, which will emphasize unity and the fellowship of the spirit.

The seventh was scientific servers, revealing the essential spirituality of all scientific work, motivated by love of humanity and relating to science and religion, which must be brought into a moral-based relationship. And then the eighth group is the group of psychologists, concerned with relating soul and personality leading to the revelation of divinity. And then the ninth, which is again a very practical one, is the financiers and economists group, working with energy through interchange and values of commerce dealing with the laws of supply and demand and the principle of sharing.

Lex Hixon: You could say the politics or the economics of the Arcane School was one of sharing, and finding a better way to keep wealth accumulation fair.

Mary Bailey: Yes, I think the principles of cooperation and sharing really are dominant here, and they should, and hopefully will, learn to control our economic and political matters in the future. Cooperation and sharing are two principles that will come into very pronounced manifestation in the opening of the New Age, which is now, of course. We're already beginning to see that a bit, aren't we?

And then there was a 10th group that was synthesizing all the others. The Tibetan called them the creative workers, because creative work is needed in all groups. Those 10 groups were the first ones organized by the Tibetan, and he selected the individuals to work in each one. In 1931, when he first started organizing these groups through Alice, there were 41 members. They all lived in different parts of the world. The Tibetan himself selected the members for various reasons—not because he necessarily thought that each one of them was of outstanding capacity as a disciple, but, in some cases, because they had an old karmic link; in other cases, as he put it, they had earned the right to the opportunity to try the work.

He gave the personal instructions to each member of the group through Alice. Alice wrote them down, just as she wrote down the teaching in the books that he communicated to her mentally, and then mailed out these communications to the different group members. Each one received the instructions of the whole group, so that they could learn to sort of understand one another and begin to integrate and work together more as a group.

This helped some, but it proved rather disastrous for the personalities of others. When he finally disbanded the group in 1946, there were only 22 members left. In the course of that time, several of the elderly had died. Some had dropped out of their own accord because they simply could not sustain the energy the Tibetan poured into the group. Others, the Tibetan himself suspended.

But it was an experiment, after all. He emphasized that from the beginning. Therefore, while in one sense, the effort to establish an outer projection of the ashram may have failed, in another sense, it was highly successful because since then and, as a result of publishing the actual instructions given to the members of this group, thousands upon thousands of people have benefited.

This is a communication from the Tibetan to a man who continued to work right up to the end of the released instructions. He says, My brother, I have thought for you today naught but a happy recognition. You have proceeded with your life task with patience, serenity, and foresight. The dual life of a disciple covering personality obligations in the chosen field of soul service has been successfully attempted.

"It amuses us at times to note that some disciples believe the masters pry into their daily lives, know their petty faults and silly little failures, and are fully aware of all they think and do. We wonder sometimes where they think the masters find the time, and why they should be so interested in the habits of thought and action and speech, which the disciple is rapidly overcoming."

Lex Hixon: That's unexpectedly humorous and delightful. The hierarchy, as I understand it, is the ultimate group of realized beings. The fact that one can contact them and be under their guidance puts a new picture on people seeking for teachers in the outer world. We tend to forget that the hierarchy is always available inwardly, and they are the finest teachers.

Mary Bailey: And of course, they are completely available. We can make that connection. We can establish that alignment. The Buddha taught this, of course, and the Christ taught it. The kingdom of Heaven is within you.

Joseph Goldstein
October 12, 1975

Joseph Goldstein was born in 1944 and grew up in the Catskill Mountains of upstate New York. After he graduated from Columbia University in 1965, he joined the Peace Corps and was stationed in Thailand, where he first encountered Buddhism. In 1967, he began a serious study of Buddhism that led him to India, Burma, and Tibet, and by 1974 he was teaching insight meditation retreats all over the world. He is a co-founder of Insight Meditation Society (IMS) in Barre, Massachusetts, and is still a guiding teacher there. He envisioned the expansion to IMS's Retreat Center and Forest Refuge, and in 1989 he helped establish the Barre Center for Buddhist Studies. Goldstein's many books include *Mindfulness: A Practical Guide to Awakening*, *One Dharma*, and *Insight Meditation*.

Lex Hixon: Joseph Goldstein represents the tradition of insight meditation. He has studied extensively in India and Bodh Gaya and is now sharing these techniques—perhaps "teaching" them is too strong a word, because he definitely is not on a guru trip. How did you make that connection with Buddhism, Joseph?

Joseph Goldstein: The thinking that led me to the connection really started at university. I was at Columbia here in New York, studying philosophy, particularly interested in Plato and Spinoza. By the time I got to my senior year at Columbia, I had the strong feeling that I wanted to start living some of the philosophy rather than merely studying it in an academic way. At the time, the most exciting prospect for traveling and having some new experiences seemed to be the Peace Corps. So I joined and was sent to Thailand, where I spent two years teaching English at a school in Bangkok. I came into contact with quite a few Westerners who had become Buddhist monks in Thailand. They were having discussion groups and different kinds of classes in Bangkok, and I started going to these meetings originally to make my own connection between Western philosophy and the teachings of the Buddha, which were quite new to me. I saw the value of a lot of the practical teachings of the Buddha, and I found the teachings expressed by these Westerners opened up a way of actually living a philosophy by integrating it into my life.

After two years of volunteering in Bangkok, I came back to America, where I went through a somewhat difficult time trying to find out what kind of work to do, and how to further the meditation practice I had just barely begun there. I went off for a retreat by myself, trying to practice meditation intensively, and I found that it was very difficult to do without guidance. I was tapping into different kinds of energies that I didn't know anything about.

Lex Hixon: Did you have any training in meditation while you were in Bangkok?

Joseph Goldstein: I'd had some very basic instruction, but not any kind of intensive practice, so I was really just at a very beginning stage. When I went off by myself and tried to meditate all day long, I found I was really in over my head, and I realized that I needed a teacher to help me along.

Lex Hixon: At this point, had you done any reading in spiritual things?

Joseph Goldstein: I had done some reading but it became very apparent that it is very difficult to practice meditation out of a book. It can be a beginning, but you need more guidance to go on. That was in 1967, and there was not so much happening in this country, as far as meditation or spiritual practice. So I went to India to look for a teacher. First I went to the ashram of Charan Singh. He is a very powerful spiritual master with a very beautiful ashram. But it didn't feel like just exactly what I was looking for.

Lex Hixon: In retrospect, do you think that you were a Buddhist from the very beginning?

Joseph Goldstein: I think that's probably so, although as my practice in Buddhism deepened, I began to realize on a deeper and deeper level that actually the label of Buddhism or Hinduism has less and less meaning, because many spiritual practices have the goal of understanding who we are, and that's beyond any of the words or concepts.

Lex Hixon: That's a very good thing to point out. I think that it's an accepted idea, by now, that all the disciplines are moving in the same direction. But less commonly understood may be the idea that there seems to be some sort of deep destiny that people have to practice a certain way, and that it's not just a matter of choice.

Joseph Goldstein: I think that's true. It depends very much on temperament and personality, and that's why it is very beautiful that there are so many different traditions and styles of practice, because people can find one that's suitable to their temperament. After having traveled around India a little bit to different teachers and ashrams, I ended up in Bodh Gaya, the place of the Buddha's enlightenment. It turns out that there was an Indian meditation teacher there who was teaching the method called Vipassana, or insight meditation. As soon as I came into contact with that teaching, it felt like I was coming home.

When I first met my teacher, the quality that most impressed me about the practice was its purity in terms of not adding anything else to our conditioning or to how the mind is working. It's simply watching. Learning to sit back and watch what's happening. Watch it in a way that's free of greed, which is the clinging to what's pleasant; free of hatred, which is the condemning of what is unpleasant; free of delusion, which means not really seeing clearly. It's a practice which leads to a perfectly balanced state of mind, seeing in every moment the arising and passing away of all phenomena of mind and body without the clinging. It's all a process of change. Everything is in flux. Instead of blocking the flow by our reactions to it, we get into harmony and become the flow. So the mind achieves a very rhythmic balance with what's happening

Lex Hixon: I'd like to go back to your connections with Plato and Spinoza. It's interesting that the Greek word *gymnosophist* is the word that is found in ancient Greek literature for yogis because the Greeks did have contact with India. Spinoza's contemporaries used that term to describe him. He lived alone and there's every reason to believe that he had a concrete mode of practice, along with his intellectual work. Now the trouble is that we read his ethics, his intellectual work, and don't have any connection with his mode of life. And similarly, Plato emerged out of the Pythagorean communities, where he received a practical spiritual training. Yet again, when we read Plato's dialogues, we're not aware of those communities and their structure and their rules. So it's my own feeling that the so-called Western intellectual tradition had their roots in the same kind of concrete spiritual practices as are found in the East. But all we have are the written works of these thinkers.

What do you feel now about Plato and Spinoza? Do you still feel any kinship to them? Would you consider writing something of a philosophical nature?

Joseph Goldstein: I think my connection with them has been weakened as I have gotten more into the practice of meditation, in a non-conceptual way, so there's not the same force in their words. At the time, however, they had a very profound influence on me.

Lex Hixon: I happen to be a student of philosophy, too, as you can probably tell. If Western philosophy is going to grow and produce a new stream of work, I think one of the ways it could happen is through people who have rediscovered this spiritual training in the Eastern traditions where it has been maintained. They can then come back and write in the Western philosophical tradition and not necessarily be confined by it. And Eastern traditions are not without concepts because when you read Buddhist philosophy there's a tremendous intellectual tradition there. Even in Zen, that's supposed to be totally anti-intellectual, there are long treatises, which have tremendous philosophical value, as far as I can see.

Joseph Goldstein: There's an interesting Zen story that points to the role of concepts in spiritual practice. A man is standing outside on the night of a full moon. A friend comes out and points with his finger at the moon. If the friend is wise, he'll see that the finger is pointing at something and look up at the sky and see the moon. If he's not so wise, he'll see the finger pointing, and keep looking at the finger. Concepts and words, represented by the finger in the story, are used to point to a direct experience of the truth, they are not the experience of the truth. In that respect, the words and the concepts are useful and helpful, but not if we cling to them.

Lex Hixon: If I could expand on that metaphor a little bit, we have this finger, which is part of a hand, pointing at the moon. Now, suppose you had a culture that then forgot the finger and just gazed at the moon. But then, what would be the connection to the hand? How could the hand build all the useful technical things of the society? So I feel that we have to be careful not to say, "Well, that's just the finger. Now that we've seen the moon, we can forget about it."

Joseph Goldstein: No, no. That's a common misconception of people who don't yet understand really what the spiritual practice is about. It's not throwing out the conceptual or intellectual level of mind. Anybody who has sat even for a short while and watched their minds has seen that the mind is pretty much involved in a running conceptual commentary of dialogue and chatter. The practice is to bring the mind to a certain level of peace and stillness, when we can use the words and concepts when it's appropriate to do so, but reside in a place of stillness and balance.

Lex Hixon: And presumably, philosophers of the Western tradition have, one way or another, achieved that stillness and balance, and so they write out of that space. I guess I'm arguing about this because I don't want to see Western culture being thrown overboard in the enthusiasm for the practices from the East.

Joseph Goldstein: I agree.

Lex Hixon: I think it would be marvelous if someone like you would write about this. Maybe it's not your destiny.

Joseph Goldstein: I think it's probably more yours, to write the treatise on Spinoza and Eastern philosophy.

Lex Hixon: It's really the responsibility of all of us, isn't it, to maintain Western culture from this point of stillness that we also find in these Eastern practices? But I was just talking about this last night with some friends who are psychoanalysts and have developed their scholarly and critical faculties. They are all interested in meditation. I was trying to indicate that this skepticism and this intellectual acumen that they've developed is not something to be thrown away.

Joseph Goldstein: One of the things that interested me so much in my own teacher, in Bodh Gaya, is that he is one of the few people who had mastered both aspects—the theoretical and the practical side—of meditation. He was a very great scholar as well as being a very great yogi. So his understanding of the Dharma was very broad. He wasn't trapped in any narrow sectarian view because he had a broad base of understanding. I appreciated very much that quality of openness.

Lex Hixon: I'm so glad you feel that way because I feel strongly that way myself, and I think that after four years of doing this program, if anything is emerging, it is this idea of stressing practice and intellectual understanding with the feeling that both in isolation could be a problem. Everyone admits that just intellectual thinking in isolation is a problem. The big head trip. But fewer people among those who are beginning spiritual life and practice have a critical sense of how narrowing focusing only on practice can be.

Joseph Goldstein: Yes, that's a liability. But I met students of my teacher in India, who probably didn't have a very great amount of education, who were at very high stages of purity and enlightenment. So it's not a prerequisite for spiritual practice or enlightenment that one have a theoretical understanding, although when you add that understanding to the practice, it makes your experience very rich.

Lex Hixon: And perhaps helps with the teaching of it in the West. How deeply do you still feel identified with your role as an American? Or do you just think of yourself as a teacher of Vipassana?

Joseph Goldstein: A lot of the practice has to do with coming to understand the basic selflessness of the mind/body process, not solidifying any one aspect of one's life or experience as constituting our essence, or self, or ego. So a lot of the practice has been to settle back into the moment in flow, not holding onto any particular past image or concept we have of ourselves. But it is also about allowing it to express itself in the moment. So I don't really think of myself in terms of being this kid out of the Catskills, now teaching Dharma. It's just an ongoing evolution.

Burmese meditation master Mahasi Sayadaw with some of his monks and his four Western teachers (from left: Sharon Salzberg, Joseph Goldstein, Jack Kornfield, and Jacqueline Mandell-Schwartz) at an Insight Meditation Society ceremony in 1979

David Dellinger
February 1, 1976

David Dellinger was born in 1915 in Wakefield, Massachusetts. While at Yale University, he was arrested for demonstrating for the trade union movement. After graduating Phi Beta Kappa in economics, he worked in a factory and lived among the homeless. As a fellow at Oxford University, he drove an ambulance in the Spanish Civil War. Back in New York, he enrolled at the Union Theological Seminary. He spent three years in federal prison, starting in 1940, for refusing military service, and was physically abused during solitary confinement. As a radical pacifist, Dellinger opposed the bombings of Hiroshima and Nagasaki and the Vietnam War. His friends included Dr. Martin Luther King and the Berrigans, and he was one of the notorious Chicago Seven. In 2001, at age 85, he protested against the NAFTA treaty. His books include his autobiography, *From Yale to Jail* (1996). He died in 2004.

Lex Hixon: We've got David Dellinger with us this morning, and we're going to be talking about how the world might get around to understanding on the worldly level and the spiritual level— we hope there's no gulf between those in the final analysis. I want to read a little bit, before I start talking to David, from his recent book, *More Power than We Know,* published by Anchor Press. It's a paperback.

"*In my view, abolishing capitalism is an absolutely necessary condition for human liberation, but it is by no means the only condition. Genuine revolution requires a politics of transcendence, as well as intimate illuminance of love and joy, sometimes in the midst of struggle and confrontation, sometimes apart from it. The danger in attempts to achieve fulfillment and freedom through spiritual awareness is that we might isolate the spiritual from the political.*

"*There are reasons to believe that the spiritual enlightenment being cultivated so assiduously by thousands of people will be as revolutionizing for the next hundred years as scientific Marxism and its rival anarchist cousins have been for the past hundred. This is most apt to happen, it seems to me, if it draws on the lessons, both positive and negative of the secular revolutionary movements that have helped bring the search for human liberation to its present stage of development.*"

There may be some of you listening who conceivably might not know who David Dellinger is. Of course, he's known nationally in contemporary history as a defendant in the Chicago Eight trials in the Sixties. But for many, many years he's been connected with the non-violent revolutionary movement to liberate oppressed people. David, can you tell us just a little bit about how you grew up and how you got involved in this kind of work? Were you given the gifts of love and faith in childhood? Did you have that kind of richness?

David Dellinger: I grew up with a father who was, at the risk of sounding too exalted, love incarnate. He was one of the warmest, most loving human beings I've ever known. The interesting thing is that he was chairman of the Republican town committee. So I had adopted his politics early on. I was a freshman in college the year that Franklin Roosevelt defeated Herbert Hoover in the election. I remember walking through the streets of New Haven, almost depressed that all of those "Communists" were now in the government. And of course, very soon my politics changed, and it reached a stage with my father when we could almost not communicate. I remember one time I was going off to an anti-war conference, which led to my refusal to register for the draft and to accept an exemption. He saw the handwriting on the wall and was very upset that I was going. He took me to the train, all the way trying to tell me not to go. He thrust a few dollars into my hand and said, "If I never see you again, take this." He thought all my political ideas were wrong, and I thought all of his political ideas were wrong, and yet in his life, he just kept expressing an almost transcendent quality of being able to relate directly, humanly, warmly, lovingly to individual human beings of whatever class, race, sex, age, anything. It helped me to realize that whatever political or religious differences we may have, we impoverish ourselves if we cut ourselves off from other people, if we don't reach out to them in love and openness to understanding their hopes and fears and aspirations.

Lex Hixon: Did your father use religious language to describe his lovingness and transcendent feelings? Was he a religious person?

David Dellinger: He was a member of the Congregational Church, and I did attend church regularly as a child. Most of the time, I was totally offended by it. It was the most boring and the most hypocritical place for me. I don't think that my father was enriched greatly by the Church. It's always hard to tell about other people. In my own view, he wasn't using religious words, but he was living it.

Lex Hixon: It shows that this loving quality doesn't necessarily translate into liberal politics.

David Dellinger: No, but of course I have to feel that it was a tremendous condemnation of the system that a man with as much innate love and warmth as my father could end up doing things institutionally as a lawyer which I'm sure were very harmful to people, because he was operating within the existing institutions, was dealing with the existing courts. He was often—I'm sure, for all of his best intentions—what objectively might be called an oppressor. He would do work free for people. But on the other hand, he would receive, for a week's work settling a will, what a worker in a factory would get paid in a year. One has to see the flaw there.

Lex Hixon: When did you begin to find in Marxist philosophy and other places a kind of confirmation of your innate feelings about these things?

David Dellinger: I guess it happened that same freshman year in college, when everything was changing in my thinking—even before I walked up and down the streets of New Haven, wondering how to face the fact that the "Communist devil" Franklin Roosevelt had been elected to the White House.

I had seen a notice in the Yale University Christian Association, that anybody interested in bettering the conditions of the university maids and janitors should come to a meeting. So I went. It was the beginning of a campaign to unionize the university employees and to raise their wages. I think I did this because I was upset the very first day on campus by having a black janitor say, "Yassir, yassir" to me. I couldn't get him to relate to me as a person. I had an Irish maid who was a little closer, but nonetheless quite distant too. So even before the election, I'd gone to that meeting, and then I'd spoken to the janitor and the maid and asked the questions we were supposed to about how much they earned and what hours they worked. The next day I was called into the dean's office. He said that it was really nice that I was concerned, but the university knew what was best for them and that if they had more money they wouldn't know how to use it anyway. And he wanted me to know that, actually, the meeting had been organized by Communists and I should stay away from them. Obviously, I didn't.

Lex Hixon: Years later you went to Union Theological Seminary. How did you start getting interested in Christian issues? How did you make the connection with the Church? What got you there?

David Dellinger: When I was, I think, in junior high school, my closest friend and I sort of discovered the New Testament and I fell in love with Jesus, or with the Sermon on the Mount. That friend was also attracted to the New Testament. So we used to read it and say, "Goddamn it, goddamn it, isn't this wonderful? Why is it so different from everything that has to do with the Church?"

And when I did go to seminary, I went there out of love for a way of life, a revolutionary way of life, which later I'd come to identify with the Communism of the early Christians. They sold all of their goods, and there was neither rich nor poor amongst them. So I went there to find out more about that revolutionary way of life and its sources of inspiration and strength and insight. I did field work, and in the summertime I acted as a minister. But in a sense, I was saved from that fate when the first peacetime draft came. Along with everybody else, I was supposed to register. A bunch of us talked it over, and 20 of us announced that we weren't going to register for the draft. The next morning, we received telegrams from the president of the seminary expelling us. They succeeded in whittling down the number of non-registrants from 20 to eight. But if I was, in a sense, getting hooked on the Church, that broke the umbilical cord and saved me. Forgive me if this sounds irreverent. It's heretical, thank goodness.

I went to prison as a result of that. But also, I got married between my first and second prison sentences, and during the time that I was in prison having certain experiences, my wife was staying in a commune with Teresina Raul, who had studied Buddhism in Japan. I think my wife was the first one to understand the limits of Christianity as a kind of imperialism that insisted that this was the one God and the one Christ and the one path, in contrast to the idea that there are many paths and there are many different ways of relating to what some people call "God."

Lex Hixon: But you say that you still do consider yourself a Christian in some sort of deep sense.

David Dellinger: Did I say that? Yes, if you take away the imperialism—namely, that Jesus was the only Son of God. And if you stop excluding not only the Buddhas and the Muhammads and the people whose names we don't even know, and if you consider the life and teachings of Jesus—then that's the kind of Christian that I was. That does not mean, Lex, [that] I opposed the professors at Union Seminary who preached what they called "the social Gospel." I hope I was as much of an anti-imperialist, anti-capitalist, anti-economic-sexism-and-racism person as they were, but I felt that they were teaching something which was only half the story. In other words, they were attributing all awareness, all human love, all human interpenetration to simply fixing up the institutions, or changing them. I felt they were missing what was the main theme in the seminary, which was that Jesus was much more than a revolutionary. I think that what Jesus taught was that everybody is capable of being a son or daughter of God.

Lex Hixon: How do you get along with fellow people in the political movements, with this kind of openness? Do you make enemies this way? I have a little difficulty getting along in my field, which is the spiritual movement. My openness tends to really bring out some insecurity on the part of certain people. Sometimes I have to even hide that openness a little bit.

David Dellinger: I guess what I think is the best thing is not to hide the openness but not to use the words that offend people, which is really in the spirit of what I'm trying to say anyway, that these things can't be put into words. One of the problems is that most churches, including Marxist-Leninist sects and fundamentalist Christian sects and certain Buddhist or Hindu sects, put things into words, and then insist on the words, and shove the words down your throat instead of letting the person unfold from their own experience.

But sometimes it is a two-way thing. But you see, there's more that I want to say on that anyway. Take this time around the Chicago trial. Now, we had a wide range of attitudes, lifestyles, and political philosophies among the defendants that the government selected to be co-conspirators.

Sometimes this was a source of conflict, but if you were fighting against the same oppression, even in slightly different ways, if you were sharing the struggle, then you respected each other even though you disagreed. And so, a lot of things in the "Yippies" [Youth International Party members] were very far from my lifestyle, but I remember once in court when something happened and Abbie Hoffman said that I was the first Yippie. It felt like a compliment because we were sharing something together, he could see beyond our superficial differences to our basic unity. In the same way, although there were some things that bothered me about their actions or attitudes, I thought that it came like the breath of enlightenment, when Abbie Hoffman and Jerry Rubin and Paul Krassner and others burned money on Wall Street, burned dollar bills. It was beautiful; it said more about the money system in American culture than any of the speeches I'd been giving. I think if you share the struggle together, and if you get away from the idea that there is a single correct line, whether it's the line of Jesus Christ our Savior, or of Marxist-Leninism, or of the Guru Watchamacallit, then I think you can reach across those barriers.

Lex Hixon: Would you read from the book that you are working on now?

David Dellinger: I should say that this [is about] when I was first in prison in 1940:

"Whatever the reason, I was in the hole for the first time. No light, no bed, a little prison food once a day, shivering in the middle of summer, damp like Byron's dungeon [in his poem, 'The Prisoner of] Chillon.'

"I heard, 'You won't come out until you agree to obey orders. All orders. I was scared, because earlier, when I was in solitary, one tier below, 'Tough Tony' Marcello, who terrorized the prisoners and was supposed to be a triggerman for the Mafia, had been put in the hole. In the middle of the night, when everything was quiet, they had carried him out screaming; four men carrying him screaming past my cell to the mental ward. The prisoner in the cell next to mine told me through the ventilator, 'Nobody can stand it. Don't ever do anything to give them an excuse to put you in there.' I was plenty scared, I wondered how long I could hold out before I cracked like Tough Tony cracked.

"Then it began to happen. Gradually, for no reason I can explain, I began to discover how little it mattered where you are or what they do to you. I knew that what I did to get to get thrown in there was right, and somehow the longer I was there, the better I felt. Maybe that wasn't it at all. But anyway, I never felt better in my life, even if I was shivering and wished I had something to eat, or a cigarette, and my hips ached from lying on the floor and I was trying to sleep standing in a corner because it wasn't so cold that way, but it was still too cold to sleep, and when I did fall asleep I started to keel over, and you could hurt yourself if you weren't careful. I wondered how many hours it had been. Maybe it was only a few minutes, because I remember the story by Ralph Waldo Emerson, I think it was, about a man who was accidentally locked in a sepulcher, when he went back to look at his dead fiancée one last time. And he thought he was there a week, but his friends missed him right away and came back for him an hour or two later. His hair turned white and he was shaking, just as I was shaking then. He never got over it. He shook the rest of his life.

"Then unexpectedly, for no reason at all, I felt good again and I didn't care how long it had been or would be. I felt warm inside and filled all over with love for everyone—everyone I knew and everyone I didn't know: plants, animals, tin cans, even bankers. Everything and everybody. Why did I feel so good? Was it God? Or approaching death? Or just the way life is supposed to be, if we weren't so busy trying to make it something else?

"It didn't matter why. The only thing that mattered was that it was happening. It happened when you least expected it. You didn't try to make it happen. You didn't even know it could happen, not there, not anywhere, that much. I never felt so good before. Not even when I kissed Rena [my wife]. Or when I won the two-mile run in the Yale-Cornell meet. Or fought Bobby Dean in the fifth grade because he was punching a little kid.

"I thought about when I'd been in Spain during the Civil War. The peasants and some of the student soldiers were some of the most inspiring people I had ever met, and I knew then that I would always be a revolutionary. It would never leave me. But I would be a nonviolent revolutionary, because although the other way is tempting, it doesn't work. I had almost picked up a gun on the third day in Madrid in the

People's Park, when Franco's troops were half a mile away and advancing. I thought that if my friends were going to die, I wanted to die with them. And who knows, maybe we'd win. But whoever won that way, it wouldn't be the people. I knew I had to find a better way of fighting.

"*That was the hardest decision I ever made in my life, not to pick up the gun in Spain. After that, World War II was simple. I wasn't even tempted to pick up a gun to fight for General Motors, U.S. Steel, and the Chase Manhattan Bank, even if Hitler was running the other side. Besides, by then I had lived in the slums for a couple of years, and knew the U.S. government didn't want to help the American people, let alone the German people.*

"*Now I was in the hole, and I felt the way I had in Spain, only more so. I had gone from freedom to jail; from regular jail to solitary confinement; from solitary confinement to a damp, black dungeon they called 'punitive isolation;' and I had never been so free before. For the first time in my life, I had nothing, and for the first time in my life, I had everything.*"

Lex Hixon: David has been reading from the new book that he's working on about his remarkable life experiences. I'm impressed by the way David comes across as a natural, indigenous spirituality. He's sort of like his father. I like his politics better than I would have liked his father's. There's this underlying spontaneous, naturalness, which hasn't really been brought about by any system of thought, and in fact it looks like he's spent a whole life battling not only oppression in the political sense, but the oppression of various systems of thought.

Have you ever been tempted to get out of the political movement in some sense, and just say, "Well, I've given all I can to it, and now I want to...?"

David Dellinger: Sometimes people say, "How do you keep going? You're 60 years old, and aren't you tired?" And I think it's just the opposite. The process itself is fulfilling and vitalizing. It's sort of like—I don't know if this is going to work exactly—but it's like the seasons. So there has to be spring, summer, fall, and winter, or else the cycle would not be complete. But I don't see any reason ever to get tired of winter, or see any reason ever to get over that inexhaustible surge of vitality in spring, which takes over the whole universe. How are you going to get tired of it? And yet it moves into some other season.

Lex Hixon: Do you have something like a meditation practice? Or is just your work and your life your meditation?

David Dellinger: I began to be sure that I had more solitude recently, more privacy, more chance to read spiritual things, or later when I got strong enough, to climb mountains or earlier, sit alone on a rock overlooking the sea.

See, I'm afraid that what I've been saying may sound like I'm against techniques. I'm not. I don't use any established technique, unless you can call reading and watching nature [one]. I'm only opposed to techniques when they become the substitute for the experience. While I was doing some of the radical union organizing work, I took a course at Yale Divinity School, taught by Richard Niebuhr, who was a brother of the better-known Reinhold Niebuhr, about rituals. It was so beautiful. He talked about all of the things that are supposed to be a ladder to God and how at a certain point the temptation is that they replace God. So that's my only criticism of techniques. I think people can very often plunge into a program, they become part of it, they give themselves to it, and they grow. But maybe the danger is if they get hung up there and stay there and don't move on.

Lex Hixon: Actually, [you have] attempted to bring that very particular answer out in [your] whole lifetime.

David Dellinger: And, of course, you began by reading about the fact that capitalism absolutely must go, and we can't fudge that. I had intended anyway to come back to the fact that I think that it's best to work simultaneously at attaining the kind of peace that we talked about, and doing away with or replacing the oppressive institutions of the society. It's a subject for a whole other program, but just because it is possible to achieve peace when being oppressed or when being put in the hole does not mean that one should welcome oppression or being put in the hole. I didn't come out of the hole thanking the warden for putting me there and saying, "Put the other prisoners there too," because it's a paradox that the poor and the abused can experience the highest possible consciousness and total awareness. That's a paradox, but it should not in any way gloss over the fact that the evil institutions must go. General Motors must not be allowed to exist in its present form, or the Pentagon. We can't accept the illusion that this is a democracy because we vote for the oppressor who operates as the executive head of the ruling class.

Lex Hixon: And as you said, revolution itself is the way. It's a kind of goalless process. It's a process that just goes on and on.

Eileen and Peter Caddy
February 8, 1976

Born in London in 1917, Peter Caddy was raised within esoteric Christian and occult circles, and attended Harrow boarding school. His brother-in-law initiated him into the Rosicrucian Order. In 1962, after several jobs, a failed first marriage, and 15 years as a Royal Air Force officer of catering, Peter and his second wife, Eileen Jessop Caddy (born in 1917 in Alexandria, Egypt), moved to a Scottish trailer park with their three children and their friend Dorothy Maclean. They started a garden, and found that with Peter's labor, Eileen's "inner voice"—divine messages she received daily—and Dorothy's ability to communicate with angelic beings about plants, they could produce extraordinary vegetables, including 30-pound cabbages. Their group, Findhorn Foundation, became a thriving New Age intentional community. Peter left Findhorn in 1979 after Eileen stopped receiving guidance. He married twice more, founded another community in California, and died in a car accident in Germany in 1997. Eileen died at Findhorn in 2006. In 2016, Dorothy Maclean celebrated her 96th birthday at Findhorn, which now has approximately 400 residents. Findhorn's Ecovillage currently works on new methods of wind energy and water restoration and treatment.

Lex Hixon: A woman of the spirit is with us this morning in the studio. Her name is Eileen Caddy, and she and her husband, Peter, founded Findhorn Community, a New Age community in northern Scotland. Eileen is not a metaphysician; as she herself insists, she just has simple truths that she knows and embodies. When Eileen was in Glastonbury about 22 years ago, she received a transmission from a higher, purer plane, much as Alice Bailey did, but it didn't come from a Tibetan.

Eileen Caddy: No, it didn't. It was a voice I heard, actually, and I didn't know what it was or where it had come from, but the words that came were, "Be still and know that I am God," and then it went on to say that if I followed this voice that everything would work out perfectly. I had been going through a very, very difficult time. That is the voice that I've followed for the last 22 years.

Lex Hixon: On the outer plane, that voice has manifested in the form of a community; a burgeoning, complicated, beautiful community, Findhorn Community. Eileen's husband, Peter Caddy, has had a great deal to do with building and organizing it. But what we want to do is talk more about the inner life with Eileen. At this very moment, there are about 100 people in Studio C who are watching a film on Findhorn. Peter is out there talking to them and introducing the film. Peter and Eileen are always at work and always together.

"Be still and know that I am God" sort of appeals to me because there is that kind of ultimate simplicity there, that ultimate place where this message came from. It wasn't simply a message from one of the intermediary planes. It came right from the ultimate. What do you feel the plan is?

Eileen Caddy: The plan on earth? It is God's plan. It is the divine plan, and we just follow step by step. We are not given a great, vast plan in front of us, but we live from moment to moment being guided by that inner voice.

Lex Hixon: So you don't have visions of the future of the exact events that are going to happen? It is kind of a moment-to-moment feeling?

Eileen Caddy: No. I am given the visions occasionally and especially when we were sort of building the community. I would be given quite a number of visions, and I would have to hold it in my consciousness—the vision—and then Peter would have to bring it down into the physical. He did all the hard work. I did the receiving.

Lex Hixon: Light, love, and power—can you give me just your own immediate impressions and associations with each of these divine aspects? What does light suggest to you?

Eileen Caddy: Light and power, I feel, are the same. Light is truth, really, and the strength of knowing that you are doing God's will, and love is the one that I really and truly respond to. But I feel now that it is a question of finding balance of these three in one's whole being. To begin with, when Peter and I first came together, he was light and I was love, and we worked, we complemented each other. Then the time came when we had to be split so that we could become two separate individuals—balanced individuals. That's really what we are in the process of doing now.

Lex Hixon: I get the impression that love, or the quality of love, is a kind of quiet thing, which does not necessarily have to manifest on the outer plane.

Eileen Caddy: It is a question of being, I think. That is what I feel. It is a demonstrating, a living.

Lex Hixon: Do you feel that the community and the outer work, say, the University of Light that you are engaged in building in Scotland, is essential to your being?

Eileen Caddy: I think it's absolutely essential, yes. But I do think you need balance though, and that is the thing I am finding now.

I have to find the balance, really, of the will and purpose as well as the love.

Lex Hixon: Do you feel any contact with any particular one of the masters, or do you really relate more to the ultimate beloved?

Eileen Caddy: That's right—the power behind everything—that's what I really relate to. That's who I relate to.

Lex Hixon: I feel the same kind of feeling about that—it's all very well to have the divine focused in various ways. It is very useful, but I feel a kind of impulse to relate to the very source of the whole.

Eileen Caddy: Well, I think it helps a lot of people to have these other different spokes to the wheel, but the hub is God.

Lex Hixon: Eileen, were you born with this kind of openness to the ultimate, or did you have to be transformed?

Eileen Caddy: I had to be transformed. I think the awful thing is that one has to have one's back against the wall before one really turns to the God within, and that's the state I was in. I was in a very, very low state, and that was when I really found the God within.

Lex Hixon: Did you have any training as a child?

Eileen Caddy: No, none at all. I was just brought up in an orthodox way, in an orthodox religion, the Church of England.

Lex Hixon: Do you remember any childhood experiences?

Eileen Caddy: I had no imagination and I had no experiences at all until 22 years ago, when things really started to happen, and have gone on happening ever since.

Lex Hixon: Would you say when you were in Glastonbury, were you praying for guidance, were you really opening up in longing?

Eileen Caddy: Yes, I was really asking, "What can I do? What *can* I do?" And then I heard this voice. It was very distinct. Soon after that, I did hear several other voices, but always, they came back to that one voice. And that is the one voice that I've held onto and have followed.

Lex Hixon: Could you say that it was a male or female voice, or was it neither?

Eileen Caddy: I would say neither. It was just a voice. I call it "the still, small voice," and I know that everybody's got that within them. It was very clear with me.

Lex Hixon: Do you think that voice might be focused through what is called the Christ-spirit?

Eileen Caddy: Very much so, yes.

Lex Hixon: When one says, "the Christ-spirit," what do you feel inwardly?

Eileen Caddy: When I hear that word, I feel a tremendous joy, actually, and I feel the need, no matter where I am, to evoke the Christ presence and the Christ-spirit, and it's there.

Lex Hixon: "When two or three are gathered..." and there are two of us, so...

Eileen Caddy: That's right.

Lex Hixon: We've fulfilled the bare minimum requirement.

Eileen Caddy: I feel that, yes.

Lex Hixon: After you received this initial guidance, can you say a little bit about the kind of disciplined meditation that you did?

Eileen Caddy: Oh, I had a very rough time after that. I had thought that everything would be smooth sailing, but it wasn't. Yes, one has to learn self-discipline, and I used to spend many hours in meditation and just being still. I always had to do it at night because I have a family, and I was a very busy person during the day. So it was at night that I had to really take time to be alone and listen to that still, small voice.

Lex Hixon: Did most of your meditation hours consist of the voice speaking, or was it mostly silence?

Eileen Caddy: No, no, silence, and sometimes I was told to read something and sometimes I was told to just be. I just did whatever I was told to do. I learned to follow this voice no matter what it told me to do.

Lex Hixon: Was it simply a verbal communication or was there more?

Eileen Caddy: No, what happened was, I had to write it down and I wondered for a long time why I had to write everything down. But now I can see so clearly, especially after we acquired and went to Findhorn where the community is—I have written about 30,000 pages of guidance—I can see now this clear picture running right through what went on in the community because every single thing has been guided by this inner voice. There's a most incredible pattern and plan running through it.

Lex Hixon: So rather than hearing the voice inwardly in an audible sense, by just writing it?

Eileen Caddy: I just wrote it down. Whatever I heard, I wrote down.

Lex Hixon: The main focus of this guidance was to build a community.

Eileen Caddy: No, it wasn't. It was really and truly to help us through our lives. After all, I heard this 22 years ago, and many things happened before we went to Findhorn. We have only been at Findhorn for 14 years. But it is really in the last 14 years that there are these 30,000 pages of clear directions on how to run the community, and so on.

Lex Hixon: But looking at the whole thing from this perspective now, don't you feel that the community was the fruit out of all of this guidance process?

Eileen Caddy: No. Peter was manager of a four-star hotel just outside Forres, and we ran that hotel under God's guidance, too. So that was really and truly where we got our practical work, because no matter what I was doing, whether I was bathing a baby or whatever I was doing, I had to drop everything. If Peter came and said, "Please, would you get some guidance on such and such a situation in the hotel?" then I would have to do that. It was a good training.

Lex Hixon: Did you find it easy to enter into the meditative state in order to get that?

Eileen Caddy: Very often I was very busy and I just had to sit quietly and as soon as I sat down quietly, the whole thing just flowed and I knew the answer immediately.

Lex Hixon: In a community, there is this sense of joining the individual lights of people into a single light. Do you feel that individual beings are basically separate, or do you think that really there's only one light in the first place?

Eileen Caddy: I think that there is one universal mind and I feel that we can all tap that universal mind—divine mind, call it what you like—because four years ago I was told I was no longer to get any guidance for the community. I used to get it every night and then it would be read in the sanctuary in the morning and people were beginning to lean on me. I was becoming a prop, and

I was told, "You must stop it," because people must learn to turn within and get their own inner direction. That's really what has happened now, so that I get my own inner guidance, but not for the community, because the community have got to learn to grow and stand on their own feet and become strong within themselves.

Lex Hixon: It seems that we could call Jesus one of the clearest manifestations of the Christ Consciousness that ever occurred on the planet. His guidance, if you could call it that, seemed to focus on this idea of the Kingdom of God, of a dawning, say of a New Age on earth. Christians both ordinary and esoteric have been living in that expectation of the New Age, from St. Paul, who felt it was imminent. What do you feel about that?

Eileen Caddy: Well, what I have been told is, "Bring down my kingdom on earth." I feel that is what we are really attempting to do at Findhorn; bringing down God's kingdom on earth, because it's a living demonstration, really. It's a working community and we are living and demonstrating a way of life.

Lex Hixon: This concept of a community being the joining together of the different lights of individual minds into a single light which will create a new world, in other words, bringing this kingdom down is expressed beautifully in a song from Findhorn. All these songs that we'll hear are composed, except for the invocation, which was composed by "the Tibetan," but the others were composed at Findhorn and sung at Findhorn. So in the spirit of this transformation, which occurred to Eileen at Glastonbury—it's a ruined abbey now, isn't it?

Eileen Caddy: No. There is a ruined abbey there, but that is not where I was. I was in a private home and they had a small sanctuary there.

Lex Hixon: Eileen, I want to ask you how in the community and in your own personal life this radiance of Christ—we could call it the radiance of Buddha nature or Allah or Jehovah or the Tao, or anything—how this radiance of the ultimate can be invoked.

Is formal meditation necessary, or can one invoke it simply just in living?

Eileen Caddy: I think in living, actually. That is what I feel. I mean, I do evoke the Christ many a time during the day, no matter what situation one is in, because you can evoke it out of every soul in a room. That's what I do.

Lex Hixon: Do you also do formal meditation? Do you have a regular time when you sit?

Eileen Caddy: Yes, I do. I like that. I need it. Some people do and some people don't, but I do.

Lex Hixon: Can you describe the process of attuning, which is a technique, you might say, or a custom at Findhorn?

Eileen Caddy: We usually sort of hold hands and attune to "the One" and attune to each other. It brings unity and oneness in every situation.

Lex Hixon: I understand that occasionally there are interesting sights at Findhorn, such as people standing around in a circle with brooms and mops and pails and they are all holding hands and attuning before getting to work.

Eileen Caddy: Yes, and why not? I mean, whether it is gardening or in the kitchen or whatever it is, we attune to the One Mind, really, to the One Source, so that there is unity and oneness in whatever work we are doing, no matter how mundane it is. You can do it to the glory of God, anyway.

Lex Hixon: When you were sitting in the studio here, before we went on the air, I noticed that you had your eyes closed, presumably attuning in some way or another. Can you describe that process?

Eileen Caddy: I was just evoking the Christ presence really, and I feel the Christ presence here in the midst of us.

Lex Hixon: Is it a kind of a general evoking, or do you hold in your mind certain people or situations?

Eileen Caddy: No, it was this situation, actually.

Lex Hixon: What I am trying to ask is, is there a difference between a kind of general attuning to the ultimate which is not asking help for any specific situation and a more prayerful focus on a particular problem or situation? Are there two different ways of doing it?

Eileen Caddy: Yes, I suppose there are, really. I just sort of sit and I allow myself to be used in any situation. Supposing there is somebody in very great need, I ask to be used as a channel to radiate love and light to that person in need and I have seen such incredible things happen that I know that it works.

Lex Hixon: This is a beautiful balance, which I am trying to strike, too, between relating to the ultimate, which is formless, the source of all, and which has everything in mind, you might say already, without being reminded of any specific need. But then there is the other dimension of it, which is an occasionally specific focus in prayer is important. Why is that? Why does the divine need that?

Eileen Caddy: I don't know. Sometimes I feel as if somebody is placed on my heart and I know that I have work to do for her/him, really, and so I just ask to be used as a channel.

Lex Hixon: Could it be that this ultimate spirit or consciousness needs the human being to express it on this plane, or is it just a matter of choice, choosing to express the human?

Eileen Caddy: I have no idea. I just sort of sit sometimes in the morning when I am meditating, and a name is given to me. I realize that perhaps that person is going through difficulties, perhaps there is a negativity in them, and I just ask to be used as a channel to radiate that Christ love to them, and I can feel it going out from me and that is when change comes. "In the twinkling of an eye," as the song says.

Lex Hixon: Do you feel—again, I'm just asking your impressions of things you probably never thought about in this way before—when you feel that divine grace flowing, let's say, from your heart to the heart of another person, do you feel that it originates somewhere beyond you?

Eileen Caddy: It is within me. I feel that it is the God within. That is what I accepted—the Christ within—the all within, really.

Lex Hixon: So the center of this radiating energy is within you?

Eileen Caddy: Yes, within my being. It is not a body, but it's a being, really. That is what I really feel, yes.

Lex Hixon: Are there times when you no longer feel like an individual being?

Eileen Caddy: Yes, I've had some incredible experiences of just losing one's whole identity and just becoming one with all life. Those are heights that one touches, but then you have to come down, and really and truly, you can't help your fellow man if you are living up in the heights, so you have to come down and be at one with him so that you can communicate. At least that's what I have been told. That's my way of working.

Lex Hixon: When you say, "I have been told," do you mean from guidance?

Eileen Caddy: From this inner voice. I have been told that you can rise to great heights, but you've got to come down. You can't live on the top of a mountain all the time. You've got to come down into the valley to be able to communicate with your fellow man.

Lex Hixon: Do you feel that your soul will decide to be born again on this planet to do that and continue that process?

Eileen Caddy: I wouldn't have any idea. That's all in the good Lord's hands.

Lex Hixon: If you were given a choice, what would you say?

Eileen Caddy: I am here to serve, and if I am needed, I shall say, "Use me."

Lex Hixon: I guess you haven't really been given a choice for the last 22 years though, in a certain sense.

Eileen Caddy: I think that I have been given a choice, yes. I could choose anything, but I wanted to do only God's will. I wanted to follow that voice and do what I was asked to do and that is really what I have followed. Sometimes it's been right against the grain from a human point of view. We've had to do some pretty crazy things, you know? But it's been so right because everything that we've done has worked out in the most wonderful way. So I know that it is the divine hand in all that we have done.

Lex Hixon: Do you feel that people have to go through a process of purification before they can have this feeling of every instant being guided?

Eileen Caddy: I don't know that everybody has to, but I certainly had to and it is not comfortable. I am even now in the process of change all the time. That is what life is really: a constant change. I know for myself this is what I am feeling now, that I am just changing, changing, changing, and it's darned uncomfortable at times.

Lex Hixon: There are various words for divine qualities that I want to get your impressions about. I have asked you about light and love, and power. What about joy? The quality of joy?

Eileen Caddy: I think that is terribly important because, at one time, when we first started the community, there was very little joy. It was all work, work, work. Then we reached the point when something just sort of broke, and now there is tremendous joy in the community, and that's what we need, I feel. All work and no play makes Jack a dull boy, and I can assure you it does, too.

Lex Hixon: What about the quality of peace?

Eileen Caddy: Yes, I think that it's very necessary too. These are all the qualities that I think one needs.

Lex Hixon: Can you give your impression again, just spontaneous subjective impressions about the quality of peace?

Eileen Caddy: For me, peace is just learning to be, not trying to strive for anything, but just learning to be—to be oneself, really, and that creates an inner peace. You are not trying to be anything, anybody else, but just yourself. I have been told to do this many times when I've been sort of striving and wanting to do this, that, and the other. Just *be*. That brings a tremendous peace, really.

Lex Hixon: You could almost say that your guidance originated on the note of peace: "Be still and know that I am God."

Eileen Caddy: Yes, indeed.

Lex Hixon: You said to me that love is what you especially feel expressing [itself] through you, but it seems to me that the basis of that is peace.

Eileen Caddy: Yes, peace and love. They go hand in hand, I think, too.

Lex Hixon: These terms can so easily become just a cliché in the New Age language, and we have to try to reexamine them again, and kind of open them up, take off the husk, and really find what's there. Your description of peace as being yourself is interesting because it doesn't have a quietist flavor to it. You could be in the midst of intense activity and be yourself, and therefore be peaceful.

Eileen Caddy: And we could always have that peace within, yes.

Lex Hixon: Are you able to feel that pretty much all the time?

Eileen Caddy: Oh, no, no, not all the time. I have to seek it. I have to seek grace many a time.

Lex Hixon: What about life? Jesus, reflecting the Christ consciousness, was supposed to have said, "I am the way, the truth and the life." What does "life" mean in that context? In other words, it's not simply the biological conception of amoebas in the ocean gradually evolving out and becoming living beings.

Eileen Caddy: When you say the word "life," I feel a sort of fullness. Fulfillment. I don't know quite what I mean by that, but I feel a fullness, really. That's life.

Lex Hixon: That's a beautiful thing, that fullness itself, divine fullness is life. It's not a question of different life forms on different planets, necessarily. We see maybe just reflections of that fullness. I don't mean to lead you into a metaphysical discussion.

Eileen Caddy: No, don't, because I wouldn't be much help to you there.

Lex Hixon: I love your immediate responses to things, because you're tuned into such a deep source. I think they're valuable. So I think, again, let me ask you one more time of these different qualities, and perhaps you can respond to me with your impression. Now, "joy," when you hear the term, "joy," what do you...

Eileen Caddy: I don't know, I just sort of feel a bursting out of a shell, really, I think, with joy. I feel an opening up. It's tremendous, actually.

Lex Hixon: That's lovely. I feel the strength of that, because you communicated to me a sense of intense strength there, rather than simply sort of a joy in playing games.

Eileen Caddy: No, no, I meant an inner joy.

Lex Hixon: Really, almost volcanic. What about peace? Again, free associate.

Eileen Caddy: Well, the peace, as I say, is just being oneself and just *being*, really. What else can I say about peace? It's so important in one's life, too, to be at peace.

Lex Hixon: I think this idea of *being* is it—to be at peace. It seems like peace and being are fundamentally expressive of each other. What about love? You said you had a special feeling about that. What do you associate when you think of love?

Eileen Caddy: Well, I feel a pouring out of my being to my fellow man, I think. It's a tremendous feeling, really. I can actually feel it going out from me.

Lex Hixon: You gesture to your heart center.

Eileen Caddy: Yes, I do.

Lex Hixon: So that's where it's coming from.

Eileen Caddy: I suppose so, I hadn't even thought about it, but that's where it seems to come from.

Lex Hixon: I mean, as long as we're aware of a body.

Eileen Caddy: I'm sure it's more than that, though.

Lex Hixon: As Ramana Maharshi locates it, two fingers to the right of the breastbone.

Eileen Caddy: It's funny, isn't it? I didn't even sort of think about it.

Lex Hixon: And then in life, you felt a kind of fullness. These are really divine names, and Eileen has given us, from the depth of her spirit, kind of new versions to these divine names. Joy is opening, peace is being, love is pouring out of being and life is fullness. And these names are the divine name, and by invoking the divine name, we can become the divine name.

Eileen, it's such a joy to be able to talk to you about these spiritual matters, and not have to really worry about talking about the nuts and bolts of community life, although I think that's really a very, very important aspect. I want to ask you, what is the relationship of, say, the spiritual seeker, the human being to Jesus, who Himself was a human being who fully manifested the Christ consciousness? Is it possible for the rest of us to manifest this, to be the Christ?

Eileen Caddy: Yes. And I think that's really and truly what we are. If we can accept the Christ within, the God within, we are moving from that center.

Lex Hixon: Do you have any feeling that this is not a part of Judeo-Christian tradition? Do you have any feeling about what other traditions call the Divine Mother, the concept of that focusing of the ultimate, which is feminine?

Eileen Caddy: I think the feminine aspect is coming out more and more now, and it's not only just being drawn out of women, I feel it's the feminine aspect in men, too, that is coming out. I mean, for example, Peter was light and I was love. There was a sort of will and purpose in Peter, and there was love in me. But now that we've sort of been split, and we're two individuals, balanced individuals, we are finding that balance of light and love and wisdom within our own beings. You see, we've always complemented each other, and now we're two individuals, finding that completeness within our own beings, which hasn't been so easy, I can tell you. So we're still in the process of change in that way.

Lex Hixon: "The Word"—we hear the phrase from the Gospel of John, "In the beginning was the Word." 'Til this moment, I never really saw the full impact of that concept of the Word, because in the case of your spiritual life, words have been the medium of your development and growth.

Eileen Caddy: Yes, because I've heard the Word. The Word has been put down in writing, really, and been followed out and lived, and demonstrated.

Lex Hixon: Do you think that these words that you've written down under guidance, do they have the stature or the status of the scripture, for instance, of a revelation?

Eileen Caddy: Oh, yes. Some of the words are very much from the Bible.

Lex Hixon: I meant, in that sense, a fresh Bible.

Eileen Caddy: Oh, very much so, yes, and also every now and again, there's sort of a phrase from the Bible.

Lex Hixon: Obviously, the biblical tradition is part of your karmic makeup that's being expressed through you.

Eileen Caddy: This, remember, is just the last 14 years, so far more than that [exists].

Lex Hixon: Out of these thousands of pages, there is probably a large percent of things saying, "You should pay the cooks at the hotel a certain amount."

Eileen Caddy: Yes. The whole thing has been very practical.

Lex Hixon: But I imagine there are some [entries] that are purely spiritual in nature.

Eileen Caddy: It's all spiritual. Don't separate anything!

Lex Hixon: Oh, I made that mistake! You caught me. There are some, though that might bear reading and rereading by people who are not connected...

Eileen Caddy: Yes, well, actually there is a book coming out on me, on my life, that's being published by Harper & Row, and it's going to be called *The Spirit of Findhorn*, because, I suppose, with me, it's the spirit that's coming out there.

Lex Hixon: Will that contain selections from the guidance?

Eileen Caddy: Yes, it will, and I hope there'll be a sort of sequence of books on the guidance I've received. Really, they are just very simple teachings.

Lex Hixon: It's beautiful to see the process of revelation going on. We tend to canonize scriptures, and very arbitrarily. We think of the Bible or the Quran as something very, very far in the past that we need, that we can turn to, and we can savor it. We never imagine that we would meet someone who actually had that kind of revelatory experience. Meeting you, I can say that I feel very comfortable, and [there is] absolutely no pretension on your part whatsoever. If anything, you are a servant of this guidance. When Christ said, "I come among you as a servant," I can really feel in you that servant feeling.

Eileen Caddy: I am here to serve my fellow man, and if I can be used that way, I say, "Thank you, God."

Lex Hixon: This power of the Word coming through in different cultures, different times, and so richly through you, and the Findhorn family—it's a beautiful thought. When we read in the Gospel of John, "In the beginning was the Word," it sounds so far back there.

Eileen Caddy: It's not. It's right here.

Lex Hixon: It's right here.

Eileen Caddy: Now, I no longer write it down. I have to learn to be it and to live it and to demonstrate it, which is not as easy as writing things down.

Lex Hixon: It's true, and as you pointed out, you became a prop to the community, that your revelatory words—the same is true of all religions—they become a prop, and people are really afraid to venture out beyond them and to embody them. I want to return to the idea of the Divine Mother and the feminine aspect. I feel myself a worshipper of the Divine Mother, and [I am] maybe 90 percent feminine, myself. I don't know if you get that impression from me, psychically. Do you?

Eileen Caddy: I feel a wonderful balance, actually.

Lex Hixon: Well, it's beautiful to discover the Divine Mother, to put it in that metaphor, within oneself. It's exciting if one is a man, because it's unlocking the whole aspect of one's feminine nature, and it's exciting if one is a woman, because one already has been focusing on this feminine nature. To find that it's actually a very deep force in the universe, it must be delightful for a woman, too. How do you feel about that?

Eileen Caddy: I feel with myself sort of like a universal mother, really, because I seem to have so many children in the community. And everyone is my child, actually. I have many children myself, too, so...

Lex Hixon: That's true. You should stress that you're a Christian mystic who's also the mother of eight children.

Eileen Caddy: Yes, and nine grandchildren.

Lex Hixon: And you've raised them all and worked with them and seen them all through every little detail of life. I feel that. But Peter has a strong male energy, in a sense of a creative—

Eileen Caddy: He's becoming far more feminine. His feminine aspect has got to come out in him, and that is what is happening now. There is a tremendous change in Peter, so it is beautiful to see it.

Lex Hixon: I don't want to project my own theology, but as someone who meditates on the Divine Mother, I always feel that the feminine is going to be the salvation of the planet.

Eileen Caddy: I agree.

Lex Hixon: Getting away from male-centered concepts in spiritual life is really a work of the New Age. But there is the tradition of the goddess, and there is that kind of tradition of the mystical feminine coming through all the traditions. So it's not that we have to invent it anew. But we have to reattune to it. I feel that the quality of love is the essence of the Divine Mother.

Eileen Caddy: I quite agree with you there. That's why I feel, with Peter, there's so much more love coming out in him, which wasn't there before. There was a sort of will and purpose, which was a hardness. And now there's a gentleness coming out. But then, you see, I've got to develop my male aspect, too, which is where the change has got to come in me.

Lex Hixon: What do you feel the male quality is?

Eileen Caddy: Strength, actually, and faith.

Lex Hixon: But no one could say that you haven't been strong in your life. There is a feminine strength. I don't want to get into stereotypes.

What we're talking about here is basically spiritual qualities. We're not talking about personality qualities, things like that.

Eileen Caddy: Well, I had to go through an experience, really, of the will and purpose energy coming up in me, in the community, which is something I'd never experienced before. And I found it was so powerful that I upset all those in the community that I was working with. So it was an unbalanced energy that was coming out. The love had always been there. They suddenly found something that was not me at all, or they thought was not me, but I gather there is the balance, and now what I'm trying to balance is the love and the light and the wisdom, all together.

Lex Hixon: They thought that Eileen was just a sweet, mild mystic, and they didn't know the wrathful side. This is the beautiful thing about the Divine Mother, as she's portrayed in many profound meditative traditions. She has wrathful forms. People don't realize that that wrathfulness—it's actually that joy that you expressed. Do you remember when you said that joy had that kind of volcanic feeling of breaking out?

Eileen Caddy: Yes.

Lex Hixon: That's actually what I feel the wrathfulness of the Divine Mother is. It's not wrath in the sense of anger. It's a kind of tremendously cutting through energy— explosive, as you said. It's almost an explosive feeling of that joy.

Eileen Caddy: Well, I feel very close to the Divine Mother.

Lex Hixon: So, the theme, then, of our talk is this turning to the feminine. Of course, the building has to go on; the building activity, the creation on the level of manifestation. But it seems that this can be done through the ultimate activity, which is love.

We've been talking with Eileen Caddy. Her husband, Peter, has now joined us. His strong, clear feeling has definitely entered the space. There's a new feeling here. Peter, can you say something about one of the most available manifestations of Findhorn spirit—the Findhorn garden?

Peter Caddy: Yes, that's one of the reasons why we're over in the United States, to introduce and promote *The Findhorn Garden*, which has been written by members of the community. Paul Hawken's book, *The Magic of Findhorn*, sort of prepared the way with a chapter on myself, Eileen, David Spangler, Roc, and Dorothy. In *The Findhorn Garden*, there is a chapter by myself, Eileen, Roc, David, and Dorothy. Its full title is *The Findhorn Garden: Pioneering a New Vision of Man and Nature in Cooperation*.

Lex Hixon: I imagine you're still as dedicated as always to manifesting the spirit outwardly, and building and building.

Peter Caddy: Yes, although I've been going through changes within myself, to develop more of a consciousness of drawing out what is within people, others. But when necessary, my initiating energies are still required. For example, we've just acquired Cluny Hill Hotel, the place where we were for five years before coming to Findhorn. We can accommodate about 160. And those energies of mine are needed to get the whole thing going.

Lex Hixon: I'm glad you still have that rough energy power thing. It's coming from a very pure source. I consider that your irrepressible energy is coming from the same ultimate source as Eileen's.

Peter Caddy: Absolutely. It's from God.

Lex Hixon: Isn't it kind of artificial and unfortunate that people in other parts of the world have to travel to Findhorn? Or do you think there's some kind of value in a kind of a pilgrimage to a power point on a planet?

Peter Caddy: At Findhorn, we grow people as well as plants. It's like a greenhouse. The energies there are very potent, and people experience rapid spiritual growth and change. The only thing that's required of them is to change. But that, of course, is not easy, and it's very often very painful. So don't come to Findhorn just thinking you're coming for a holiday there. [It] can speed up spiritual growth. From Findhorn, go seeds to be transplanted to other parts of the world. But this is part of what's happening all over the planet. There are other places. Not everybody is right for Findhorn, and Findhorn isn't right for everybody. It's a new consciousness that is emerging on this planet—the New Age. Findhorn is a center of demonstration of this consciousness.

Lex Hixon: I understand that Findhorn and Cluny and those places that you have are related to actual spiritual power points in the planet itself. So it's not as if it could have happened anywhere. Are there such power points over here in this area?

Peter Caddy: Yes, that is true. Findhorn is a place of magnetic center. It's a cosmic power point; it's on many ley lines. There are these centers in Britain, but there are also these centers in other parts of the world. In North America, as elsewhere, it is those who are near to the soil, near to Mother Earth—like many of the North American Indians—who know where the sacred places are. They know where the places of spiritual power are, but they won't always reveal them. I think the American Society of Dowsers have done quite a bit of research in it. And "sensitives," too, know where these places are. So the place is also important. It's easier in a place of spiritual power and spiritual energy.

Lex Hixon: Presumably, there must be different spiritual temperaments, and some very, very serious or profound spiritual seekers might not get in the Findhorn atmosphere what they need—or do you think that what everyone needs is there?

Peter Caddy: Let me make it perfectly clear. Findhorn is not for everybody, and everybody isn't for Findhorn. There are other centers, there are other paths, there are other movements. There are many different people in the world, and we see that each religion, each movement, each teacher has something to give.

We see the wholeness and the oneness in the divine plan. People should choose which is the right path for them, which is the right center for them. In any case, Findhorn hasn't got all the answers.

Lex Hixon: Peter, you mentioned to me in one of our previous conversations that you felt Findhorn, although it looks very simple and childlike, is actually a place for fairly advanced spiritual seekers that already should have done years of meditation and training.

Peter Caddy: Yes. Findhorn is a place for those that have come along on some spiritual path, some discipline, because there's no particular path at Findhorn. A guru, a master, a teacher, a discipline can only take you so far along the path. Then there comes a time when you have to turn to the God within, the Christ within, the guru within, the master within; call it what you will. Findhorn is for those people who are ready to seek within.

Lex Hixon: As the material of Eileen's guidance in future years becomes available and published and people [will] come out, sort of [like] seeds come out, from Findhorn, to establish other communities, I hope that same thing will be true, that there'll be a sense of pilgrimage to Findhorn as a beautiful experience, but in no sense a necessity. There will be in every place on the planet [an] accessible center of light, not necessarily directly related to Peter and Eileen's work, but associated with it. Peter, did you want to say something?

Peter Caddy: Yes, indeed, a whole network of light is becoming established all over the earth, so that each country does have a center of light meeting the needs of that country; each one different, but the principles are the same. We see Findhorn as rather a mother center with a lot of daughter centers in different parts of the world, linking up with other movements, other communities.

Lex Hixon: I like your feminine imagery.

David Spangler
February 1976

David Spangler was born in 1945 in Columbus, Ohio, and lived with his family in Morocco from ages six to 12. He attended Deerfield Academy in Massachusetts and Arizona State University, leaving in 1965 to move to Los Angeles, where he began lecturing on spirituality. In 1970, he went to Scotland to help establish the New Age community Findhorn. Returning to the U.S. in 1973, he and Dorothy McLean founded the Lorian Association and he and William Irwin Thompson founded the Lindisfarne Association. He and Thompson wrote *Reimagination of the World* (1991), criticizing the New Age movement's commercialism, faddishness, glamorized spirituality, and guru figures. Spangler is considered a transitional thinker who bridges early esoteric theosophy and incarnational spirituality. His autobiography, *Apprenticed to Spirit* (2010), traces the development of postmodern practical spirituality. He is active as a lecturer and on the Internet.

Lex Hixon: This morning we will hear from a person of great importance in the evolving culture of this country. His name is David Spangler, and he was one of the leaders of the Findhorn Community in northern Scotland. While he was there, he received communications full of wisdom and sensitivity from revelatory beings of a high nature. Some of these communications have just come out in published form. The book is called *Revelation: The Birth of a New Age.*

David, you have a ready source of wisdom that is flowing into your conscious mind. When did that begin for you?

David Spangler: When I was very young, before I was six, I used to have out-of-body experiences and the awareness of people around who were not in physical form. When I was seven, my parents and I were living in Morocco, where my father was working. My parents were extremely ecumenical, particularly my father, who worshipped as a Muslim and as a Buddhist and as a Baha'i. Our home was actually like a sanctuary of universal religiousness.

I remember one day we were driving to Casablanca, and I was in the back seat of the car. Without any warning, my personality as David Spangler began to dissolve. I felt a tremendous rush of energy, and the next thing I knew, my identity just ceased to exist, and blossomed out into something else.

It was an experience of waking up. The closest analogy is the tremendous sense of relief, felt by someone who has been caught in a dream and suddenly awakens. But the content of the experience was entirely formless. I found myself in an identity with no barriers between me and the universe, and it felt like this identity reached to the farthest ends of the universe. It was accompanied by a deep peace.

It didn't last very long. And then I recollected myself very consciously, saying to myself, "All right, I have awakened to this; now I have to recreate David Spangler." I remember distinctly that it was an act of will to pull that identity back together. My human identity did not appear like a cage in which the spirit was enclosed, but as a co-created reality. It was something that had its own purpose, and whatever greater identity had ordained my birth was working on it in partnership with me.

When I came back to myself it was with a sense of how natural it all was. I never talked about the experience. It didn't seem to be something that I should talk about, and I didn't really have any language to explain what had happened, although I had a deep intuitive understanding. My particular experience of spirituality has always been towards what I call "divine ordinariness" and the ability to integrate it fully and deeply with human life.

Lex Hixon: Did you keep having experiences?

David Spangler: Throughout my childhood and adolescence, I was aware of this other dimension, but I honestly didn't know what to do with it. When I was 14, my father got a job in Phoenix, Arizona, and we moved there. While we were living in Morocco, my mother and father had experiences of UFO sightings. So they found a UFO group in Phoenix, and for three years before I went into college, I was involved with the UFO subculture out in Arizona, which can get pretty wild. It offered me a whole set of concepts concerning New Age spirituality, none of which I was particularly comfortable with, but they were the first concepts that spoke to what was happening to me. Then I had a few mediumistic experiences that started to be unsettling and I realized that I shouldn't be doing that. So I ended up dropping it all and going off to university.

In university, I put all my concentration towards my studies, and that seemed to naturally cause this other aspect of my life to begin to come into focus. In my first year, I also met Myrtle Glines, who has been my co-worker for 11 years now. Meeting her was a catalyst that awakened in me a sense of the work, which I couldn't verbalize, but suddenly I knew I had to do. In my junior year, I had a strong intuitive impression that I should leave. When I didn't act on it, I actually began to lose my ability to study and I realized that I would have to leave.

I withdrew three weeks before final exams and went to Los Angeles, where Myrtle joined me, and I started lecturing to a group there. One thing led to another and I never did get back to university.

Lex Hixon: What was the quality of the experience that passed between you [and Myrtle]? What did you two work out together to refocus your spiritual experience and plan the correct spiritual work for you?

David Spangler: It was like meeting an old friend because we recognized each other, having been together in other lives. We would talk about possibilities of combining my spiritual insights with her insights into human relations and personality. We talked about creating some kind of educational process, and for the first time I seriously considered the idea of actually being an educator in spiritual matters because I was still thinking of being a research geneticist.

My spiritual orientation was still very abstract because I had no effective language for the information coming from higher levels. Myrtle, on the other hand, came into the relationship with me with a great deal of practical experience. She was born Mormon, had raised a family, and had trained as a human relations counselor. She had built a flourishing practice in Salt Lake City, where she intuitively realized that to really help people have insights, you have to work with them holistically, as spiritual as well as emotional beings. We knew that we were both entering a new cycle and that we would have work to do in it. That also struck us when we first met.

Lex Hixon: How can we evaluate and discriminate between different levels of revelation?

David Spangler: The simplest answer is that it is a matter of individual resonance. Is it something that will begin to affect my life in positive ways? In Western culture, we are people of the book. It means that we value the word as being true. We're accustomed to giving greater weight to words than they actually deserve. The Eastern traditions are more shamanistic—that means it's a person who is actually embodying a divine process. Of course, that has disadvantages, too.

Lex Hixon: We're all witnessing those disadvantages now with the problems of blind guru worship that gives a human being more weight than they deserve.

David Spangler: I feel that part of the problem of guru worship is that we in the West do not know how to deal with a shamanistic manifestation. We've just transferred our devotion from the printed page to a guru. The New Age is all about coming to terms, in a realistic way, with human divinity and universal divinity. The vast number of revelations that are coming out, the many different gurus, and the various ways in which we can image the divine are confronting us with a chaos of divine revelation. If we're going to be able to discriminate and deal with this explosion of epiphanies, we will have to really look at what this divine manifestation means.

Lex Hixon: Is the solution for everyone to appreciate themselves as an instrument of revelation?

David Spangler: The challenge here is that we think of revelation as words. But, to me, revelation is life. We are revelators of the divinity of our life. We all need to see ourselves as revelators, not in a prophetic or verbal sense, but to recognize that the universe is an ongoing negotiated reality. I am co-creating it with you and with all your listeners, and especially with God.

God represents the transcendental force beyond space and time, beyond definition—that is the ultimate source of what we are experiencing. If I can hold in my being the paradox that I'm distinct, yet at the same time, I am not separate from God or from you; if I can be both separate and not separate, like a particle and a wave in quantum mechanics, then I'm in a position to understand clearly what it means to be a revelator.

When I was in college I realized I was in touch with something that was both part of me and yet not part of me—an intelligence that was group mind. This was a very profound experience because I don't feel any less an "I," but I do feel part of a group mind. I believe we need a new concept. I like the concept of a *synarchy*, which is a blend of synergy and hierarchy, where you have a group of beings who are creating a wholeness that is greater than the sum of their parts.

Lex Hixon: The scientist in you is very present. You mentioned the theory in quantum mechanics that light, for instance, can behave both as a particle and a wave. The science of microparticles has been discovering greater and greater complexities and pluralistic structures within what they thought were the simple building blocks of the universe. At the same time, there has been movement toward a unified field standpoint. There's such immense complexity that we no longer feel we can even build a satisfactory model of the atom.

Similarly, after our conversation, I feel we can no longer build a satisfactory model of the spiritual sphere. It's just too complex. It's transmuting. It's different to itself, from different perspectives, yet at the same time, as you said, there's a kind of inexpressible Tao, a kind of unified field aspect to it. Could you talk more about this? Perhaps it will develop into a meditation on this inexpressibly unifying ultimate.

David Spangler: Something about nuclear research and high-energy physics that I read the other day was very interesting to me. The authors were commenting on this very point that you raise. Each time they think they've found the last particle, they find another one. What they're beginning to speculate [about] and hypothesize is that the very act of searching for the particles creates them—that within the complexity, there are certain basic essential relationships that are probably very simple. But the relationships or the dynamics can be expressed in so many ways that their particularizations are almost infinite.

I feel that our spiritual search—our attempt to get down to the ultimate parts of the universe—keeps creating more and more things to experience within the universe. And in that sense, we are making it highly complex. What we are really saying is that the universe is dynamic enough and universal enough and perhaps simple enough that it can throw off all these combinations. If the universe were truly complex, like a highly interlocking machine, chances are this wouldn't happen, because it would run the risk of breaking down.

The point I'm trying to make is that the more complex a system becomes, the more vulnerable it becomes, and the less actual real freedom there is for growth. The simpler a system is, but the more dynamic, the greater the chances there are for growth, and the less vulnerable it is.

I always come back to the sense that the divine source is essentially inexpressible in its wholeness. That is true in terms of space and in terms of time. In terms of time, it means that there is no cessation to its becomingness, no point where we can say, "This is it. We've now encompassed the whole thing." And if this synarchic divine is going to express itself in space through form, it will have to be in the dynamic patterns between forms! The dynamics of structure need to have a rich diversity that is relational, although, like the Tao, this divine wholeness can never be totally embodied, like the Tao.

At some point in my development, I will have to reach out to you, because I realize that I can't express more of what I am unless we express it together, unless in some way a dynamic field is created, a relationship is created that is greater than either of us alone.

David Spangler in the present day

St. Teresa of Calcutta
April 18, 1976

Mother Teresa was born Agnes Bojaxhiu in 1910 to an Albanian Catholic family in Skopje, Macedonia. At 18, she joined the Loreto Sisters of Dublin in Ireland. After her novitiate in Darjeeling, India, she taught at a Catholic high school for girls in Calcutta, and in 1937 took her final vows. She went on to become the school's principal, before leaving in 1946 to answer a second calling to serve the poorest of Calcutta. In 1950, she founded Missionaries of Charity with 12 members. Throughout the 1950s and '60s she established an orphanage, leper colony, nursing home, and health clinics. In 1971, she opened the first American House of Charity in New York. She was awarded the Jewel of India and the 1979 Nobel Peace Prize for her work in "bringing help to suffering humanity." When she died in 1997, there were 4,000 Missionaries of Charity sisters and 610 foundations in 123 countries worldwide. Mother Teresa was canonized as a saint by Pope Francis on September 4, 2016

Lex Hixon: We are moving now into another dimension entirely, maybe [into] an even more comprehensive dimension—that of Mother Teresa of Calcutta, a saint of the highest order; a living, breathing, total realization of Christ's presence within her and within all other beings. We will begin by hearing an address that she gave recently at the 30th Anniversary of the United Nations, and at the Temple of Understanding Conference there. From that point, we'll go to a brief interview that I did with her after the address at the Missionaries of Charity, St. Rita's Convent in the South Bronx, in which she talks a little bit about the Christ in everything, and reads from scripture and prays.

It is rather rare even to meet a saint like this, but to be able to record her words and listen to them together is probably the most ultimate blessing we could share together.

A very, very intense being, Mother Teresa was a nun for 20 years in Calcutta, and then suddenly it dawned upon her that she was living in a rather comfortable convent and teaching and serving in that way. Suddenly she realized that Christ—[in the form of] the hungry, the poor, the suffering, the dying—was around her in Calcutta. So she got permission from the Catholic Church hierarchy and began her own order and just went out and lived in the slums of Calcutta and began gathering children and people to her. Now she has various homes like this all over the world. She has, in particular, a house for the dying in Calcutta, a most powerful place—Kalighat, the Home of the Pure Heart [Nirmal Hriday]. It is an old Kali Temple, strangely enough. The compassionate Mother Kali is supposed to whisper the words of liberation in the ears of the dying. It is more than just a coincidence that this old Kali Temple is now Mother Teresa's home for the dying, where she brings people in from the streets and treats them with gentleness and love and tenderness, and also with a great amount of respect and joy. She has a way of treating suffering people so that they no longer feel the kind of personal diminution that suffering can bring. Mother Teresa, with her touch of divine grace, can restore a person's sense of being a whole person. Sometimes they recover, but if they do die, they die in a kind of spiritual delight, which is something that money can't buy—we all know that. So, with great reverence, I present Mother Teresa's talk at the United Nations:

"I am grateful to God to be able to be with you today, because I stand here for our people, our brothers and sisters who have been created by the same loving hand of God, one God, God of love. And

He has created us in His own image, therefore we have been created to love. Faith in action is love, and love in action is service. God loved the world so much that He gave His own son, Jesus Christ, to us, to be amongst us, to be one of us, to be like us in all things except sin, that we may be able, with this human body, to come as close as possible to the divine and love Him as He has loved us.

"Christ spent the few years of a human life with us going about doing good and continually stressing that one point; that we are one, that we are His, that we'll belong to His Father, and that His Father has made us for Himself. Continually, He kept on saying, 'Love one another as I have loved you. As the Father has loved me, I have loved you.' And we know how He loved us, dying on the cross, and from the cross, you and I stand and look at each other and we wonder, 'Do we really love as He has loved us?'

"Thousands and thousands of people today are hungry and naked and homeless. They are our brothers and sisters. They belong to the same family, to the same loving God. To make us realize, Christ has said, and Christ cannot deceive, 'I was hungry and you gave me to eat. I was sick and in prison and you visited me. I was naked and you clothed me. I was homeless and you took me in." He made Himself the poorest of the poor so that at the hour of death He may be able to tell us—to tell you, to tell me—"Come, you blessed of My Father, because when I was hungry, you gave me to eat. Not only bread, but I was hungry for love, to be wanted, to be known, to be somebody to somebody. I was naked and you clothed me; not only with a piece of cloth, but with human dignity. And I was homeless and you took me in, not only in that little room made of stones, but in your heart. You covered me with that understanding love. You took me as your brother, your sister. You did it unto me.'

"How wonderful is the greatness of Christ's love for each one of us? Let us today, when we have gathered to prove to the whole world that we are one, let us be one in this love to the poorest of the poor in the world, that we recognize Him in them, that they are our brothers and sisters. Do we know where they are? Do we know what it is to be hungry? Do we know what it is to be lonely? To be unwanted? To be uncared for? To be helpless? To have forgotten what it is to smile? To have forgotten what is that human touch? Do we know? Do we know our poor here in the United States? Do we know our poor in our own

home—the lonely ones, the unwanted ones? Do we know that that child, the unborn child is the unwanted one—that 'I, the poorest of the poor, I don't want that child'?

"*How terrible it is to think that our little brothers and sisters, created by the same loving hand of God are unwanted, unloved. This is the greatest poverty. Let us today pray together that you and I bring peace into the world, not by just doing small things and forgetting. Our poor people don't need our pity. They need our love, our compassion, for they are very great people. They are very lovable people. We don't know them. That's why we can't love them and because we do not love them, we do not serve them. That's why Jesus, again and again and again, He repeated Himself, 'Love one another as I have loved you!' He has loved us until it hurt Him.*

"*Do we love—do we really want to love until it hurts, recognizing our brothers and sisters that live in the gutters and [living] with them. Like one of them, when I picked him up, said, 'I have lived like an animal in the street, but I am going to die like an angel, loved and cared [for].' Just a few weeks ago, I picked up a woman from the street, from a drain, an open drain, and brought her to the Home for the Dying. And I knew she was at her last, that she was dying. And after I did whatever I could do for her, she took hold of my hand. There was a very beautiful smile on her face and she said one [thing] only: 'Thank you.' She gave me more than I gave her. Her love was greater for me than mine for her. God bless you.*"

And now, welcome, Mother Teresa, to "In the Spirit."

Mother Teresa: There is a very beautiful prayer of Cardinal John Henry Newman, and also St. Francis of Assisi: "Make me an instrument of your peace." Yesterday [at the United Nations], I wanted to [pray], but it just went off my mind completely. It would have been just beautiful.

Lex Hixon: The talk was very good, though. I think everyone felt moved by it.

Mother Teresa: That's the truth, you know; we can't make up these things. These are the people, and this is the truth of Christ. There is a very beautiful prayer of Cardinal Newman's:

"O Jesus, help me to spread Thy fragrance everywhere I go. Flood my soul with your spirit and life. Penetrate and possess my whole being so utterly that all my life may only be a radiance of yours. Shine through me and be so in me that every soul I come in contact with may feel your presence in my soul. Let them look up and see only Jesus. Stay with me and then I shall begin to shine as you shine; so to shine as to be a light to others. The light of Jesus will be all from Thee. None of it will be mine. It will be You shining on others through me. Let me thus praise thee in the way you love best, by shining on those around me. Let me preach thee without preaching; not by words, but by my example, by the catching force, the sympathetic influence of what we do, the evident fullness of the love my heart bears for Thee. Amen."

Lex Hixon: Okay. Very lovely.

Mother Teresa: His [cause for sainthood] I believe is going [on and] is coming up, so I think if we live this prayer to the full, we will be only Jesus to the people, and they will be able to see religious life, they will see only Jesus. If we only live life of prayer and sacrifice.

Lex Hixon: Even the microphone is hiding away.

Mother Teresa: [Laughs.] But people are more and more hungry for God. You can see that everywhere. The poor have no difficulty, because there is nothing to suffocate them. [With] the richer ones, it is more difficult. The riches suffocate them and become an obstacle for them. So it becomes very difficult for them. Even Jesus said that it was so difficult for them.

But people are beginning to get more and more awakened to the presence of the poor in the world. They are getting more concerned and more desirous of sharing and bringing new hope and new life into the lives of those who have lost hope. And I think that we are the same family come from the same loving hand. It is penetrating more and more in the world. And for us who know Jesus and who know what He has said, and that He will not deceive us, He said very clearly: You did it to me [quoting from the Parable of the Last Judgment in the Gospel of St. Matthew: Chapter 25: 31-46].

So, we are, [for] 24 hours, touching Him—for me, knowingly, and the others, maybe unknowingly, but they are touching the body of Christ. But it is the same thing because at the hour of death we are going to be judged, all of us—Christian and non- Christians—on what we have been to the poor, to the hungry, to the naked, to the homeless. And that is for all of us. It doesn't matter who you are or what you are. People are beginning to realize that more and more, and that is when better understandings come amongst the people. And I think only this works of love that will produce peace in the world. But it's very beautiful that we get so many young people joining and giving their life totally to God to bring hope, light, and joy into the lives of so many unwanted, unloved, uncared people, and they know exactly what they want. They want the challenge, the young people today. They want the life of poverty, they want the life of prayer and sacrifice that will lead them to the service of the poor, which is very beautiful, and it is a very, very, very deep thing, knowingly to choose like that. It is not the work that they are, emotionally or anything. The work is only a means. What they want is only Jesus and to find Jesus you need to be completely free.

To be able to love Him with undivided love in chastity, to be free through poverty is very difficult. So unless there is that freedom, you cannot have that clear: "Blessed are the clean of heart, for they shall see God." That is when cleanliness of heart comes—that freedom through poverty. Only our poor people are forced to be poor, but to choose to be poor—that is very difficult.

Lex Hixon: What is meant by "poverty of spirit"?

Mother Teresa: There is a spiritual poverty, that emptiness that you feel, that you are nothing— that is poverty of spirit. There is spiritual poverty knowing God, and not loving Him. In this Western world, there is much more of that than there is material poverty, which we face in Africa and in India, which is easy to satisfy. If there is a hungry woman, I give her a plate of rice—it is finished, I satisfied. But for people like that here, or in Rome or London or anywhere, a plate of rice is not going to satisfy.

They don't need that. That terrible loneliness, that helplessness, that unwantedness, that complete darkness is very difficult [to satisfy]. It is great poverty.

What is holiness? To allow Christ to live in us, in whatever form He wants; passion, joy, success [are] the gifts of God, so suffering is a means to share in the redemption of the world.

Lex Hixon: Do you feel greatly saddened by suffering, or do you feel that you are untouched by it to some extent?

Mother Teresa: Not untouched, but you feel that, for example, when we had the refugees and had this terrible famine, things like that, you feel that the passion of Christ is relived once more, then you try to share in your own way. When you see the people suffering so much, like here, now, in this area, you see so much suffering, so much pain, so much loneliness, so much hurt; it is like Calvary—I mean, in a different form. It is Christ going through His agony again, and it is so difficult to live.

Lex Hixon: My wife and I were very moved by Padre Pio. We've read of him—

Mother Teresa: Yes.

Lex Hixon: —and the fact that he felt the pain all his life. He didn't transcend it. He didn't leave it behind.

Mother Teresa: Yes, he felt all the pain. And he shared. That was his way of sharing in the passion of Christ. And you, each one of us, if we really keep close to Jesus, then the nails and the crown have to hurt us a little bit. The closer you get, the greater is the hurt. That's natural. "I and my Father are one. I have come to do the will of my Father." Christ again and again has insisted on that the whole time, that we have to make God the center of our prayer, of our life, of our everything. Unless that [happens], there is no question of coming together or understanding each other or accepting each other. We cannot choose something outside. We have to choose something from within, and that within must be one.

Lex Hixon: Do you, [in] your very active life, have times when you take retreats and just pray?

Mother Teresa: Yes, once a year, we have an eight-day retreat and we have three days' triduum [of prayer and silence, in preparation for the Missionaries of Charity's annual feast, celebrated on August 22]. And every week we have one day of recollection and we spend four hours a day praying and every day, one hour of adoration after we finish the work. We begin in the morning with maybe two hours of morning prayers and meditation, then Mass and Holy Communion. The work is only our love for God [turned] into action. The work is our means, it's not an end. It is only that we use our service to the poor to put our love for Christ into action. Without the life of prayer and our life is very much woven with the Eucharist because if we can't see Christ in the appearance of bread, it will be difficult for us to see Him in the appearance of the Poor. That's why we need our life to be completely woven into the Eucharist. Then each step becomes very simple, then we are contemplatives in the world because we are touching Him 24 hours. That is the beautiful part. And He cannot deceive us. Without all that, I don't know what would become of us. We wouldn't be able to stand it. We wouldn't be able to continue even to work if we did not have this continual oneness with the Christ. Impossible! He explains that very beautifully with the vine and the branches and the Father, the gardener, the fruit and all that. It's very beautiful. Just exactly what our life needs to be, just the branch. But He does everything. We have only to say yes.

Lex Hixon: Could you give us an example of some of the prayer and meditation that you do? Are there any prayers that you say to yourself inwardly, that we could hear? Would you be willing to share anything like that with us?

Mother Teresa: That is very difficult. But I think everything is in Christ, no? That He is God from God, Light from Light, He is equal to God in all things, that He is the same substance with His Father, and that He has chosen us for Himself. That's it, that repetition [in the Nicene Creed] that He is: "God from God, light from light, true God from true God, begotten, not made..." [This], I believe.

Lex Hixon: Do you visualize the radiant Christ as you repeat those words or is it formless?

Mother Teresa: He is there, no?

Lex Hixon: You don't have to visualize Him. He is there.

Mother Teresa: That is why it is difficult to speak of prayer, because all of us have a different way of touching God and being touched by God. Each one. Some people find it easy to speak about it. Some people find it difficult. And so, He is glorified in both ways. Both ways are for Him only. But we have the Gospel, and the scriptures are always there. And very often, by repeating, for example [in the Bible], the 15th Chapter of St. John, repeating it again, that is a most beautiful prayer. Just repeat again, and slowly, word by word.

Lex Hixon: Would you be willing to read a little from the 15th Chapter of St. John?

Mother Teresa: You want me to read?

Lex Hixon: Would you be willing to read a little from it?

Mother Teresa: I will have to put my glasses; thank you, sister [to a WBAI assistant]; I'm calling you "sister." Very good. [Laughs.]
    "I am the vine. I am the true vine and my Father is the vinedresser. Every branch in me that bears no fruit He cuts away, and every branch that does bear fruit, He prunes to make it bear even more. You are pruned already by reason of the Word that I have spoken to you. Make your home in me as I make mine in you. As a branch cannot bear fruit all by itself,

167

but must remain part of the vine, neither can you, unless you remain in me. I am the vine, you are the branches. Whoever remains in me, with me in Him bears fruit in plenty, for cut off from me, you can do nothing. Anyone who does not remain in me is like a branch that has been thrown away. He is with us. These branches are collected and thrown on the fire and they are burned. If you remain in me and my words remain in you, you may ask what you will and you shall get it."

Lex Hixon: Very lovely.

Mother Teresa: This is the place, also, where it says: "Love one another. It is to the glory of my Father that you should bear much fruit. And then you will be my disciples. As the Father has loved me, so I have loved you. Remain in my love. If you keep my commandments, you will remain in my love, just as I have kept my Father's commands, and I remain in His love. I have told you this so that my own joy may be in you, and your joy may be complete. This is my commandment: Love one another, as I have loved you."

Lex Hixon: Thank you so much.

Mother Teresa: Very beautiful, that chapter; you can read and reread [it], and say it again and again and again. Yes.

Mother Teresa (front row, second from right) and
members of the Missionaries of Charity order she
founded

Ram Dass
June 6, 1976

Ram Dass, one of America's most beloved spiritual figures, has made his mark on the world by teaching the path of the heart and promoting service in the areas of social consciousness and care for the dying. Ram Dass first went to India in 1967. He was still Dr. Richard Alpert, an eminent Harvard psychologist and psychedelic pioneer with Dr. Timothy Leary. In India, he met his guru, Neem Karoli Baba, affectionately known as Maharajji, who gave Ram Dass his name, which means "servant of God."

On his return from India, Ram Dass became a pivotal influence in our culture with the publication of *Be Here Now*. In fact, those words have become a catchphrase in people's lives for the last 40 years. With the publication in 2011 of *Be Love Now*, Ram Dass completed his trilogy that began with *Be Here Now* in 1970 and continued with *Still Here* in 2004. In 2013, he released a new book with co-author Rameshwar Das, *Polishing the Mirror: How to Live from Your Spiritual Heart*.

Ram Dass's spirit has been a guiding light for four generations, carrying millions of people along the journey, helping to free them from their bonds as he works his way through his own. He now makes his home in Maui, teaching worldwide through his website at RamDass.org, and continuing the work of Neem Karoli Baba through his Love Serve Remember Foundation.

Ram Dass: If you're in your living room, Volkswagen Microbus, meditation room, beach house, office, or bathroom, you are here with us in the community of the spirit. What we share together is a sense of our being, and that being transcends all boundaries of time and space. This is our gathering place. This [radio show] is the place of the heart. And the music and the words are merely the temporary adobe bricks that we use to build the walls of a space where we can meet. And then, a moment later, the walls crumble back into dust, and the spirit loses that form to take another form.

We come and go, geographically and through life and death. But we stay together in the spirit. We're just getting to appreciate who we are. What a joyous, light, spacious quality. How free. We're incarnations, and we are having the fun of *lila* [the Sanskrit word for "delight"], the play of forms. It's the dance of keeping it together, recognizing the formless and the form. We can keep it together all at once. We can keep our earthly game together. Just call in and give a few dollars to make our time here together feel right on every level. Okay?

Let's keep it all together. Keep the joy of it. Keep the humor of the big cosmic joke, that we can play in forms and yet know that we're formless.

Lex Hixon: Thank you, Ram Dass. That was a perfect pitch for contributions in the context of this program. We're here together at "In the Spirit," raising money for the annual drive to support listener-sponsored radio in New York. It's all right to deal with money in this situation. If you give to WBAI, you know it's not going to be used for some nefarious purpose.

Now, since Ram Dass is here with us for a while, and since I'm an incorrigible intellectual, I'm going to ask him this big question about theism and nontheism. Do you feel that there is a personal God, or is there just pure consciousness? Would you start by letting us hear something about your attitude toward God as it developed in your autobiography?

Ram Dass: I have a suspicion that intellect—which you're so fond of, Lex—will never be satisfied because God hasn't deemed it necessary to be comprehensible to the rational mind. My historical trip may not shed much light other than being similar for many people to their own trips.

Initially, as a Jew, I was Bar Mitzvahed, confirmed, and went to temple for holidays and occasionally on Friday night or Saturday morning. My conception of God was mainly that of a grandfatherly figure with a great deal of power who was judgmental and supportive but to be feared. Every now and then, I'd get a little feeling, in the psalms or the songs, of some of the softer or more loving aspects of God, but that was downplayed in my tradition of Judaism.

The kind of Judaism I was involved with just didn't feed me. That's all I would say, right? I don't think I ever put down the Jewish concept of God. My involvement with temple was mostly to please my family and for sentimental reasons and a strong identity with Jewish emotionality and love of learning. I still felt that strong identity. That's all.

Lex Hixon: What happened to your practice of Judaism when you went to college?

Ram Dass: In college, I became very involved with the Quakers. I went to Quaker meetings, and while the inner voice never prompted me to stand up and speak, I could identify with that concept of looking inward. That was the quality I saw in the Quaker tradition and later found in meditation.

Dave McLellan and his wife Mary took me to my first meeting. Dave was later my boss at Harvard. He was the head of the department of social relations, and was one of the leading Quakers in the country. He was a super scientist too, and there didn't seem to be any contradiction for him. I was a computer programmer-type scientist, dealing with statistics and methodology and teaching courses in them. Also, I was teaching Freud, as a trainee in the Psychoanalytic Institute in California, and I was being analyzed. I saw everything spiritual and religious as sublimated sexuality. I treated the patients that came to see me who talked about God as having a neurosis! I have a lot of karma to work out for that.

Lex Hixon: From your present perspective of knowing about Kundalini energy, don't you still see an intimate connection between sexuality and spirituality?

Ram Dass: There is a connection. But it is only a part of the way in which the energy of the universe manifests through a human being.

Lex Hixon: It's interesting that since our Judeo-Christian tradition is theistic, a lot of us who have been turned off or, as you say, not fed by those religions, are reawakening to spirituality through the East in nontheistic traditions. After we have immersed ourselves in them, we seem to be able to come back and appreciate our theistic traditions.

Ram Dass: Because the heart wasn't flowing enough. See, a lot of people move toward very dry techniques. And then they feel that they are limited, because their heart only opens when they're playing with their dog, or when they're with their husband or wife, but not in relation to the spirit. Then they go back into a flow.

Lex Hixon: In Buddhism, it seems that what they call compassion, which might be better translated as a sense of solidarity with beings, seems to have that heart-chakra function, as the devotional prayer does in a theistic tradition.

Ram Dass: Buddhist meditation teachers who seem so absolutely exquisitely impersonal, when they get around to the *metta* [loving kindness], their meditations turn into these very lush *bhaktis* [devotional worshipping], in terms of the love for all suffering, sentient beings. So it sneaks in everywhere. And my feeling is that to come to God fully, one must come with heart and head. If you are pushing away anything, if it's a personal concept of God, or an impersonal concept of God, you will be losing out. Ultimately, we have to find the way through in every method.

Lex Hixon: To me, there is a problem when people talk about the theistic approach as being a rung of a ladder that you climb up beyond, because it seems to put a hierarchy there, where theism is on a more primitive level, and if you see beyond it, then you see the forms of God dissolve and disappear. But for St. Francis, or for Mother Teresa, the Christ was not dissolving and disappearing.

Ram Dass: I understand that. But I like to conceive of it much more as a circle, where you go through dualism into a non-dualistic relationship to God, and then you come back to functioning in dualism, seeing God everywhere, but recognizing that you and God are in a relationship that isn't seeable or knowable, but is only "be-able." In other words, I see that both of them exist simultaneously. It's not a hierarchy. It's merely a temporal ordering, okay?

Lex Hixon: Let's continue now, from the scientific phase of your biography.

Ram Dass: I got into drugs—or, as I prefer to call them, psychedelic chemicals—because science wasn't feeding me any more than my brand of Judaism had fed me. Science was feeding my intellect, but I was feeling cut off from the world, and very dry and empty.

I had experienced marijuana, but it hadn't ever broken through my intellectual barriers because my defenses were very strong. But the first time I took psilocybin I was catapulted out of my space, and experienced another level of relationship to the universe. That changed the whole meaning of my existence, but after I tried unsuccessfully to stay in that space, for six years, I was led to the next thing.

Lex Hixon: Do you think that the psychedelic space was just as limiting in retrospect as the conventional Jewish space or the conventional scientific space?

Ram Dass: It took me an awful lot closer to transcending my own model of myself than anything else. There were moments in the High Holidays, like hearing the *Kol Nidre,* that were transcendent in Judaism. Science could have taken me beyond my mind if I'd been a real disciplined scholar doing problem solving like an Einstein.

Lex Hixon: But you don't really have to go all the way to Einstein. It seems that science does get some people high, to use that terminology?

Ram Dass: It takes the discipline of problem-solving. It takes someone who stays with the problem until they are eating straw. They have to be so deep into solving their problem that their one-pointedness allows them to pierce a barrier of consciousness.

Lex Hixon: Which is actually meditation, or yoga.

Ram Dass: That's meditation in action, sure. Absolutely.

Lex Hixon: Do you think that if you had the good karma to meet your guru, Neem Karoli Baba, after just having experimented with marijuana, you would have been able to recognize him as well as you did after six years of psychedelics?

Ram Dass: Well, Lex, what you're touching on now is something about social responsibility about drug usage in America and young people. I've got to do a very straight scene about that. My way through definitely involved the use of psychedelics. That doesn't mean it's useful or necessary for any other human being. Nor is it necessarily not useful or not necessary. I am not in a position to judge about another human being.

I've observed, in the past 10 or 15 years, that the Beatles, the Rolling Stones, Tim Leary, Allen Ginsberg, Bob Dylan, *Star Trek*, and thousands of other vehicles have given us new models of reality existing simultaneously in the culture. This means that a young person already exists in a multiple-reality situation, which is the effect that psychedelics gave me. So the drugs already did it to the society, if you will. The individual already has a support system for his mind that allows for exploration. So what I'd say is that I haven't recommended that anybody take drugs in years, because it doesn't seem necessary any longer.

Lex Hixon: Can you talk about how you made the transition from the psychedelic space to a space of the guru and the divine in the form of Hanuman? These are new concepts that are so rich and yet so strange to our culture.

Ram Dass: My attraction to teachers has been intimately related to the powers that they manifested. That was the first sign to me of something going on. This was true of Maharaj-ji, who was my guru, Neem Karoli Baba, who immediately read my mind, and looked at me in a way that opened my heart in a moment.

It turned out that it was Maharaj-ji's love that fed me. But I was initially attracted to the power. The power gave birth to the love, which drew me into the philosophy of the system, which allowed me to recognize that, ultimately, I would look right through my guru and I would find myself, and that when I looked through myself and my guru I would find God. And finally I would realize that the three of them turned out to be the same thing.

Lex Hixon: That's a very rich statement. We'll have to unpack that a little bit.

Ram Dass: I'll tell you, from where I'm sitting, Maharaj-ji and Hanuman and Shiva are all the same being, just different forms of it. That's about it! It's a lineage of total love that has at its edge a certain kind of rascality or Tantric quality of playing with the elements for the purpose of purification. It isn't the fierceness of Kali, but it has that edge to it of impersonal fierceness along with an incredible amount of love. It's the loving of the love in another being. Because that love is the mirror of God, right in there.

I'm a power-tripper, and the biggest power trip I've ever seen is love. It's like the third eye opening. Love is part of the prerequisite to see the forms that Krishna shows to Arjuna in the 11th chapter of the *Bhagavad Gita*. He opens his eye and lets him see the forms that are not seeable through the two eyes. That's what you see "when thine eye be single," as it says in the Aquarian Gospel.

Lex Hixon: Your path, as you said, is very much a path of the heart. The idea of being fed is the way you have discriminated for yourself about what has been right for you in your spiritual life. Now you can nourish a lot of seekers in our culture with a real feast. You're in a position to serve up the truth to us. It's like you've become a rabbi. You've gone full circle!

Ram Dass: Don't tell the rabbis that. They won't approve of that. Because I'm not kosher.

Lex Hixon: Well, you know, the idea of kosher is also expanding.

Dudjom Rinpoche
July 4, 1976

Dudjom Rinpoche was born in 1904 in the southeastern Tibetan province of Pemakö, one of the four hidden lands of Padmasabhava, and was considered a revealer of the treasures concealed there. As a Dzogchen master, he headed the ancient Nyingma lineage. He was also an astrologer, healer, poet, and scholar, and wrote several Tibetan histories. He left Tibet in 1958, establishing communities for Tibetan refugees in India and Nepal. In 1972, he visited London as the guest of Sogyal Rinpoche. He founded many Dharma centres in the West, including Dorje Nyingpo and Orgyen Samye Choling in France, and Yeshe Nyingpo and Orgyen Cho Dzong in the United States. Dudjom Rinpoche was a householder *yogin*. He married twice and had 10 children, many of whom are *tulkus*, including his son, Shenphen Dawa Rinpoche, a well-known Western teacher. Dudjom Rinpoche settled with his family in the Dordogne center, and died there in 1987. His body lies in a stupa at his monastery in Boudanath, Nepal.

Lex Hixon: We have a very, very special visitor with us in the studio this morning, His Holiness Dudjom Rinpoche, who is the head of the oldest lineage of Tibetan Buddhism. He is 74 years old. He made a great effort to come down to the station to talk directly to you. I think it's unique that [today], on the 200th birthday of our young country, we would have the representative of the most ancient lineage of Tibetan Buddhism appearing and speaking about the highest teachings of mind. His Holiness wants to say a few words in greeting, and then I am going to be asking him some questions. He will be responding through a translator.

Dudjom Rinpoche: We are here in New York City in the United States of America at the insistence and request of a few of my disciples and many other interested followers. These are followers of dharma, particularly in the line of Guru Padmasambhava, the great Tantric teacher. And it is very auspicious that this coincides with the 200th anniversary of the founding of America. I am very happy to be here in your midst and talking to you like this.

I have been able to talk a little bit about Dharma and give a little bit of information about it. Hearing is such an important thing in meditation—the noble quality of hearing. Because of interest initiated by the talk, many followers took refuge. And also, many have received the initiation of Guru Padmasambhava and Vajrasattva, representing all Tantric deities. The meaning and the symbolism that are connected with them were taught and explained to the recipients. I felt that it did have some profound effect.

Lex Hixon: I'd like to say that I was fortunate enough to take the initiation in Guru Padmasambhava. It was very remarkable. His Holiness gave a series of three public talks at the Community Church of New York, where he appeared in a very plain Tibetan jacket and with his hair very tightly pulled back. He looked perhaps a little bit like Dr. Suzuki giving lectures on Zen at Columbia. Then, when we went into the place where the initiations were held, he looked completely different to me. His hair looked like it was flowing in all directions, and he had a beautiful white robe with a red brocade border. It was a very remarkable experience. How many people do you suppose were there?

Dudjom Rinpoche: I think about 200 people. I am very happy to find that there is a tremendous interest here in America and receptivity to spiritual teachings generally, and not just a mere interest, but a genuine interest has been generated. And furthermore, that there is a special link felt by many to Guru Padmasambhava, this great teacher who brought Tantric Buddhism to Tibet and made it available to all, because Guru Padmasambhava is one who is especially apt in calming us down in this turbulent and speedy period that we are passing through. So, as I am one in the line of Guru Padmasambhava, I feel especially happy to see this is happening.

Lex Hixon: In the case of a figure like Guru Padmasambhava, is that just a projection of one's mind in meditation, or is he a real living figure that exists as much as we do?

Dudjom Rinpoche: Guru Padmasambhava is one with the Dharmakaya or the primordial Buddha in essence. Therefore, he is the essence of all Buddhas, but he manifested in this world of ours out of compassion in order to help sentient beings. He is, in essence, Buddha Amitaba, who manifested out of a lotus in Danakosha Lake. He is known as the Lotus-Born Guru.

It would be difficult for us human beings to appreciate Guru Padmasambhava if he does not manifest in this human form. But the essence of Guru Padmasambhava is without any limit of lives or spheres or time. So he came in physical form, yet his wisdom form is everywhere, and for all time. Historically speaking, he went away from us. But wisdom-wise, or intrinsically speaking, he is everywhere that there is devotion. If we truly realize that all this is but a mere manifestation of the intrinsic mind, then Guru Padmasambhava becomes one with our mind when this nature is truly realized.

Lex Hixon: Does His Holiness feel any special presence of Guru Padmasambhava in his own consciousness, his own awareness?

Dudjom Rinpoche: It comes in different stages or spheres. It comes in a visionary form. It comes through dreams, wherever the devotion is most receptive. When help is most needed, the presence of Guru Rinpoche is made known.

Lex Hixon: Can one begin right away from a non-dual position of regarding mind as pure, even though one still has obscurations?

Dudjom Rinpoche: At the moment, we still are grasping, we still have a problem with this manifestation. So, as a result, we have to tackle this first. In order to tackle that, Guru Rinpoche compassionately has manifested externally and through the prayer so that this grasping of manifestation may be purified. Once that is removed, the intrinsic mind will realize that it *is* Guru Rinpoche.

Lex Hixon: Is the intrinsic mind at rest or at play? Or both? Or neither?

Dudjom Rinpoche: Between the interplay of the two, we live and we exist, we think. And so, when we watch the mind, and we watch the changes and try to understand them, we may gain a certain amount of understanding. But for that understanding to be maintained, or for us to sustain it, requires a long and arduous, almost effortless effort to keep that state of mind. We have to work for it.

Lex Hixon: Since His Holiness experiences this natural mind, could he tell us what are the marks of this natural mind? By what characteristics do you recognize it?

Dudjom Rinpoche: Our mind is intrinsically empty, or *shunyata*, but due to the manifestation, we don't see it as empty. Put it this way: We put our thought or concentration more on the sparkle of the manifestation of mind, and we do not pay attention to what we really are. We would rather hang onto the manifest aspects of it. That is the problem.

Lex Hixon: What are the characteristics of the mind when it is not grasping?

Dudjom Rinpoche: When the mind is without any of our grasping, it is in its natural, selfless state, clear and all-pervading like the sky. But our grasping onto it is like a cloud which obscures the sky, like holding onto this empty manifestation almost empty-handedly. That is what our grasping is all about. And that is why it is so futile.

Lex Hixon: Is the basic, ultimate mind, which is our natural mind—when one perceives it—flowing like a stream, or is it absolutely still, say, like empty space or sky?

Dudjom Rinpoche: Although the mind is intrinsically all-pervading like the sky, in its manifestation, a problem comes, as His Holiness explained earlier. That is why, in order to realize the intrinsic nature of the mind, we have to respect the relative complication.

Therefore, both the practices must be combined; that is to say respecting the relative aspect of the practice because sometimes people forget the importance of that and try to understand mind by meditation only. That is not possible. Until the clouds of defilement are removed, no intrinsic mind can be realized. So it has to be that first one removes the clouds and then you can begin to look back. But even by removing that cloud, we should always relate within ourselves. Otherwise, it becomes a complication in itself if we just hang onto the external practice itself and don't see the intrinsic nature.

Lex Hixon: So there's a relative practice and an absolute practice.

Dudjom Rinpoche: Interrelated, both interrelated.

Lex Hixon: So even for someone who is a beginner, beginning relative practice could at the same time, in a humble, sensible way, begin an absolute practice?

Dudjom Rinpoche: It is very important even for a beginner to understand the nature of the intrinsic mind. Of course, it's easier for us to understand than to maintain it or to understand it fully. But first there must be that understanding in the background of our minds as to what mind really is so that you can relate even the relative practice in the light of that. This makes all the difference.

Lex Hixon: One of the greatest blessings is the blessing of the lama's mind, the guru's mind. Evidently there's a possibility of mind-to-mind teaching and contact. Could His Holiness explain that?

Dudjom Rinpoche: The essence of the Buddhas is out of compassion, and skillfully they manifest or take form in the external lama as the example. So in connection with him, and through learning and through following we develop our mind and ultimately through the help of that external symbol we may gain insight and understand the meaning of the internal lama. Ultimately, we unify our mind with that absolute lama, which is within our mind all the time. That is Buddha nature.

Lex Hixon: Could Rinpoche say something about his own life, how he began meditation practice? I imagine it was as a young boy. Could he say something about some of the stages and understanding that he went through?

Dudjom Rinpoche: First of all, I was very fortunate to be born in a family which is spiritually oriented or has that background, so I was brought up in the way of Dharma. I was also able to see many, many great teachers and to receive teachings from them in the form of initiations, instruction, and in a manner which is almost direct transference of understanding through guidance from the lama. I can say I've received almost all the teachings. However, as I assumed the responsibility of a lama, as a practitioner one often becomes very busy working with others, as a result I don't have that much time to follow my own practice.

Translator: By the way, this is an important point to bear in mind: In the West, everybody is very direct and people often talk of their own attainment. But it is very different in the East. A great teacher like His Holiness does not boast of his attainment. Sometimes he doesn't even talk about having done practice, as he is saying at the moment. So I think we should appreciate the humility.

Dudjom Rinpoche: Generally, if one follows the meditation and practice faithfully and properly, the effects they have, almost the side effects they have are tremendous. One is able to almost fly like a bird, you know? One can gain almost sort of spiritual wings as such. Also one can travel long, long distance in no time or cross over rivers easily almost without touching. One can live on rocks and things we normally wouldn't imagine that we could eat. Things like that are side effects of this experience that can be gained.

Translator: My experience as a translator is that people get hung up very much on these side effects and they think about how great they are. The reason I say they are side effects is because the practice is not done to attain these supernatural powers. These are just symptoms which express what has been reached.

Dudjom Rinpoche: I'm telling all this just to indicate how the practice can take effect, particularly if one follows in the line of Guru Padmasambhava. It has the extraordinary effects of bringing these kinds of symptoms of meditation. If one follows the practice properly, one can dissolve the ordinary physical body with the spirit. There can be nothing left behind. Or, in order to satisfy some people who might [not] think that well, he may have just disappeared, just to indicate that it was not just disappearing into another land, but a true disappearance: the nails and hair are left behind. So those kinds of signs one can achieve. As an example, my predecessor, Dudjom, had 13 disciples who attained this kind of spiritual attainment where the entire body is transmuted virtually into rays of light.

Lex Hixon: Rinpoche, why would someone want their body to disappear into rainbows in the first place? Why would they want that?

Dudjom Rinpoche: This body is the result of our own karmic obscurations. This body is what we call the gross body, not the subtle body. Through the power of practice and meditation, this gross body, which is the result of karmic delusions, can dissolve into the subtle body. Even if we cannot dissolve into the Rainbow Light Body through the practices like the Mantrayana [or other] practices that we have, we can find that we have the intrinsic Buddha nature in our body. We have that potential nature. Through the practice, we can perfect and purify all this into the pure perceptions, so that all appearance would manifest as the mandalas of the different deities or mantras. There wouldn't be any obstructions to going through mountains and rocks or to go into space. These are the results, the power of the practice. We can gain all these miracle powers.

Lex Hixon: Is it possible that a lama or a person who has had this highest realization and who is still living, that they might appear to have an ordinary body which functions in the ordinary way, but actually that all the nerve systems and everything have been completely purified, and actually that the body is not an ordinary body?

Dudjom Rinpoche: Yes, there are many that through internal practice have perfected everything into purity of perceptions, yet they remain very ordinary. There are many great realized beings who, even when they reach the third stage of [being] beyond practice and concepts, in order to benefit beings, they would remain because our practice and teachings are based [on] the commitment to save all sentient beings. They can benefit beings through their body, through being seen, being heard, being touched, or being remembered.

There are many great teachers, such as the previous His Holiness Dudjom Rinpoche, who had recognition of the true nature and had developed all kinds of realizations. He had the vision of Guru Rinpoche himself and stopped his practice. He explained that Padmasambhava told him, "I sent you to benefit beings. Now it's time to stop your practice. You have to benefit beings." Thus, there are great beings who remain without resolving into total transformation into the Rainbow Light Bodies.

Lex Hixon: Your Holiness, would you please pray for us who are listening now that we can tame our minds and realize that our ordinary bodies and minds are primordially pure?

Dudjom Rinpoche: Yes, definitely we all should wish that, and pray that whoever has a connection with great Guru Padmasambhava, that this may be the last rebirth in this universe, and that we be able to attain the primordial Buddha Samantabhadra's level. And even if we can't reach that level through practices yet, with whomever we have connections [to] through prayers and wishes, that we will be able to be reborn into the Buddha fields of the Lotus-Born Guru in the Copper-Colored Mountain.

Lex Hixon: Your Holiness, you mentioned the transcendental realm of Padmasambhava. Will most of us complete our spiritual practice there in that transcendental realm? Or will we be able to complete it here in this realm?

Dudjom Rinpoche: Those who pray and wish to be reborn in the Buddha field of Padmasambhava, when we go after death through the experience of *Bardo*, the intermediate stage between death and rebirth, at that very moment we would experience all the *dakas* and *dakinis* greeting us in the special Buddha field of the Lotus-Born Guru, Padmasambhava. There, we would be able to receive teachings and practice and we can attain realization there. Those who get realization there, again, Great Guru will send us back to benefit beings on this earth, saying that you should go through these practices and benefit beings.

Lex Hixon: Where is this Buddha field? Is it far from here?

Dudjom Rinpoche: That Buddha field, the Copper-Colored Mountain, just depends on our natural mind. It is just next to us if we have the inspirations and prayers. It is not somewhere we can reach on our feet. If we have the inspiration, it is just next to us. It is to benefit beings that all these Buddha fields, such as the Copper-Colored Mountain as well as Shambhala, are manifested. All these celestial realms are not places we can go by ordinary means. We have to reach them through our internal progress and the development of our understanding.

Sakya Trizin
Fall 1976

The 41st Sakya Trizin was born in 1945 into the Sakyapa, one of Tibetan Buddhism's four lineages. His parents and a sister then died in quick succession, leaving him and his other sister, Sakya Jetsun Chimey Luding, with their aunt, who trained them to teach and transmit. In 1959 he moved the family to Rajpur, India, where he established the Sakya Center, a nunnery, hospital, college, followed by many centers around the world. He married in 1974 and his two sons are also Rinpoches. Today, Sakya Trizin heads the Sakya lineage. His U.S. seat is at Tsechen Kunchab Ling in Walden, New York. Sakya Jetsun Chimey Luding settled in Vancouver, Canada, and founded Sakya Kachod Choling on San Juan Island in Washington.

Lex Hixon: We have with us in the studio His Holiness Sakya Trizin, the 41st head of the 900-year-old Sakya Order of Tibetan Buddhism. The Sakya Order has a tradition of married lamas, and His Holiness himself is married with several children.

Yesterday, His Holiness gave a seminar on the feminine principle here in the city. We thought we would continue that discussion here on the air, so all of you can hear while sitting comfortably at home. The Dharma is so compassionate that it will even come into your own home and reveal itself to you.

Your Holiness, it became clear during the seminar that the Tibetan Tantric tradition has a special feeling for the feminine aspects of reality. To explain this to the people who are listening, we'll need to use some technical Tibetan terms, but we'll try to make it very clear. There are three forms of transcendent, feminine deities: the *yidam*, *dakini*, and *dharmapala*. Could you describe each of them? Perhaps we could begin with the yidam; as I understand it, Tara is a yidam.

Sakya Trizin: Yes, that's true. Yidam means an emanation or manifestation of the Buddha. In order to help different types of people and situations, the Buddha takes different forms. Some yidams are in wrathful form, some yidams are in peaceful form, and some yidams are female deities, like Tara. Yidams are different forms of the Buddha.

Lex Hixon: Buddha nature, I suppose, must be something neutral—beyond gender, beyond name, beyond form. Why does this pure Buddha nature take the form of a feminine deity such as Tara?

Sakya Trizin: It is true that in the ultimate state, there is no such thing as female and male gender, but for people who have not reached that state, who are still thinking in terms of male and female, it may be more powerful and helpful to concentrate on female deities; and for some people, it may even be more helpful to concentrate on wrathful deities.

Lex Hixon: The other example you gave at the seminar of a yidam deity was that of the Vajrayogini. Could you describe the Tara and the Vajrayogini and their differences?

Sakya Trizin: The main manifestation of Green Tara is actually a very peaceful one. Tara is more for helping develop common *siddhis* [someone who has attained enlightenment or a paranormal power possessed by a siddhi], for instance, the power to prevent disasters and to protect you from evil on the path. If you use it for your own personal benefit, that is not the right way. It is for achieving the ultimate goal and helping all beings. You need a long life and wealth and health for that. If you are involved in Tara's blessings for that reason, that is the right idea, but it is not just for the worldly benefits. It's like asking a great emperor to sweep the house.

All these deities came, of course, from the Vajrayana or the Tantra tradition. There are four different classes of Tantra. Tara actually comes into all of the four different classes of Tantra, whereas Vajrayogini is only in *Anuttara Yoga* Tantra, which is the highest class of Tantra. They are both in reality, *Prajna Paramita*, or the ultimate transcendental wisdom, but in form they are very different. The main emphasis of Vajrayogini, of course, is only achieving enlightenment for the benefit of others.

Lex Hixon: Can you describe each of these yidams?

Sakya Trizin: Actually, Vajrayogini has many different forms, but the one we normally use is in between wrathful and peaceful. She is usually in the red color, with one face and two hands holding a curved knife and skull cup filled with nectar and she is adorned with bone ornaments. All these different ornaments and objects have many very deep meanings. The curved knife usually represents the fact that she cuts all defilements. The cup represents what in Sanskrit is called *mahasukha*, which means "the great bliss." She is in a complete state of great bliss all the time.

Tara usually has her right hand in what we call the "giving gesture." She is bestowing *siddhis* on all beings. The left one is holding the *utpala* flower, which represents the many qualities of the Buddhas.

Lex Hixon: In the Tantric meditation, there's a union or identity that the meditator experiences with these deities. Could you explain that? People might think that these deities were essentially outside or separate.

Sakya Trizin: Yes, that's right. Actually these deities are the symbol, or the manifestation of the ultimate truth. The female deities are more on the wisdom side and the male deities are more on the method [compassion] side. But the ultimate, actual transcendental knowledge of wisdom is the complete union of these two things. So they are not really separate. And this great Dharmadatu or transcendental wisdom is actually with everyone, within every sentient being. But we haven't realized this, so we are thinking in an ordinary way about everything that we see, everything we do. Therefore we cling to this present scene that we have. When you cling to this, then naturally the defilements arise because we take actions based on this present scene, and due to this, we are again and again surrounded by *samsara*.

The main method that is used in Vajrayana is to stop seeing things as ordinary. So you should see all these things as transcendental wisdom and oneself in the form of a deity, and all sounds as mantra, and every thought that comes as transcendental knowledge. Although at the moment you are just visualizing, you are just imagining, gradually your attachment to the ordinary vision loosens and you strengthen your path in the Vajrayana tradition.

Lex Hixon: You've expressed that this feminine energy or principle is somehow connected with wisdom. Can you give us some suggestion as to why the feminine energy is the wisdom energy? And what do you actually mean by wisdom?

Sakya Trizin: In the actual state of ultimate wisdom, as I said before, there is complete union. There are no two things. But out of this unity, two things arise. Not only method and wisdom, but everything, like day and night, left and right, and long and short, everything; all dual things arise, like man and woman also. Wisdom or the feminine side appeared as more passive and the method or masculine side as more active. Without the two, with one alone, you will not be able to achieve the final attainments.

Lex Hixon: I don't understand. You describe the Vajradakini as standing with the curved knife that cuts through defilements. It sounds like that's not passive. It sounds like she has a very active quality, too.

Sakya Trizin: Yes, of course, this does not mean that she has only one facet. But there is more emphasis on the passive side. Of course, she is everything—she is transcendental knowledge.

Lex Hixon: Maybe, in our culture, the word passive doesn't have the right connotation. Perhaps if you told us what you meant by wisdom we could understand what quality it has. You've mentioned the Prajna Paramita, who is another goddess, the primal wisdom that they say is the mother of all the Buddhas and bodhisattvas. What is that wisdom, precisely?

Sakya Trizin: That is the wisdom that sees the ultimate truth, and the wisdom that sees the complete final states, where you are completely finished with all the karmic defilements and the impure propensities. Everything has gone and you have realized the very final truth. It's not only that you know it, but you are completely merged with the absolute state.

Lex Hixon: That gives me a much better understanding than the word "passive." In that sense, the feminine is totally complete, changeless, encompassing everything, embracing everything. Many times we associate the feminine with the earth, or with the fruitfulness of the earth, or with childbearing, but this sounds like it's totally beyond what we think of in the ordinary sense as feminine.

Sakya Trizin: We call Prajna Paramita "the mother of all Buddhas" because all Buddhas and bodhisattvas are born out of this great wisdom. A mother gives birth, so this great wisdom also gives birth to the Buddhas and bodhisattvas; therefore, in a way it is in a motherly form, isn't it?

Lex Hixon: Yes, it is, but not a mother as we ordinarily understand. If she has really given birth to the Buddhas, could you say in a certain sense that she is the main focus of the Tantric tradition?

SakyaTrizin: Yes. But as I said, to achieve the final enlightenment, wisdom alone will not be enough. For instance, to get to the final stage, the most important thing the Buddha said to do is the six *paramitas*, the six perfections. Of these five, generosity, discipline, patience, effort, and meditative concentration are method teachings; only the sixth one is the wisdom teaching.

Lex Hixon: When you say "method," do you mean the masculine principle? So you would say that the goal in a certain sense is wisdom, but somehow the path to the goal...

Sakya Trizin: No, to achieve the goal, you need both, because wisdom is like an eye. You have an eye, but if you don't have feet, you cannot walk. You just sit. You are crippled. The method is like your feet. If you have method with the wisdom, you have eye and feet together, then you can walk and reach your destination.

Lex Hixon: Yesterday in the seminar, it was mentioned that in the Tantric tradition, veneration of all women is suggested because this great wisdom, this mother of all Buddhas and *bodhisattvas* [people who have vowed to save all sentient beings] is so much a part of the Tantric tradition that it is felt that every woman, just by being a woman reminds one of that great wisdom and therefore should be treated with veneration. And yet it doesn't say that about men, that you should give special veneration to all men because they represent method. So it seems that there's a special reverence for the female form.

Sakya Trizin: I think that is from the point of view of mother-line Tantra because one of the *samayas*, or pledges, after receiving initiation in the mother-line Tantra, is to respect women.

Lex Hixon: So in Tantrayana there is a mother line, a father line, and then the third line is the mother-father that consists of the union of male and female?

Sakya Trizin: It's called the "neutral line." It's the all-non-dual line, I think is a better way to say it.

Lex Hixon: Does everyone go through both father line and mother line in order to reach the non-dual line? Or are some people just temperamentally drawn to the neutral, to the masculine or to the feminine?

Sakya Trizin: Many people practice both or all, but most people choose one.

Lex Hixon: My friend Madeline Nold was at the seminar yesterday. We are both Alex Wayman's students in the doctoral degree program at Columbia. She has taught at Wellesley, and she ran the Kalu Rinpoche center in Boston. She has given me five questions from the feminine perspective that she didn't get time to ask yesterday. So I'm going to pose them to His Holiness right now.

What exactly is a dakini? Are they predominantly the more feminine aspect, like the consort of a male deity rather than the mother aspect?

Sakya Trizin: There are many different stages of dakinis. Usually, a dakini is one who has transcendental knowledge and who is helping sentient beings. I think many times in Tibetan [Buddhism], dakinis are translated as "messengers" who are emanations of the major deities. The consorts also use the name "dakini," so it's both the feminine who are helping sentient beings as well as the counterparts of the male deities.

Lex Hixon: What about the dharmapalas, or the wrathful side of the feminine in Tibetan Buddhism? How does one address oneself to that?

Sakya Trizin: There are two different types of dharmapalas: worldly and non-worldly. Non-worldly dharmapalas are deities. The one that is most popular in Tibetan Buddhism is called Palden

Lhamo or Mahakali. She is black in color with one face and two hands holding a stake and skull cup and riding on a mule. She is in very wrathful form with many bone ornaments.

Non-worldly dharmapalas are very much the same as deities. You can use them in practicing and visualize them like the yidams. Mostly, when you practice with a dharmapala, you do not become that deity. You invoke them in front of you and then make offerings. You request them to protect the dharma and to protect you, to have great success on your spiritual path.

Generally, these peaceful deities and wrathful deities are meant for different types of people. The wrathful yidams are meant for people who have in themselves a great defilement of anger. For the people who have much anger, it is more reliable to have more wrathful deities. I think this is not something that is only about you yourself, but in a way, all outside obstacles such as enemies are actually your own anger. To destroy this, you have to imagine and worship angry deities.

Lex Hixon: Do you feel that Western women would be more comfortable with a Tara manifestation than, say, [with] one of the masculine deities, as the introductory means of approaching Tibetan Buddhism, since there is such strong feminism in the West?

Sakya Trizin: Yes, but I am also giving male deity initiations and women are participating. I think it's purely individual choice. Now many women are taking part in Buddhist activities. When we have regular classes in our center, I see usually more women than men.

Lex Hixon: You spoke yesterday about your aunt and the training and the beautiful nurturance and wisdom you got from her. Would you share some of that with us now?

Sakya Trizin: She is a very, very religious-minded person, and she is always in meditation. She sleeps only a few hours a night, never lying down. Even when she sleeps, she just sleeps in the cross-legged position. She doesn't even have a bed. During our lifetime, she has recited many, many mantras; for instance, her main deity is Red Tara. She decided to recite her mantra 20 million times. Our mother died when we were very young; it was our aunt who brought me and my sister up and gave us our education and arranged for us to meet all the very holy lamas to receive all the teachings, and arranged all the studies and meditations. Especially when we were doing the retreats, it was she who arranged everything.

She is just living an ordinary life. She is living in a household with many children and many ordinary people, but she recited more mantras and did more meditation than people who are in complete seclusion in a cave! I think it is just a matter of one's own endeavor and efforts. If you make the right efforts, you can do it even in your own house. You don't need to go anywhere else.

My sister is now living in Vancouver, and anything I could teach, she could also teach. I think [that] as her children grow up, she is going to have more time, and I hope that she will later have the opportunity to teach. That will be a very good thing. Usually this tradition has male heredity, but as far as qualities are concerned, she could also have been the head of the Sakya Order.

Lex Hixon: Could a female become the Dalai Lama?

Sakya Trizin: The Dalai Lama is not appointed, he chooses his birth. If he chooses to be born in a female form, I don't see any obstacle, but so far, all the Dalai Lamas have chosen to be born as a male. There's nothing saying that a male is more precious in actual theory and philosophy. But so far, the tradition has been like this.

Lex Hixon: We've talked in detail about feminine deities, but I'm sure a lot of people are wondering, do these deities really exist? Are they just expressions of psychological temperaments? Or are they somehow actually transcendental?

Sakya Trizin: No, they are not something solid outside. They are the manifestations of the ultimate transcendental wisdom. For people who believe in outer appearances, things appear in an outside way. But the real truth is they are all manifestations of the great transcendental wisdom, which is everywhere. The whole appearance is this. Everything—the transcendent part and the worldly part—came out of that.

Lex Hixon: In the seminar yesterday we were talking about a Tibetan nun who was very close to Mahakali. Evidently, Mahakali would come and appear to her as vividly as we are appearing to each other now. A psychological understanding of the dharma might say, "Well, the deities are just ideas. They're just forces inside the mind." But then, how could they appear as vividly outside as other human beings appear?

Sakya Trizin: In Buddhist tradition, we have two truths: the relative truth and absolute truth. In absolute truth, there's no deity. There's nothing. It's inexpressible. In other words, it is something that is completely beyond our present way of thinking and being. But relatively, we have everything existing. We have "I," and "you," and all this. Empty it is, also. All these deities are different, with different categories. Some deities are called yidams, some deities are called dharmapalas. It is not just an idea that we have created. They are all truly like this. They protect you and they bless you, they help you, and sometimes they even punish you.

Lex Hixon: So we should take the deities as seriously as we take other beings.

Sakya Trizin: Yes, of course.

Lex Hixon: One final question on the nature of the ultimate reality. When you say that there's nothing in the ultimate reality, it sounds like you are going to the extreme of nihilism. As far as I understand the Buddhist philosophy, the ultimate is neither existence nor nonexistence.

Sakya Trizin: When I say it's nothing, it means it is neither existence nor nonexistence. It's just like space. It has no color, no shape, no sign. The absolute truth is described many times in many scriptures as completely beyond our ordinary way of understanding things. Until we realize that, it will be difficult to describe.

Lex Hixon: But in the Tantra, it describes deities and, indeed, all phenomena as rising up out of that pure open space, and not separate from it. So it seems to me that one could be in the ultimate way of looking and still even see trees and deities and people, but of course they would appear in a totally different way. They wouldn't necessarily have to disappear.

Sakya Trizin: Yes, that is true relatively, of course. And when you get enlightenment you have constant, ultimate, inexhaustible, compassion flowing to all sentient beings.

Lex Hixon: I want to thank His Holiness for being on the program with us. I hope people who are listening realize what a major cultural event this is, to be talking to a man who is the head of an ancient lineage and who is himself regarded as an emanation of Manjusri, the Bodhisattva of Wisdom. He's speaking to us in our own language, and he's so kindly accepting all of our limited questions. We're very grateful to you, Your Holiness.

Sakya Trizin: I also enjoyed it very much. It's definitely a pleasure to answer whatever I know for all the people to hear.

Sakya Trizin as a young man

Kalu Rinpoche
Fall 1976

Kalu Rinpoche was born in 1905 in eastern Tibet. At age 15, he began studying at the Karma Kargyu Palpung Monastery. After 10 years there, he spent 15 years as a solitary yogi in the Tibetan forests. He returned to the monastery for final studies and began teaching in the 1940s. When forced into exile, he taught in India, attracting Western students, and eventually travelling to the West. He established the first Western three-year retreat center in France. During the 1970s, he introduced many Westerners to Tibetan Buddhism, founding centers in 12 countries and traveling to give teachings, empowerments and Refuge Vows. Kalu Rinpoche died in 1998 in his monastery in Sonada near Darjeeling, India.

Lex Hixon: It's "Big Mind," as Suzuki Roshi would say, that we're looking for today on the program. We are going to present [a taped interview with] Kalu Rinpoche, who is the senior meditation master of the Kagyu order of Tibetan Buddhism. I had the honor of doing a short interview with him when he was in New York. During that visit, he also gave an initiation into the Buddha, the Dharma, and the Sangha—the basic Buddhist initiation, called "taking refuge," which we will play later in the program. It's probably the first time anything like this has ever been heard over the radio.

Kalu Rinpoche is 70 years old. He spent as many as 12 years meditating in solitude in Tibetan caves and is more qualified than anyone else to speak about this Mind, this Buddha Mind. I went down to a loft on Fifth Avenue, where Dharmadatu Buddhist Meditation Center has its meetings, to hear Kalu Rinpoche speak about Mind.

The elevator was broken, and it's 10 floors up. I walked up the 10 floors and was very exhausted and winded, when I got there, carrying the sound equipment. Somewhat later, Kalu Rinpoche arrived. He had climbed right up the 10 flights, and he walked right in, sat down and immediately began chanting. He was so energetic, even though he looks ancient—like he could be 100 or 200 years old. His physical looks are spare, sort of like a dry leaf. But there was such intense energy flowing through him. It was very remarkable to see.

He began his talk by saying that he took his own Bodhisattva Vow from the 10th Trungpa Tulku. The Bodhisattva Vow is basically promising that you will live your life entirely for other living beings. Kalu Rinpoche has this tremendous Bodhisattva compassion. One of his close disciples told me that he heard the Rinpoche in the middle of night, repeating the mantra of Avalokitsvara, *Om mani padme hum*, as an act of compassion for humanity.

Kalu Rinpoche gave some clues about Mind in that talk. He said that Mind is empty, and yet lasting. This is a very hard concept to follow. Perhaps it's not a concept, and that's why it's so hard to deal with, because we think of what is lasting as something substantial, with substance. But that's just what the problem is. It's permanent *and* empty at the same time.

And the other thing that struck me very much was that this is what Buddha is: Buddha *is* this Mind. In other words, we have immediate contact with Buddha in our own mind. This is the basis of our investigation—it is something we have with us most intimately. So, Kalu Rinpoche says, there is no fundamental difference between Buddha Mind and our own mind as it's presently operating. And this is very interesting and perhaps even the essence of Buddhism, you might say; it's not a question of something unknowable way off someplace that one could doubt. Mind is right here. As Descartes would say, you can't doubt the Mind, because the doubting process is Mind at work. Now, of course, Descartes and Augustine tried to apply that to the concept of God in an indirect way, and used it as an argument for the existence of God. But I feel that Buddhism goes one step further—not by totally eliminating the idea of God, but by fusing that idea with the idea of Mind. So we become that ultimate goal that we're seeking.

I was thinking about the Om mani padme hum mantra. *Mani* means jewel and *padme* means lotus. There are all sorts of interpretations of what the mantra might mean. But the jewel is Mind, and padme could be the lotus of the body, or the lotus of samsara. In other words, the jewel—the Buddha Mind—is right here in the lotus. As Kalu Rinpoche says, the immediacy of things appearing to us is a quality of the Buddha Mind, and that could be anything—whether suffering is appearing to us, or joy—it doesn't make any difference. It's the *immediacy* of that appearance which is Buddha Mind.

I wanted to ask Kalu Rinpoche about the teaching called Mahamudra, the ultimate *mudra*, which is the central teaching of the Kagyu school, the central mystery. It is basically this idea of seeing relative appearances and the empty ultimate Mind as nondual. I tried to think of an analogy. It's sort of like seeing all phenomena with perfect vividness, and yet, as if they were all fully transparent and you see nothing behind them but just the empty Mind. It's a rather crude way of putting it, kind of a spiritual metaphor. But one sees all detail with perfect vividness, and it's not that they're not there. It's not that the rice bowl that you're eating from is not there. It's not that the computer that you're programming is not there. But it's fully transparent. It doesn't impede the flow of Mind.

So I wanted to ask him about Mahamudra because to hear about Mahamudra from someone who has realized it, as Kalu Rinpoche has, is a tremendous blessing. One's intellect is not necessarily suddenly satisfied about what Mahamudra is, but simply the sounds of his words are like sparks, which really can ignite one's understanding. Concerning the Mahamudra, in our totally not perfect non-dual insight, it's not just about seeing emptiness, and it's not just simply seeing form disappear. It's seeing form and emptiness disappearing back into each other, sort of flowing back and forth. In Buddhist Tantric art, this concept is represented by male and female deities in divine sexual union. And this doesn't just occur in the Tantra. If you read the Upanishads, which are nonTantric in character, they give the analogy there that the knowledge of Brahman is comparable to a man and wife in loving sexual embrace. They know nothing inside, nothing outside. And this is kind of a clue to me: it's that those two concepts, the inside and the outside, no longer hold significant meaning. Everything is Mind. Everything is empty. Everything is appearing.

I had all these questions, and I wanted to go to see Kalu Rinpoche in person and ask for more light on the subject. So I went to the place where he was staying and had a personal interview with him, which I have on tape to play for you. So here is the tape of my interview with Kalu Rinpoche through a translator with the sound of traffic behind him on 72nd Street—a beautiful city mantra saying, "Hum, hum hum."

Rinpoche, if you think there's been enough preparation on my part, I'd like to hear in your own voice what the meaning of Mahamudra is.

Kalu Rinpoche: Mahamudra, or that which is called Mahamudra, is the mind resting in emptiness without wavering. It is Mind knowing itself.

Lex Hixon: Is there a way of directly pointing the student to this Mind?

Kalu Rinpoche: An individual who has, in previous lives, gathered tremendous accumulations of merit and cleared away many, many obscurations, and has very, very little evil karma and the very highest capability, can with little preparation receive the pointing-out instructions for the nature of Mind in this life. These pointing-out instructions depend upon the compassion of the lama or the teacher and the capability of the individual. For most people, however, it is very important that they clear away obscurations and gather accumulations in this life, because they are not at the point where they could see the Mind nature even if it was pointed out to them.

Lex Hixon: In the present case, would it be appropriate to give some indication of the nature of Mind, to point to it?

Kalu Rinpoche: A lama is always very, very happy, and always wishes to point out the nature of Mind, because this is the most direct and straightforward method by which a sentient being can realize his own Mind nature and so transcend suffering and reach enlightenment. Without clearing away obscurations and gathering accumulation, however, the pointing out of Mind nature cannot take place.

Lex Hixon: We read that the state of direct seeing of Mind is a natural, *sahaja* state [the last achievement of all thought]. Is that one way of pointing to it, to Mind?

Kalu Rinpoche: Naturalness, or lack of contrivance is an aspect of the pointing out instructions.

Lex Hixon: I really wish that Rinpoche would say something about the very highest teaching because that's our central interest and concern. I don't look upon the listeners as being any different from myself in this matter.

Kalu Rinpoche: Mahamudra is composed of two Tibetan words: *sha ja* and *chempo*. *Chempo* means "great." The word *mudra*, in Tibetan, is *sha*, which means "the transcending awareness of emptiness," and *ja*, which means "totality." By this is meant that all phenomena are Mind—all the appearances, absolutely everything, are *no things* in themselves. They're intrinsically empty. But this emptiness does not exclude anything. It is the totality and the nature of all phenomena. Nothing is excluded from this.

The sky or space is empty, yet there is nothing which lies outside of space. This conveys somewhat the idea of what Mahamudra means. It is, as you say, a most important teaching. In a sense, it is the essence of all the Buddha's teachings. All the teachings have been given to benefit sentient beings.

In the teachings of Buddha, it is said that after one has cleared away obscurations and gathered the accumulations, one should rely on a qualified lama with complete devotion and respect. When one receives the blessings of the lama in this way, then one can realize the Mahamudra.

Lex Hixon: Everything you say about Mahamudra is precious to me because I feel that this may be the last time I will ever see you, so what you say to me now will stay with me for all the rest of my existences.

Kalu Rinpoche: Thank you very much.

Lex Hixon: If you are willing to say more, I will be happy to hear more.

Kalu Rinpoche: For a person who has tremendous capability and very, very little obscuration, Mahamudra is extremely easy, almost straightforward. It comes naturally, and such a person has very little difficulty in understanding it. But for a person of less capability, it is very difficult to understand. The reason for this is the obscuring effect of unwholesome karma, which makes Mahamudra seem like trying to see your own face with your eyes.

Sheikh Muzaffer Ozak al-Jerrahi
March 12, 1978

Sheikh Muzaffer Ozak al-Jerrahi, affectionately known as Sheikh Muzaffer Effendi, was born in 1916 in Istanbul, Turkey. His father was an Islamic scholar and a teacher in the court of Sultan Abdul Hamid. His mother, Ayesha Hanum, was a member of the Ozak family, believed to have descended from the Prophet's grandson. When Sheikh Effendi was six years old, his father died, and a family friend and Sufi sheikh took over his spiritual education. Eventually, Sheikh Effendi became an imam, preaching in 42 mosques in Istanbul, including the famous Sultan Ahmed Blue Mosque. He joined the dervishes of the 400-year-old Pir Nureddin Jerrahi lineage, and became its head in 1965. As a book dealer, he owned a bookshop in the Istanbul Bazaar. He made many trips to Europe, and visited America 13 times, starting in 1978, when he was interviewed on "In the Spirit." Sheikh Effendi wrote many books in Turkish and English. His first book in English was *The Unveiling of Love* (1981). He died in 1985.

Lex Hixon: Good morning. I'm with a very revered guest, Sheikh Muzaffer Effendi, of the Halveti Order of Dervishes from Istanbul. He and some of his dervishes from Turkey have just arrived in the city, and will be performing *dhikr*, or the repetition of the name of God, at the Cathedral of St. John the Divine—for the spiritual benefit of everyone in New York City. We begin this program in a traditional manner with the chant of the opening Sura of the Quran.

Sheikh Muzaffer Effendi: *Bismillah, ir-rachman, ir-rahim...*

Lex Hixon: Effendi, can you tell us a little bit about what's contained in the opening Sura of the Quran, and why it is always chanted in the beginning?

Sheikh Muzaffer Effendi: The meaning of this chapter from the Quran is for us:

"May the compassion and the gifts of Allah be on humanity, and all thanks and all grace and all love of men is for Allah alone. He is the creator of the universe. He is the compassionate and the beneficent. He shows compassion and love to all His creation. His beneficence and His compassion extend to His servants from this world, into the next. He is the king of the Day of Judgment. He has given as a gift all that we are in this world and in the hereafter. We ask your aid to be able to serve you. If you do not aid us, and if you do not accept us, how can we pray to you? May you keep our feet firm to walk on your straight path among those who enter your paradise. Keep us on the straight path. Please do not let us be confused by those with whom you are angry. Amen. Accept our prayer. Keep us with you and keep our hearts illuminated with your love."

Lex Hixon: Thank you very much, Sheikh. We begin the program with prayer because these are intensely prayerful people who are with us this morning, and beneath these words is really the experience of the presence of God.

I want to begin right away by asking Effendi about the practice of dhikr that is the repetition of God's name and really the direct experience of the divine presence. I'd also like to introduce, at this time, Tosun Bayrach, who is translating for us, and who lives here in the United States, in Spring Valley, and is the representative of Effendi in this country. Please ask Effendi if he will explain dhikr and say to him that we are broadcasting for people who long to actually experience divine presence, only words and concepts are not enough for people anymore.

Sheikh Muzaffer Effendi: The word *dhikr*, literally speaking, means remembrance. To remember so that one knows one's Lord, one seeks one's Lord, and one finds one's Lord.

The worst of the worst, which leads people to disaster, is to forget Allah. By nature, man is created as the beloved of God and the most supreme of all his creation. The ones who forget their creator are perhaps more unfortunate than animals because the animals, like the rest of the creation, do remember their creator.

The heart in every human being is the center where Allah stays. Allah, who does not fit into heavens or worlds, fits into your heart. A heart that is with the truth of the creator is a heart that is strong and beautiful. If the heart is empty of the truth of the Lord, it invites the devil to enter. Beautify your heart so that God comes to it.

The dhikr, the remembrance, is what cleanses the heart. All existence, from the tiniest speck of dust to the furthest corners of heaven, is a reminder of Allah. All his creation remembers him and makes dhikr. The one whose ears are not plugged listens and hears this remembrance of God. And he who doesn't have the curtain in front of his eyes sees Allah in his remembrance. Wherever we look we are seeing His beautiful face.

Thus this remembrance, the dhikr, is the key to these secrets. When you remember Him, Allah will remember you. When one remembers Allah with asking forgiveness, Allah will forgive. God will show his compassion to the one who remembers his Lord at the day of last judgment. One must not forget, one must remember continuously.

Lex Hixon: Effendi, is dhikr a secret teaching that one has to be initiated into, or could people who are listening now who are sincere lovers of God, repeat a simple dhikr and, if so, can we hear what it sounds like just simply with your voice?

Sheikh Muzaffer Effendi: Dhikr could be done by oneself and also in communion. As I have mentioned, all the creations of Allah are remembering Him and making dhikr continuously. Some of you do realize and are conscious of remembering Him, and others are not conscious that you remember Him. Those who have love in their hearts find joy in dhikr and their love increases. The wind, the sound of the leaves and the plants and the sound of the water, even the fishes in the water, they have got their own way of repeating the name of their Lord. One has to see and hear that. The ones who are deaf to it, they do not hear this music. And those who are blind to it do not see this light. If you wish, the dervishes will give a sample of a dhikr.

Lex Hixon: But first, I'd like to ask one or two more questions. Over here to my left, there are about 12 or so men gathered, seated around a central microphone, and they're prepared to do various forms of dhikr with us this morning, but I'd like to ask Effendi, with his own voice, we would just like to hear the words that are used in the most simple dhikr.

Sheikh Muzaffer Effendi: *La ilaha illallah…* The famous ancient poet dervish saint Hasreti Yunus, with this poem, indicates what a dhikr is: "The sea of compassion has overflowed its bounds. The meaning of the four holy books is *la ilaha illallah.*" God's compassion is so vast that all creation, believer, unbeliever alike, is surrounded with it. Within this compassion is included the one with religion and the one without, the one who lives right and the one who does not. They are all surrounded by it.

The meaning of the four holy books—the Quran, the Bible, the Old Testament, and the Psalms of David—which are accepted and considered holy alike, is *la ilaha illallah.* The meaning of all the four holy books is to lose oneself in God, to seek God, to find God, to be with God. It is the one name of God, the most beautiful one, the most meaningful one, and the purest one. It clears the rust of your heart. All the waters of all the rivers and lakes and the clouds are not able to clear the rust of your heart, but this pure word, this pure name of Allah will. It is the best of all his holy names. What is the meaning of *la ilaha illallah*? The whole creation and the whole universe are shouting, chanting, *la ilaha illallah*. The path, the quick path, as fast as the thunder, is this word, to reach and to find God. This name instantaneously brings you close to Allah. In the Quran, Allah tells us, "I am closer to you than your jugular vein."

Lex Hixon: Effendi, for all those who are listening, I want to make sure I have this name right, and I would like to have you repeat it to me and let me repeat it back to make sure I have it, very slowly, and everyone listening can learn this. Please, I'd like to hear it in your own voice.

Sheikh Muzaffer Effendi: *La ilaha illallah ...*

Lex Hixon: Perhaps everyone listening now can make a very big dhikr circle, and those who are here in the studio, and everyone listening to this, please join in this infinite dhikr circle that Effendi has said is going on with all creatures at all times, and maybe for several minutes, we'll just try to lose ourselves in this.

Sheikh Muzaffer Effendi [and his dervishes]: *La ilaha illallah ...*

Lex Hixon: Effendi, can you tell us a little about when you were a young man and were taught this practice of dhikr by your Sufi teacher?

Sheikh Muzaffer Effendi: As my family was strong in religion and faith and familiar with the teachers, sheikhs, existing at the time, my father, when he passed away, asked as his last wish that I give myself up to a sheikh so that I would grow under his instruction. When I was six years old, I learned to read and recite the Quran. By age seven, I had memorized most of the chapters of the Holy Book. And in the meantime, with my eyes and with my whole being, I was imitating [our sheikh] and through this imitation I had been learning many things. The Quran, in its outer form, is in the Arabic language, but its essence is in the language of Allah. This applies to all the holy books—to the Bible, to the Old Testament—so that in appearance it will be in various human languages, but to understand it, one has to read it in God's language. The ones who are friends of Allah may understand the holy books. Those books will not speak to those who do not have in their hearts the fear and love of God.

In my youth, I had to learn Arabic to at least familiarize myself with the exterior form of the Holy Quran. And I was attending the public school at the same time. My mother wished me to be an officer, so I was contemplating to be an officer in the Turkish army. The two branches from my mother and father's families are quite different. My father comes from a long line of military people, my mother's side, came from Bulgaria and her father was a Halveti sheikh by the name of Sayed Hussein. My mother wanted me to be a military officer to follow my father, and because it would help our financial state. But a holy personage appeared to my mother in her dreams and he gave this message: "Do not make him a soldier of men, make him a soldier of God."

That holy personage followed me all my life. Whenever I wanted to leave school or wanted like all other children to go and play and do mischief, that person has always followed me, leading me to the right path. This person—my master by that time, the master which my father has willed me to before he had died— this person taught me the traditions of the Prophet and all the religious knowledge that I possess, at least the basics.

Lex Hixon: This [is an] inner person we are speaking about now?

Translator: Well, this person who appeared in the dream to the Sheikh's venerable mother and the personage who evidently could be his original teacher seem to be one and the same.

Sheikh Muzaffer Effendi: Later in my life, I dreamt one night of a beautiful holy person—I had never met this person or seen him before. The next day, he walked in front of a shop where I was. When I saw him passing in front of the shop, I felt that it was definitely a sign, but I did not rush to him because I had hoped that he would come and seek me. Two days after, I dreamt of him again, and two days later I dreamt another dream, again concerned with him. And each time I dreamt about him, I saw him again during the next day. But I insisted on waiting until he would seek me out. Finally, one day, when he passed again in front of the shop where I was, he went about 200 meters and stopped. He came back and he stuck his head through the door of the shop, looked at me, and he said, "Aren't you going to have faith yet?" So I rushed to him and I kissed his hand and hugged him and he accepted me as his dervish. So then I started seeing everything through his eyes, and I started seeing the signs of truth.

My connection with this teacher continued for 15 years. He prophesized that I would be known in five continents and, indeed, I have friends in the five continents of this world. When he passed away, I waited to see who would take his place. And again, through the divine hand, I was led through a dream to my actual teacher whose place I have taken now: the venerable Faharadin Effendi of the Nureddin al-Jerrahi Order of the Halvetis.

Lex Hixon: Maybe we should have a period of more extended dhikr. Tosun, can you explain the different changes that we'll be going through in the dhikr, the way it unfolds?

Translator: A ritual of dhikr continues at minimum two hours, and sometimes much more. And those of you who will come to the ritual in St. John the Divine, and hopefully participate, will see how this length is really necessary to achieve some kind of a connection with God. But time does not permit, so we are going to offer you a little dose of dhikr here and try to include various facets of it: the hymns, the breathing exercises, the various names of Allah will be done in a much shorter form than they are usually recited. The dhikr starts in a sitting position on your knees, and the head moves from right to left, and the body slightly waves. Then, after the repetition of various names of Allah in this position and chanting of various hymns, then one goes to the dhikr in a standing up position, but still standing at one point. Finally, one forms a circle and the circle starts to move. Now we will put all this into one tiny little pill and try to offer it to you within the next half an hour.

Lex Hixon: One thing I'd like to say before we begin. For half an hour, everyone should take their phone off the hook and just sit in the quietness of their own space. This is the beauty and blessing of radio—this is possible. One can have a true experience of divine presence that is, as Effendi so beautifully said, something that's flowing all the time, through our breath and through life itself, but this will allow us to become conscious of it.

...I thank Effendi very deeply. I couldn't think of a more beautiful gift to offer the people of New York City. We feel blessed, like we've been sitting in our shop and he actually came and put his head through the door of the shop to give us an invitation, and we all of us embrace him and thank him.

Sheikh Muzaffer Effendi: We are so touched with the love for God, and for truth, which we have seen in the eyes, in the hearts of the American people. I am living the most joyous moments of my life in your country. I pray to God that this dhikr affects you and makes your path clear. And may God bring you together with other human beings, through dhikr and may you all drink the wine of love. May God's peace be upon you. May his compassion be upon all humanity.

Sheikh Muzaffer Effendi [and his dervishes]: *La ilaha illallah... la ilaha illallah...la ilaha illallah...*[Thirty minutes of chanting and singing followed.]

Lex Hixon: Nobody can walk into the presence of Sheikh Muzaffer and remain simply curious. Effendi, I want to ask you about the ultimate goal of the path. I know that we're just barely beginning the path, but maybe there will be some value in asking about the goal.

Sheikh Muzaffer Effendi: The beginning of the path is Allah, the center of the road and the way through the road is Allah, and the end of the road is Allah. We came from Him and we seek to go to Him. Joyful is he who knows this, and who thinks about it, and who strives about it and feels it in his heart.

I would like to tell you a story about this as a gift to the American people. There was once a person who knew the truth of God and who had reached Him in his heart, but appeared like a poor creature to the eyes [of those] who did not know. He had only one dervish. This person applied to the religious order, asking them to give him a building for himself and his one student. The official who assigned buildings to teachers looked at his poor appearance, tattered clothes, weakened condition, and could not see the treasure in his essence. But in the end, they decided that there was a dilapidated little house which they did not know what to do with, so they decided to give that to him, hoping that he might at least repair it and at the same time live in it with his one student.

So he took this little house and repaired the exterior. And soon people who, like bees, know which flowers to take their honey from, came to him, and the building became crowded and shining with light and the interior of the house became transformed by the light of love. More and more, it became honored because of the one who lived in it. So the office which gave housing to the teachers at the time saw the students crowding to this sheikh whom they did not think much of, and decided to test his knowledge and his spirituality. He said, "Fine, I am ready to be tested." The examiners asked him, "The first lesson of a dervish is *la ilaha illallah*. Tell us what it means." He asked the examiners, "Shall I give you the answer which you expect, or shall I answer what I really know?" They said, "Tell us the way you understand it." He said, "Well, if you wish to hear it the way I understand it, I cannot do that by myself. I will need my one dervish."

So he stood with his one dervish in front of all the religious scientists and began to repeat the dhikr as you have heard. He repeated it once as the officials watched. But the next time as he chanted the first part of that phrase, *la ilaha*, his dervish disappeared, and when he said *illallah*, he reappeared. At the third time, when he recited *la ilaha*, he and his dervish both disappeared and both reappeared at *illallah*. At the fourth time, when he repeated *la ilaha*, the whole crowd, including the examiners, disappeared, and when he said *illallah*, everybody reappeared! Then they understood that hidden under this miserable appearance, the dervish was a bright treasure. He showed the meaning of *la ilaha illallah* this way.

Lex Hixon: [The people disappear because *la ilaha* means "there is nothing," and they reappear because *illallah* means "only God."] So, Effendi, if everyone appears when you say *illallah*, then everything must be Allah.

Sheikh Muzaffer Effendi: Yes. There is no doubt that everything is God, wherever you look, He is there. There is a poem which is recited which says that there is nothing but God, which is the literal meaning of *la ilaha illallah* and the one who loses himself in that truth becomes eternal. There is no end to his existence. He becomes the one who belongs. He is joyful, and together with his creator. My peace and my salutations to the ones who lose themselves in God, thus finding true existence.

Lex Hixon: Please accept all of New York City as a little broken-down house. And please accept everyone who's listening as that one disciple.

Sheikh Muzaffer Effendi: Amen.

Sheikh Muzaffer Ozak al-Jerrahi with Lex Hixon

Pir Vilayat Inayat Khan
October 8, 1978

Born in London in 1916 to renowned Sufi master Inayat Khan and Ora Ray Baker (second-cousin to Mary Baker Eddy, founder of Christian Science), Pir Vilayat was truly educated in an East / West inclusive manner. In addition to completing his studies at Oxford University and the Sorbonne, he pursued the guru hunt—the search for meaningful contact with enlightened spiritual masters, and was eventually initiated in the same order as his father had been: the Chishti Order of India. He was eventually named a Pir (guide) in that order. Pir Vilayat, as he was commonly known, went on to lead a movement his father had created specifically for Westerners, the Sufi Order of the West, which taught a universalist approach to Sufism thought most suitable for those in the West (as well as globally-minded people). Rooted in a unification theory of the major world religions plus science, its metaphysics included the latest theoretical findings of science with nods to relativity theory and quantum physics. Pir founded the Abode of the Message, a residential community for Sufis in the Berkshire Mountains of Massachusetts. His close students, inspired by his holistic teachings, in turn founded the Omega Institute, a leading holistic adult learning center in Rhinebeck, New York. Pir Vilayat died in 2004. His son, Zia Inayat Khan, succeeded him in leading the Order, which was recently renamed the Inayati Order.

Lex Hixon: Today we're going to be playing a tape of a conversation I had with Pir Vilayat Khan last week at his community up at the Abode of the Message in New Lebanon, New York. Pir Vilayat Khan, as you may know, was born in the West. He had an American mother and an Indian Muslim father. He had the full mystical training of Islam, yet he was educated at Oxford University and other Western institutions. What we have in him is a very interesting mixture of East and West, particularly now that he is interested in what he calls the coevolution of science and spirit. He makes some very, very interesting remarks about feeling that he is a member of all religions, yet that the traditional forms of all religions are passing away and that something else is emerging.

Now, in this interview with Pir Vilayat, I'm practically debating him like a younger brother on many points. He is a deeply trained and awakened spiritual master who doesn't have any outer pretensions to that position or to that station, and speaks very informally. It's due to his depth and his humility that he made me feel so much at home. I don't want anyone to think that this is just an intellectual conversation, because when you are in the presence of a meditation master such as Pir Vilayat, there's a certain deep level of communication that goes below the words. After [my wife, Sheila, and I] left and were driving home, we felt intense joy. Something happened there, deeper than the words.

And, of course, my questions are not simply intellectual either because they come out of my own deep concerns about spiritual life and how to work it out between different cultures and different points of view. So I would just introduce the tape that way—it is a spiritual document; it's not a classroom discussion.

Lex Hixon: Pir Vilayat, I came not really to interview you, but to seek guidance from you. You've been laughing and putting us all at ease. Maybe that's part of the guidance, that I shouldn't be so serious about certain things. But I just spent a month in Istanbul living with an orthodox Muslim dervish community. I had a very, very overwhelming experience of the power of Islam and the power of the argument of Islam, which includes living a life based on the life that the Prophet lived, including the five-times-a-day prayer and the ablutions and the ways that He lived. The impression that I received there was that the mystical life of Islam that we all feel so drawn to, and that we think of as Sufism, is not really easily separable from the life of orthodox Islam.

I was overwhelmed by this feeling, and I began practicing the orthodoxy in the environment there. It felt very good and very inspiring. But at a certain point I realized that, as a contemporary American, I couldn't really fully embrace orthodox Islam. My sympathies go to a broader scope of all the world religions. One of the first things I wanted to do, coming back to this country, was to come to see you. After all, your father was a member of the Chishti Order of India. Perhaps he also practiced the five-times-a-day prayer. And yet you, with an American mother and a liberal, humanistic Western education, have not opted to teach the traditional way of Islam. So maybe you could guide me on this matter.

Pir Vilayat: Well, I can give you my opinion. I think you hit the nail on the head when you said that you found it very comfortable to adopt the formal adherence to the ritual of Islam when you were living in its environment so that you were in harmony with the environment. When you came back to the United States, however, when you looked upon it in retrospect, you felt that you couldn't very well continue the same practices in this environment. That is very typical, I feel, because the religions have developed in the course of the growth of civilizations very much like the plants develop in the course of evolution, or different species of animals develop. They had their part to play in the whole. In the particular climate, in the particular environment, a certain plant grows naturally, and if you try to acclimatize it somewhere else, you run into difficulties.

Lex Hixon: But Pir Vilayat, excuse me for interrupting, the fact is that you can and do transplant plants from one country to another and they grow essentially in the same way. For instance, your father's and your background were that of an orthodox Islam that had moved all the way from Mecca to India, but still retained such practices as the five-times-a-day prayer.

Pir Vilayat: Yes, I think one can be more specific and one can indeed transplant plants, but now, of course, scientists are finding out that when one does, they do undergo some kind of mutation in order to adapt themselves. Now, there's always been, in the past, a dichotomy between those who observe the external forms of a religion and those who don't. In Islam, it's called the Shariat. The mystics basically do conform to what I call the religious background in which they unfold, but, let's say, maybe they have their roots in the tradition but they grow their branches of their trees into further dimensions. I would say that I am a Muslim and a Christian and a Jew and a Hindu and a Muslim. I don't think it's just a way of talking. I think that it's part of what Hazrat Inayat Khan called "the message of our time." In fact, he puts it very well. He says, "There's all the difference between the followers of the Prophet and the followers of the followers of the Prophet."

The Prophet was giving the message in his time to a people to whom He gave a new impulse through the very severity of the discipline that He imposed. He gave them a rule of life that was absolutely indispensable, to bring about the growth of a new civilization. But there's a deeper aspect of Islam, which is the mystical side. And that is beyond the formalism of the Shariat.

Lex Hixon: But strangely enough, in the particular community where I was in Istanbul, there was a tremendous and deep harmony between the Shariat, what you refer to as outer form, and the mystical side. The sheikh who leads this community doesn't simply go through the motions of the daily prayer and the various formal aspects of Islam. He does it with such joy and ecstasy that it actually doesn't make any sense to call it the mechanical outer form anymore.

Pir Vilayat: No, when it is an expression of an inner experience, then, of course, it's very, very beautiful. Actually Hazrat Inayat

Khan, my father, said, when he was asked something like this, "There's not one drop of blood in my veins that is not Muslim."

That's a very strong statement. And actually, if you look for the deeper teachings of Hazrat Inayat Khan, you'll find them in the mystical significance of Islam behind the external side. But, as I said, most people simply observe the dos and don'ts instead of really understanding the real depth of Islam.

Lex Hixon: You say that you are a Muslim, you are a Christian, you are a Buddhist, and a Hindu. Could you say that you would be more Muslim than the others? Do you feel some sort of special basic root there? Since your father, after all, who was your teacher and the founder of the Chisti Order, said that there was not a drop of blood in him that was not Muslim? How would you respond to that?

Pir Vilayat: I would say that I do not feel myself apt to make any comparison between religions. I'm not qualified to. You're asking me, of course, also a personal question, how I feel about it. Of course I feel very moved, as you have experienced yourself, when I am amongst very deeply mystical Muslims, as I often am in Hyderabad, for example.

Lex Hixon: As I say to people since I've come back, I understand now why Islam spread from Spain to India and beyond. It has an inner-conquering force. It conquers one's heart. It conquers one's spirit. I felt myself being more and more profoundly absorbed in it, just in the brief month I was there.

Pir Vilayat: I realized that in Islam are the seeds of the trend of the thinking which nowadays we would call holistic. A lot of Muslims think it is being untrue to the Prophet to speak about the unity of all the prophets, and yet it's right there in the Quran.

Lex Hixon: Also in the Quran, the tremendous feeling for the creation and its unity. That seems to me a wonderful basis for science and for deep scientific investigation.

Pir Vilayat: There's an emphasis which I find in Hazrat Inayat Khan's teaching on the importance of what is achieved in the world. But it doesn't prevent me from still appreciating what other traditions have to teach. I think that we should appreciate what all religions have to teach.

Lex Hixon: I'm very happy to hear these words because I myself, in some way, have been drawn to try to accept the various spiritual traditions and not simply study them from the outside, but somehow merge with them in a real way. But my faith in this process was shaken this summer when I realized that perhaps one really needed to be rooted in a single tradition in order to really do it authentically.

Pir Vilayat: I've often found that people who are too eclectic, as one says, can lose their sense of loyalty. But, on the other hand, I have sometimes found there are mystics who could have been considered to be rather narrow-minded.

I remember consulting a Mujahideen in Hyderabad for whom the only way was Islam, as though all other religions are quite on the wrong path. So it is curious that people whom I would really quite seriously consider narrow-minded in expressing [their] opinion can, on the other hand, display very deep spiritual mystical attunement. I would say that some people can reach the top of the mountain better when they are following a very defined path. But I would rather sometimes leave the trodden paths and go through the brush and reach the top using, perhaps, paths that are not too well defined.

Lex Hixon: I myself have met a few people that I consider living saints: Mother Teresa of Calcutta, for instance. I touched briefly on the possibility of harmony of religions with her and realized immediately that that was not something that she would particularly understand or sympathize with. For her, Christ is the way, but for her, Christ is a very compassionate and vast heart that somehow mysteriously embraces Muslims and Hindus and Buddhists also. A person with a heart as vast as hers can't be exclusive in any ordinary sense.

Pir Vilayat: Of course she speaks in terms of her religious background. And that's precisely what I am saying, that people you may meet in the course of your visits or pilgrimages are always talking in terms of their background. Therefore, one can follow a narrow path, but there are those who feel that the time is coming when the paths will be converging, will be uniting. So those are the people who are working towards unity of all religions.

Lex Hixon: One of the interesting things is to become aware, really, of what is one's background. For instance, in our culture here in the West—and I have to include you as having a Western mother and having been educated here, largely—what is our background? We think it's just the ordinary way of looking at things. But it might be very much a cultural background that would include science and humanism and various forms of Christian and Jewish thinking.

About backgrounds, one of the things I returned to when I came back to this country, being very disoriented, is my provisional spiritual teaching that I, so to speak, grew up with. I was an agnostic as a child. My family was not members of any church, but when I was in my early 20s, I met Swami Nikhilananda of the Ramakrishna Order and spent seven years with him studying the Vedanta and meditating on Ramakrishna, who was a kind of all-embracing, I'd say, Sufi. I returned to this, and I realized that perhaps this is, for some strange reason, my background, and that perhaps I am really rooted in that particular tradition and I'm seeing all the other traditions somehow subtly and in the light of that. I wondered, in your case, perhaps you are really completely rooted in the teachings of your father, Hazrat Inayat Khan, and that really you are seeing everything else in the light of that in a subtle way. In that sense, you could say you are not eclectic at all. You're completely focused in a certain way.

Pir Vilayat: That is perfectly true. But I think the reason is not because he happened to be my father, but because that teaching is so much in tune with, let's say, the thinking of the planet. Beyond the thinking of the individuals, there is the thinking of the planet. And what is more, there are trends. Like, sometimes, there are only a few minds that are able to see the next step. It's their duty to be pioneers and to open new perspectives and then the other people follow. It's very amazing when one studies science to the extent that I've been doing quite recently, to see to what extent the holistic approach now confirms exactly all the things that Hazrat Inayat Khan had said a long time ago.

I'll give you an example. Until the present, it was always thought that the cells of the body were homeostatic, i.e., they sought to maintain a certain balance. Now it is found that they are heterostatic. That means that they are always seeking to improve their condition. One of the things that strikes me very strongly in Hazrat Inayat Khan's teaching is that it's entirely purpose-oriented, goal-oriented. Quite honestly, I feel that we must move forward. The whole purpose of our lives is to keep on breaking to new horizons. The whole of evolution is just exactly that.

Of course, it's natural that people get feeling more secure when they conform to patterns. That's the purpose of religions. But at the same time, behind the religions, there is always the point of showing the next step.

Lex Hixon: I notice quite an interesting similarity between Swami Vivekananda and Hazrat Inayat Khan. Vivekananda came to the United States for the first time in 1891 for the Parliament of Religions. Hazrat Inayat Khan came early in the 1900s. When exactly did your father first come?

Pir Vilayat: 1910.

Lex Hixon: So they really were contemporaries. Just possibly Vivekananda had received such wide publicity in India for his trip West that it's not entirely beyond the bounds of possibility that your father may have heard about this trip.

Pir Vilayat: My father gave me a picture of Ramakrishna to put on my wall. And when Swami Siddheshwarananda, of the Ramakrishna Mission in Paris, who had tremendous success, visited the house of my father in Paris and he was, at my invitation, giving a lecture, there were two brass plates on the chimneypiece, and as soon as he spoke about the link between Hazrat Inayat Khan and Ramakrishna, the two plates hit each other. Then he invited me to speak in his center in Gretz. At the very moment, when I spoke about their relationship, again, two plates hit each other.

Lex Hixon: We're looking nervously around here in case two things are going to hit each other. May our minds and hearts touch each other on this point, Pir Vilayat. I've always felt that Hazrat Inayat Khan and Ramakrishna had this. Vivekananda, as the younger man who came West, which is actually what Hazrat Inayat did, had the kind of courageous, visionary act. They both recognized that there was something here in the West, more than just materialism and affluence, but there was a potentiality here.

Pir Vilayat: You see, the interesting thing was that here was someone coming from the Hindu tradition who had reached this sort of multireligious attitude, and someone from the Muslim tradition who reached the same point of view, and here they were meeting. It's so meaningful to what's happening on the planet at this time.

Lex Hixon: It seems possible that this kind of harmony of religions may not have been able to arise any place but India, because of the nature of India.

Pir Vilayat: Exactly what I was thinking. You see, you have spent some time in Turkey, as many of our people have done. I know a few people who have visited the Sufis in North Africa. Now, you must understand that in those countries the official religion is Muslim. Now, if you go to India, you find a totally different climate. You find that the Hindus and the Muslims have [coexisted] together for long decades or even centuries. In fact, it was only political propagandas that divided them.

In my family, my great-grandfather, Maula Bakhsh, had two wives—one Muslim and one Hindu. There were a lot of intermarriages and friendships between Hindus and Muslim and, as you know, there were many people and mystics who tried to find common measure between the two. There is a story of one such mystic. After he died, it was not clear whether he was Hindu or Muslim. Both the Hindus and the Muslims came to bury him. While they were quarreling, he rolled out of his coffin and disappeared into the forest so that he could die in peace.

Lex Hixon: Are you going to be cremated or buried?

Pir Vilayat: I want to offer my body for science.

Lex Hixon: Wonderful! That's a new, totally Western development.

Pir Vilayat: You know, there's the story that when I visited Professor Massignon, I realized that, in fact, I am both a Christian and a Muslim. Now, this is something that appeals to me very much, because he didn't say, "I'm not a Christian" or "I'm not a Muslim." He said, "I am a Christian and a Muslim," and that's exactly how I feel myself. And I'm not only a Christian and a Muslim, but I am also Buddhist and I am also Hindu and I'm also a Jew and I'm also a Zoroastrian. I really believe in the great value of what they have to teach.

Lex Hixon: I can't say that I ever met anyone who said so clearly my own feelings as you just did. Do you think there should be people who do keep the independent traditions of Christianity and Judaism and Islam? Or do you think gradually those things will fall away?

Pir Vilayat: They are bound to fall away.

Lex Hixon: Are they? Are they?

Pir Vilayat: Well, as much as different costumes, clothes that people wear...

Lex Hixon: But religious beliefs and whole spiritual so-called forms are deeper than costumes.

Pir Vilayat: Of course they are much deeper. [But]I think definitely there will be more and more [religious forms] merging. I think that's absolutely certain.

Lex Hixon: I would say that there is a clear point of disagreement between us, because I would look to the fact of these independent traditions existing also in their purity, kept up by people who have that form of destiny.

Pir Vilayat: Yes, I think that's very beautiful, to the extent that it is done. I think the same thing applies to clothes. I like very much an Indian to wear a sari...

Lex Hixon: But that's an aesthetic matter, Pir Vilayat. Clothes are—we're talking on a terribly serious level of a person's spiritual worldview.

Pir Vilayat: I certainly wouldn't encourage people to leave their religion and believe in all religions together or a new synthetic religion or anything like that, no. But I think that it's bound to happen.

Lex Hixon: This place where we are now is called the Abode of the Message. Is that the abode of the Sufi message of Hazrat Inayat Khan? Or is it the abode of the message of the Prophet? What message is this the abode of? It could be "the Abode of the Message in Our Time." It's not referring to some message of the past. It is a totally contemporary message coming down right now.

Pir Vilayat: Yes, but it is the same message as ever, just assuming we're always moving ahead.

Lex Hixon: I like that.

Pir Vilayat: That's my credo.

Lex Hixon: I want to switch gears in our conversation now and speak about the Symposium on the Coevolution of Science and

Spirit that is sponsored by the Sufi Order in the West. Perhaps you could say something about this relationship between science and spirituality.

Pir Vilayat: Maybe it wasn't coincidental that when I was younger I studied science at a college in London and even in Paris in university. But the reason why this particular subject is important at this time is because I think we are passing a real landmark in the evolution of human consciousness or maybe prefiguring what will be a landmark in the year 2000, but is already happening now in anticipation. I think that maybe the axial thought coming [from] the whole thing is to be found in the holistic approach.

The starting point is, of course, discovering that a crystal is made from molecules, and if you break it up, you can break it up into as many pieces as you like, up to, let's say, one molecule. You'll find that every fragment behaves just like the entire crystal. So what it really means is that man is not just a fragment of the totality, but also carries within him the characteristics of the totality. If you use religious terms, you would say that man has within him the divine perfection. In other words, we've reached a point now when we can't go on any longer simply thinking of ourselves as being "me," as a separate entity and a fragment of the totality and limited by my "I-ness," but we have to be aware of the divine and universal dimensions of our being. That's the holistic message. The scientists are beginning to realize the limitations of what they [believed to be true] in the last century or the beginning of this century.

Lex Hixon: But suppose one finds a scientist who already has a predilection towards being a visionary, and begins to get over the edge and feels this awe and maybe has certain perceptions? Isn't there a long way between there and the way of the mystic?

Pir Vilayat: Well, if a scientist is able to maintain his spiritual ideal while dealing with matter, I think it is a great achievement.

What I am saying is, as time goes on, people are giving up forms, although they have value. That's what I'm really saying.

For example, it isn't possible today to build a cathedral like Notre Dame. Why? Well, people have given up whatever it is that it takes to build a cathedral like Notre Dame. They're building other churches and so on that are technically rather wonderful in their way, but they are unable to do the same as they were able to do then. I think that the same thing is probably happening with forms. Even in the Catholic Church, they're changing their forms. That's because the forms have their value; one shouldn't devalue the forms, but they do have to change. They do have to.

I'll always try and see both aspects of every problem. What I call the holistic realization of our time is that we are not just fragments of the totality, we are also the totality. There's no way grammar allows us to express this. Grammar is entirely built on the assumption that we individuals are the subjects, and therefore our grammar doesn't enable us to say what he is trying to say, which is that it is he who knows himself through this part of himself. But, as we said, this part is also the totality. It's quite perplexing, but that's the whole thing. Now, as I say, I am excited by science because it is saying exactly the same thing. It says that the molecule has within it the quality of the whole crystal. It says the DNA structure of the cells has within it the code of the whole past of creation, not only on the planet. It says that, in fact, you cannot consider one phenomenon without considering all phenomena because they are all involved; in fact, there is only one being. No, one cannot say anything more ultimate than that. It's quite true. And this is exactly the meaning of what Hazrat Inayat Khan says when he answers the question, "What is the message in our time?" He says it's the consciousness of the awakening of the divinity in man. In other words, it's the discovery of this perfection. It's the real "me."

Lex Hixon: Would you express this just for a few moments through a dhikr? Because you said that this, in a sense, is the real meaning of the *la ilaha illallah.*

Pir Vilayat: Yes, that says it much better than words.

Lex Hixon: There's not a drop of blood in you that's not Islam. Thank you very much, Pir Vilayat!

Pir Vilayat Inayat Khan in meditation

Michael Murphy
October 16, 1978

Michael Murphy was born in 1930 in Salinas, California. He earned a B.A. in psychology from Stanford University in 1952. After military service, he returned to Stanford for a short time for postgraduate studies, then left in 1956 to spend 18 months in India at the Aurobindo Ashram in Pondicherry, which shaped his ideas about humanity and the direction of his future work in the field of transformational energy. Back in San Francisco, he lived at the Aurobindo Fellowship, where he met Dick Price. Together, they founded Esalen Institute in 1962 on the Murphy family's land in Big Sur. Murphy ran Esalen as an educational center until 1972, when he retired to write. He remains chairman of the board and continues to direct projects at the Esalen Center for Theory and Research. In the 1980s, he organized the Esalen Soviet-American Exchange Program in citizen diplomacy. He remains an important figure in the human-potential movement, contributing spiritual insights and research to the medical, scientific, and sporting worlds. His book *Golf in the Kingdom,* a fable about a golf game with a wizard, was published in 1971 and made into a movie in 2010. His many other books include *The Future of the Body* and *An End to Ordinary History.*

Lex Hixon: If you happen to be a sports fan or an athlete, don't tune out right away because you think of this as a spiritual program. This morning we are going to be doing an interview with Michael Murphy, who has just written a book, with Rhea White, called *The Psychic Side of Sports,* and we're going to be talking about the spiritual dimensions of athletic training and what this could mean to our culture. Michael was a co-founder of the Esalen Institute in California and he has been in the vanguard of various forms of new thinking in this country for a long time.

I've read this book very closely in the last couple of days. It brings together a tremendous amount of material from a wide field of sporting events, including yachting, mountain climbing, and martial arts as well team sports like baseball and football and basketball. It's woven together with the deep understanding of what the analogies might be between athletic and spiritual discipline and between the experiences of athletes and mystics. I'm not surprised, because Michael has studied at the Aurobindo Ashram, and practiced meditation for many years.

Now, would you tell us, Michael, what the genesis of this book has been?

Michael Murphy: Well, the book grew on me for many years. I've always loved sport and I've been interested in the religious traditions and in Sri Aurobindo for about 28 years, but I had not appreciated how much there was in the world of sport that cohered with the religious traditions until I wrote a book called *Golf in the Kingdom* in 1972. It's a humorous and sometimes fantastical fable, an adult fairy story in the spirit of C.S. Lewis, about a round of golf with a wizard named Shivas Irons. After the book was published, I started to get stories from athletes, the most notable being San Francisco 49er quarterback John Brodie, who asked me to come with him down to the 49er training camp.

Lex Hixon: This was on the basis of his having read *Golf in the Kingdom*?

Michael Murphy: Yes. He wanted me to take a look at professional football. I had been a season ticket holder for a long time, and this is the ultimate offer that a fan can get! We spent about 10 days at the training camp and I heard some things that made me think seriously that there was an unrecognized spiritual element in athletics.

For example, one of the big defensive linemen told us that in the national football league there was a myth that some players had a command over their bodies that defied natural explanation. The next day I saw him and I asked him to continue the story, but he backed away, saying that he had been exaggerating. I realized that he was afraid to talk to me about this. I must have seemed like somebody from the press. During the next eight days, he would tell me a story one day, then back away from it the next. It was a clue that there might be a lot of this in the world of sport that isn't talked about so when experiences happen there's no recognition for them. That was what got me started. It turned out to be a marvelous rationalization to be able to call my love of sports basic research. I could go to all the football games and golf tournaments I wanted and say it was all in the interest of science.

After a couple of years, Rhea White, who is the chief archivist for the American Society for Psychical Research, wrote to me and suggested that we do a book. We put together our knowledge of this realm for six years, and gradually this book has emerged. I was a little reluctant to publish it, thinking that we had overdrawn the connection between these two worlds, but it has become more and more self-evident that there are incredible connections.

Lex Hixon: I think that your book is going to reach deep into this culture and touch not just people who don't have spiritual languages, but people who *do* have various spiritual languages but who haven't really connected their daily physical life with these languages.

Intellectuals or spiritual seekers may tend to play down what is essentially a very rich spiritual component of sports. What you said about the football player who was reluctant to share these types of experiences points to something that doesn't just happen in sports. These mysterious experiences that might happen in any situation don't always fit into the religious language that we have. Do you think these transcending or mystical experiences happen more freely in sports simply because one thinks they shouldn't happen in that context?

Michael Murphy: Exactly. And this is why I think some coaches and some athletes refuse to talk about this. It's a kind of Zen wisdom, you know. If you have *satori* [sudden enlightenment] chopping wood, keep chopping wood. It's a combination of wisdom and fear that prevents people from taking a look at this phenomenal situation.

Lex Hixon: My feeling is that the book will enrich the experience of athletes *and spectators*. The spectators of sporting events have very rich experiences too.

Michael Murphy: The more I got into this research, the more I had a sense of the uncanny. I don't know if you've ever read Freud's great essay analyzing the idea of the uncanny. The word in German is *unheimliche*. It can mean either very familiar, or very strange, and the shadings of these meanings.

Freud felt that in all phenomena of repression, where we have forgotten something that we secretly know, there's a lurking sense of the uncanny. He was presenting that idea in the context of his therapeutic concerns, but you could argue that, in the world of sports, it's the sublime that is repressed. And that you watch these games being played like vast theaters of the occult, and the fans sense that something is lurking there, and then suddenly it bursts out. That's what it's been like writing this book. I've felt that kind of uncanny sense at times in games, that there's something else going on, and that's why it was a revelation to me after watching the 49ers for 27 years, ever since they started, to hear players talking in that language. It was mind-blowing! It seems clear that many athletes and adventurers have, however inadvertently, touched into spiritual experience.

Lex Hixon: Charles Lindbergh, who must be counted as an adventurer in this research, had experiences that seem to be full-blown mystical experiences.

Michael Murphy: There is a huge representation of experiences that we explore in the book. It ranges from extraordinary moments of clarity of perception, to time slowing down or speeding up, to the perception of auras to experiences like Lindbergh's—which sounds so close to some of the great Hindu or Buddhist scriptures that you can put them side by side. Lindbergh's experience went unrecorded in his first book, in 1927. It wasn't until he wrote *The Spirit of St. Louis* in 1953 that he could own it in public. I think he was helped to process it by his wife, Anne Morrow Lindbergh, who was a very deep student of religious lore. Then, in his autobiography, which was published after his death, he explores it even more. It was a continuous evolution of his understanding, growing to meet his experience.

He writes that there had been such a tremendous amount of focus on preparing for the flight, that by the time he took off, he was already at the edge of his resources, and then he was awake for 24 hours or so when this experience started to happen. As he describes it in *The Spirit of St. Louis*, he felt the boundaries between himself and another world growing thinner and thinner. Suddenly, immaterial forms appeared in the cockpit around him, beckoning to him to come across, and he felt that just by nodding a little bit, he could cross into their realm. He had to make a decision whether to stay here, or cross over. He decided to stay here, but he realized then that his perception had changed dramatically. His mind had become as large as this planet he was flying over, his skull felt like a single eye, and he was seeing in all directions at once.

Lex Hixon: In the book, juxtaposed to that, is the experience of a certain safetyman in football who was able to follow multiple players at the same time. Not knowing how he did it, he says that it suddenly just clicked in and he entered a new dimension where his head was an eye that could see both the quarterback and the pass receivers wherever they were on the field at the same time.

Michael Murphy: Yes, and Macarthur Lane, one of the great running backs in the National Football League, said he never learned to be a great runner until he stopped looking through his eyes. When I heard that, it made my hair stand on end because when you're running on the football field, there are many large bodies flying around with the thunder of their pads whacking into each other, and he was weaving his way through all of that without using his physical eyes, as he says.

Lex Hixon: So *The Psychic Side of Sports* may give people courage to seek out the language to describe these experiences, and possibly to open themselves up more to having them—and not only in sport, but in all dimensions of their life, at any sort of highly-concentrated crisis moment that life might bring.

I want to go back to talk about the philosophy of Aurobindo, which is something that is so deep in your background.

Michael Murphy: Great. Aurobindo's vision did inspire me. When I was at Stanford doing post-graduate work, I read in his writings that physical life, because it contains the divine, is meant to express that divinity, and that the whole evolution of this cosmos in which we find ourselves is in the service of this progressive manifestation.

Lex Hixon: To play the game of embodiment.

Michael Murphy: Yes, to play it, and he said it was just getting started. It's a vast expression of the divine and it's progressively unfolding.

At the ashram, they had quite a sports program. I coached the basketball team there, and introduced softball and taught swimming. Recently, there's been a huge proliferation of sports. The Greeks could never have imagined the hundreds and hundreds of sports that we now have. If you look upon sport as part of this progressive manifestation of the divine, then what we have to do to keep progressing is to make conscious the inner elements of the physical. I think it's going to be seen historically as a very important experiment.

Lex Hixon: It's important for its influence on you, Michael! If you hadn't spent the time at the Aurobindo ashram, you wouldn't have as deep an understanding of spiritual life as you do.

Michael Murphy: Absolutely. It was Aurobindo's writings that got me oriented to looking at things this way. And going over to the ashram for a year and a half really confirmed my practice and discipline, and I decided I wasn't wired up in a way that I could do the academic life and explore these things at the same time. So, Aurobindo has been crucial for me.

Lex Hixon: There is a strain of Hindu philosophy that teaches that ultimately there *is* no physical body, that the idea of a physical body is an abstraction. How would you respond to that? What if what we call the body is actually inside the soul, and what we call the physical universe is actually inside the divine?

I can see where you're coming from—you're celebrating the body and its accomplishments. But from the highest standpoint, don't you have to come back to the sense that the body is really made out of love and wisdom? It's not merely a physical entity.

Michael Murphy: Well, no. It's not *merely* physical, and it's not *merely* a body in any sense that we may hold those images. It is always something beyond our definitions. As we collect the lore of this bodily experience, we find more and more that people have access to different levels of embodiment, and the second book I wrote, *Jacob Atabet,* was another way into this material, where I tried to imagine the future of embodiment.

As you take seriously this entranceway into divinity and explore it, you find that there are levels upon levels of experience that are accessible to you. One way that it unfolds is through a progressive focus on finer and finer structures of the body. It seems that some people can catch glimpses of the different levels of bodily structure, and we're collecting these stories. For example, marathon runners who will be running along and suddenly will see, for maybe three seconds, pictures of capillaries bursting and red cells bursting out. This happened to me once, and it was a frightening experience, so I began to explore this with runners. When I give talks to university groups, I ask people to share experiences. I'm generally finding that about one-third of an audience will admit to having some glimpses of bodily structures that seemed frightening. They say it was more than mere imagination. You can penetrate to the level of cellular and molecular existence, where what you see gets to be more like what you can see through an electron microscope. You're seeing a shimmering light show, because, as we know now, there are 40 trillion cells in this body. Most of them include up to 200 trillion or 300 trillion molecules. The molecules on the membranes of the cells are either oscillating or spinning at the rate of several billion times a second. People in a very advanced state of meditation begin to see these things, and people taking LSD sometimes see these things too.

Lex Hixon: But let's take Charles Lindbergh. As you said, the veil between this world and another world became very thin for him. And when you were talking about these trillion spinning molecules, I thought of the diaphanous veil. The body is just a diaphanous veil between this world and other worlds.

Michael Murphy: No, I'd want to take exception with the "nothing but." You see, it's a diaphanous veil, but it is also an entity that we have to take seriously. There's something tremendous going on here, and if we can learn to play the body game more beautifully, that's what this life is all about. We don't know what it can do. This week, Lex, a great event happened in world history that will not be recorded as a great event for some time. It was revealed to the public that through instruments we can now see atomic patterns. I don't know if you happened to see this on television.

Lex Hixon: I was too busy watching the World Series.

Michael Murphy: Well, there are many ways. So, the electron microscope is getting down into finer and finer resolution, and I think that physical science is the sunrise of our ultimate remembering and seeing what this body is. You see, we're being led by the instruments of physical science down into the well of physicality, down into this cosmic light show that we inhabit, but we don't know about it.

I see we're out of time, but I have to finish.

Lex Hixon: Keep going! I'm jumping up and down. I'm levitating off my seat. We'll end the program with this.

Michael Murphy: Okay, so it's not just a veil, you know, we're all living in these bodies that are incredible light shows. We're here, and we can gain access to this, and that is what some of these athletes do for moments. Or, it's what certain painters see. Nine people have sent me paintings on the basis of the *Atabet* book, saying that it helped them understand that they were painting these interior structures. Okay, now, so you're right about something. We are seeing only one-millionth of one percent of what you and I call our body, but we must take seriously what we do see because it's our particular stargate into these mysteries. We mustn't just go zipping through our stargate and just throw it away, you see. We need to explore it, and reveal it. We need to learn how to manifest more of this glory in more and more ways. Let's open our perceptions so that we can see the whole cosmic light show!

Bernie Glassman
November 19, 1978

Bernie Glassman was born in Brooklyn, New York, in 1939. After receiving a degree in aeronautical engineering at Brooklyn Polytechnic Institute, he earned a Ph.D. in applied mathematics from UCLA. In 1963, he married Helen Harkaspi (they later divorced), and had two children. Glassman studied meditation with Taizan Maezumi Roshi, and helped found the Zen Center of Los Angeles in 1967. He took vows as a monk, but later returned his robes and began working for peace as a layperson. In 1976, he became a Zen teacher in the White Plum Asanga of the Soto School of Zen Buddhism in Los Angeles. He returned to New York in 1980, partly in response to being interviewed on "In the Spirit" in 1978, and founded the New York Zen Center. He and his second wife, Sandra Jishu Holmes (1941-1998), established the Greyston Foundation to facilitate employment projects like the Greyston Bakery in Yonkers, New York, which is now a Harvard Business School social-action case study. As a teacher, Glassman utilizes street retreats, council work, clowning, Buddha family studies, baking, Bearing Witness Retreats, and social activism, along with a rigorous sitting practice. In 1996, he co-founded the Zen Peacemaker Order and led the first annual Auschwitz-Birkenau Bearing Witness Retreat. Glassman's many books include *Hazy Moon of Enlightenment* (1977), co-written with Maezumi Roshi, and *The Dude and the Zen Master* (2013), co-written with his friend, actor Jeff Bridges. Today, Glassman and his third wife, writer, and Zen teacher Eve Myonen Marko, live in Montague, Massachusetts, and work together toward peace in places of trauma around the world.

Lex Hixon: Bernie Glassman is here from the flourishing Los Angeles Zen Center. It's great to welcome Bernie back to New York City because he was born here and his cultural base is here. He went to California for school and work, and met his teacher there. Then he went on to do a tremendous amount of Zen practice and study, and his teacher, Maezumi Roshi, has given him full permission to teach Zen. The book *The Hazy Moon of Enlightenment*, which they wrote together, includes questions and answers between students at the Los Angeles Zen Center and Sensei Bernie Glassman— conversations between American Zen students and a true American Zen teacher. I don't think we should underestimate the tremendous value of this for all of us. We don't know what an enlightened Zen master who was raised Jewish in Brooklyn is going to be like. Maybe this hasn't happened before in the history of world religions. So we have something here that is very unique.

I was drawn, Sensei, to one of the questions and answers in the book. It puzzled me. The questioner says, "Every day is a new day. Every moment is a new moment. Sometimes I'm very sad and don't know why. Sometimes I feel very alive and intelligent, and I don't know why. I used to think that enlightenment was trying to embrace all these moments in some way, but that's become totally impossible."

Sensei's answer was simply, "Thank you." Now, Sensei, why would you thank a person for saying something like that, which seems to describe such an impasse?

Bernie Glassman: Because the first step in our practice has to be this impasse. The reason that we seem to have problems is that we have the idea that we shouldn't have any problems. We have a lot of ideas, like there is such a thing as enlightenment. We start going all over the place, looking, reading, experiencing, and trying to get from the place where we are right now to some other place which we see over there. Finally, we come to an impasse because whatever we do, whatever we read, whatever we study, we find that we still wake up one morning happy and we wake up another morning feeling sad. Something happens and we feel great about it. Something else happens and we feel terrible. We think that we've studied so much that anger is completely gone, and something happens and we get angry. Eventually, we're led to that place where there's nowhere to go, and the reason is that all of this has been based on our concepts, our thinking. Once we get to that impasse, *then* we can make a break to realizing where we are, independent of the mind. Getting to that place is very important for everyone, and so I just naturally say thank you.

Lex Hixon: When you said thank you, I got the impression that you were thanking this person for seeing the impasse as a gate to go through. Was there something of that in the question too?

Bernie Glassman: Not quite. If they really saw past that point, then they wouldn't be talking about it. The student shows where he's stuck. Everything that we say points out where we're stuck.

Lex Hixon: It seems that this particular student has at least freed himself of some sort of attachments because he says, "I used to think that enlightenment was trying to embrace all of these moments in some way, to make some effort to include them all." How would you lead a student like this forward from this position?

Bernie Glassman: That's right. In Zen, the idea is always to let go of the place where you are. But if I told the person where to go next, that would be adding a new idea, not helping them let go. There's really not much to do. Whatever you do from the outside tends to leave something else to grab onto. The student will realize from the only place they can, from inside of themselves, what this life really is. They have to just see it.

The point is for the person to let go, and in Zen, the basic way to do this is meditation. That is where they have the best chance to see where they are right now, because where to go next *has* to be seen by letting go of where you are now. Zen has a nice analogy for this, and it's called "The Man on the Top of a 100-Foot Pole." It's a *koan*, one of the Zen stories that are used as teaching techniques. You imagine yourself balanced on top of a 100-foot pole. The question is: How do you go further? Where you are at this very moment is always on top of a 100-foot pole. You think you've accomplished something—whether it's success in life, success as a parent, success as a child, success in business—and now you stick to that point because if you don't, you're afraid you'll fall off. You're clinging to something, see, you're clinging to your happiness, to your sadness, whatever it is; we are all clinging to something, our positions, our ideas, our way of life. Anything that you stick to, whether it's good or bad, traps you. You have to keep going.

And the point is: How do you keep going? Well, obviously, just let go. Let go of that point, let go of that position. What do you see when you've let go? It's just boundless! It's complete freedom. That doesn't mean just doing whatever we want to do. It means that we're completely free to meet whatever situation comes up and take action in the most appropriate way.

Lex Hixon: How is this position distinguished from a wild, free, existentialist point of view with no positions? The Buddha's teachings speak of right understanding, so there must be some correct positions.

Bernie Glassman: The basis of practice rests on what we call "The Three Treasures"—the Buddha, the Dharma, and the Sangha. We could look at the Buddha as being the oneness of life, and the enlightened state. We could talk about the Dharma as being the "manyness" of life, all of the phenomena and the teachings, and we could see the Sangha as the harmony, the fact that the differences and the oneness are really the same thing. They're two sides of the same coin, that's why they're in perfect harmony. Okay, that's the rudder by which we steer.

Lex Hixon: And that isn't a 100-foot pole that one can get stuck on? Is that really something of permanent boundless value?

Bernie Glassman: Yes, but if you get stuck to the idea of Buddha, Dharma, or Sangha, then you're back on the pole. What we have to see and experience is the real fact that *we are* the Three Treasures, see? *We are* the Buddha, Dharma, and Sangha—this very moment is that. All options are open. We're not fettered by these concepts. Let me give a more concrete example of what this means: We have two hands. Now imagine that each of these hands had an idea that it was separate from the other. If somebody comes along with money, and the right hand reaches out for the money, the left hand becomes jealous. Why is the right hand getting money? If there's a fire and the left hand is caught in the fire, the right hand stops for a second and thinks, "Should I save the left hand from the fire? Maybe somebody will see me and I'll get sued."

Okay, now imagine that something happens and the ego that was in the right hand is gone, and the ego that was in the left hand is gone. The ego has now popped up to the head, and I realize that my body is just one being. I'm Bernie, I'm Sensei, and I see myself as separate from you. My hands are just part of me, but I can see that I'm different from you.

Okay, now if somebody comes along with money, it doesn't matter which hand takes it, and if the left hand is on fire, *automatically* the right hand grabs it out of the fire. Some insight has occurred so that the idea of the right hand being separate from the left hand is gone. I now know that I am one entity. Taking care of that entity is the functioning of the insight. Now, the ego is in *my* head, so I view myself as different from you. If somebody comes along with money and gives it to you, I'll get upset. Or if you're in an automobile accident, before I help, I'll stop and think, "Well, should I go over there? They might say I caused the accident."

Now we have to take another step. Something happens, causing the ego to pop out of my head and start to fade. I realize that you and I are still here, but we are the same. Then the last step happens and the ego disappears completely and I just see oneness, and I will take care of you because you are me. That is seeing life from the wisdom perspective.

So you could say that the Dharma aspect means there is a right hand and left hand or there's a "you" and there's a "me." And then the Sangha viewpoint is that we are in harmony, that the "you" and the "me" are the same thing, at the same time that we are Lex and Bernie. Then, from the wisdom perspective of the Buddha, it's just One. That's the full realization. At this point, the compassionate response is automatic—it's the functioning of seeing oneness. Compassion is automatic as long as we see from the wisdom perspective. It's definitely not nihilistic and definitely does not mean that anything goes.

Lex Hixon: That sounds like a really strong argument for an intense social concern and social action. Ordinarily, people think of Zen as being a contemplative practice that leads one into the quiet of the Zendo, but what I suddenly heard you say was that the realization of oneness automatically could lead someone out into the world to want to help in the most appropriate way and they would be expressing their realization.

Bernie Glassman: Yes, I think so. Automatically, you become involved in what you think is the best thing to do. Buddhism has the figure of the idealized person called a bodhisattva, a person who has realization of the Buddha perspective and then works for others even though it's never ending.

One of the exaggerated examples that gives a sense of the role of the bodhisattva is the image of the man who is trying to fill up a well for people. He goes up the mountain and gets a spoonful of snow and he comes down and he drops it into the well. Then he goes back, and he fills the spoon, and goes back down and drops it into the well. So, knowing that we can never fill up the well, knowing that we can't resolve all the issues and fix the world, we still automatically do what seems necessary.

Lex Hixon: When the Zen student comes into the formal interview situation it creates a certain intense focus. It's not just like bumping into my old friend Bernie. It's going to see the

Sensei. This encounter isn't necessarily verbal, is it? But there is some sort of leap of communication?

Bernie Glassman: Yes, definitely, that's true. The exchange between student and teacher is not limited to any particular form. There is a very formal situation setup for what we call *dokusan*, the private study between the student and the teacher, and that particular format does get the student into a space where everything is there and it's very easy to see. And the teacher's role is to help point to what is there, and sometimes that's done verbally, sometimes by some sort of action, sometimes by silence.

Lex Hixon: You are a person who has seen that there's no separation between you and the student, so whatever you do or say, whatever you don't do or don't say, everything is coming from the student, so you're not really offering the student anything from the outside. You are the triple treasure, reminding the student about something that is already theirs.

Bernie Glassman: Yes, but that may sound confusing to people. In a way, certainly, that's true. That's looking at it from the Buddha side. Then there is the Dharma side too, where the fact is that we *are* different, that each person is in a different place. And so although what you're saying is very true—that whatever we do, it's one thing really happening—still, somehow we have to help each of us to see that.

Lex Hixon: And, granted, you will be different in each meeting, but it would be spontaneous. You wouldn't try to look at the person psychologically to make an analysis; you would just automatically do the most appropriate thing to help them let go of the 100-foot pole.

Bernie Glassman: Definitely, that's true. There's no thinking going on here.

Lex Hixon: When you are functioning in this spontaneous teaching mode, do you feel that you're in a different state of consciousness? Do you feel a more vivid awareness than you do as just an ordinary day-to-day, walking-around human being?

Bernie Glassman: No, not particularly, because, of course, that's what I am—an ordinary human being.

Lex Hixon: If I were talking right now with an experienced rabbi or priest about their pastoral work, would they say essentially the same thing that you are saying?

Bernie Glassman: I would think so. See, we're all talking about life. Life is this moment, right? No matter what direction you come from, if you really see what this life is, it *has* to be the same. So we may have different ideas and different religious languages, but if you mean that the rabbi or priest or Buddhist or Catholic or Hindu or Muslim *really sees* what this moment is—what life is—then it *has* to be the same thing.

Lex Hixon: In fact, now that I think about it, as I talk and ask questions, I feel I am the voice of however many people are listening, and when you are answering, Bernie, you are the wisdom and insight of those people. So, in a certain sense, we have a unique demonstration right here in this radio station of what that you mean. The conversation that we're having doesn't seem to be an isolated one between two individuals, but it seems to be a conversation occurring in the minds and hearts of all the people who are listening.

Bernie Glassman: And vice versa. All the conversations going on anywhere are part of us. Everything that's going on is us. It's just a wonderful world, a wonderful fact, and if we don't see that, we force ourselves down to a little drop of water.

Lex Hixon: But at the same time, I think that the clarification you've made a couple of times is so important—that part of reality is that we *are* separate people, that there is the right hand and the left hand. I think that it's reassuring to say that we are not dissolved in a vague, mystical all-is-one statement, that what you're speaking about is not some trance state where everything disappears and there's just a shimmering light where New York City used to be.

Bernie Glassman: Then I'll say it again. What we're talking about is just life. It's just this moment, which is very ordinary, there's nothing strange about it. What we imagine can make it very strange. But this moment—it's just this. This morning we get up, we wash our faces, we eat our breakfast of coffee and bagels if it's New York, and we come and talk to you.

Lex Hixon: Let's shift gears now. I'm going to ask Sensei to lead us in a short meditation. It's coming through an ordinary scientist and mathematician, Bernie Glassman, who was raised and educated in Brooklyn. He's come back to New York, bringing these precious Zen treasures for us. Each of you, in a natural way, can imagine going into his presence, and he's saying something *to* you, *as* you.

Bernie Glassman: If you would, be seated. If you have to lie down, it's okay. Lie down. Sit in a chair if that's what's comfortable. Let your breathing be natural. It's amazing how many of us can't breathe naturally. We force our breathing. So sit naturally. Breathe naturally. What is breath? Breath is life. In many languages, breath and spirit are the same word. Breathe naturally. Sit naturally. And then let the mind be natural. Let the mind sit. In Zen, we call meditation zazen. We use zazen to allow the body, the breath, and the mind to sit. We say that we sit every morning for a half hour or an hour, and we sit in the evening, but it's not just casual sitting around. It's letting everything sit—the body, the mind, and the breathing. Let everything sit.

You know how a top spins? If you can really spin it well, then it looks like it's just sitting still. It's moving so fast and balanced so perfectly that it's just sitting, motionless. But that motionlessness, that sitting, is extremely active. It's perfectly balanced, moving at a wonderful speed. But if it's a little off balance, what happens? It falls over. And that's what we do. If we're not really sitting, then something comes up and we fall over. A problem comes up and, emotionally, we get disturbed. So the first thing we should do is just learn to sit like a top. Sitting still, breathing is natural.

What do you see? The words in your mind are nothing but us. The silence, is nothing but us. And so when we really sit, we see that this very moment *is* ourselves. It's simple. Life's ordinary. But yet we can't accept it, so it becomes difficult. You want the mysteries of life to be special, you want enlightenment to be special, and that traps us. So just sit. Forget all that, and realize that this very moment, what's happening is all there is. That's it. That very fact is mysterious and wonderful. Now I'll shut up for a few minutes and we'll just sit. Realize that everything you hear, everything you see, everything you think, is you, is me.

Perle (Epstein) Besserman
February 4, 1979

A descendant of the Baal Shem Tov, Perle Besserman (aka Perle Epstein) was born in New York in 1948. She holds a Ph.D. in comparative literature from Columbia University, and studied Jewish mysticism with Rabbis Zyi Yehuda Kook and Aryeh Kaplan. She has written several books on meditation and mysticism, including the groundbreaking *Kabbalah: The Way of the Jewish Mystic* (originally published in 1978). She has taught literature and writing at New York University, Southwest China University, Briarcliff College, University of Hawaii, Rutgers University, and Illinois State University, where she is professor emerita. She is a a recipient of the Theodore Hoepfner Fiction Award, past writer-in-residence at the Mishkenot Sha'anamin Artists Colony in Jersusalem, and Pushcart Prize nominee, and she has been praised as a fiction writer by Isaac Bashevis Singer for her "clarity and feeling for mystic lore" and by *Publisher's Weekly* for her "wisdom [that] points to a universal practice of the heart." She has presented workshops on Kabbalah, Zen, and women's spirituality around the world, including at Princeton Area Zen Group, and has appeared on radio and television. Today, she and her husband, the University of Hawaii political science professor Manfred Steger, divide their time between Hawaii and Melbourne, Australia.

Lex Hixon: We have Perle Epstein in the studio with us this morning and we're going to be giving what one might playfully call a Kabbalistic manifesto. I'd like everyone to call up your Jewish friends. A lot of people don't listen to the program regularly, particularly Orthodox people. If anyone in my family is listening, call up the Dreisingers, Moshe and Miriam. Call and tell them they should listen. It's a very special program because it is a special book. It's been published just recently, Perle? In January?

Perle Besserman: Friday the 13th.

Lex Hixon: It's called *Kabbalah: The Way of the Jewish Mystic*, and we're going to take one section of it—you might say one of the most radical sections of it—and talk about that in detail and depth, rather than trying to cover the range of the whole book. The book is brief. It's about 157 pages. At first, I was kind of put off by that. What can you say in 157 pages? But I think it's very condensed, very rich, and it has the value that you can read it through without a great deal of wading through things, so you can get an immediate, full picture of Jewish mysticism.

Perle Epstein and I are friends because we've met each other in various contexts and studied the Vedanta and the Mahayana. I know her to have had real, practical experience in various spiritual traditions, but if I'd had any sort of third eye I could have seen that she's really called to the Jewish mystical tradition. We're going to talk later in the program with her about how that can be worked out, not only by observant Jews and non-observant Jews, but also by non-Jews. This is perhaps the radical nature of the program. As [an example of a] leader in this radical quest, we're going to take Abraham Abulafia. Perle, can you say something about Abulafia to give people an idea of his cultural setting and time and what sort of a personality he was?

Perle Besserman: He was a 13th-century Spanish Jewish mystic. But I think I'd better start by saying that he's totally unacceptable to practicing Kabbalists today, and he was from the time that he started. And he will continue to be, so that if you go to a Kabbalist, which is hard enough to do anyway, but if you find a Kabbalist, a real one, say, in Jerusalem, and you ask that person to teach you Abulafia's meditation, they'll send you away. Most of the expressions I've heard were in Yiddish, like, "Heaven forbid I should teach you Abulafia."

So, typically, Lex, you picked the most radical and least acceptable of the Jewish mystics. But I think you picked him because he is also the most wide-ranging. And he was the only mystic I know, of the whole gamut of Jewish mystics from the first century onward, who taught people of other traditions. He was very, very involved with the Sufis and with Christian mystics. And he taught Kabbalistic meditational techniques to these other people, and got into trouble for it.

Lex Hixon: But this is exactly why we chose him, because our manifesto is simply that Kabbalah is just too rich and too beautiful a tradition to be kept [only] to Jewish people.

Perle Besserman: There's a big problem about that, and I've had the problem myself in two situations. Just the other day it came up in my home. We were having a sort of Jewish meditative group experience with Reb Zalman [Schachter] at the house. I had just finished doing yoga with a friend, and the friend is a Catholic. I stood there at the end of the yoga class and asked her, "Do you think you would want to stay for this? They're doing some Jewish meditation." She said, "Of course I'd like to stay." I deliberated for a few minutes and had to send her home because of what had happened to me in Israel when I met non-Jews who came to Kabbalistic groups and [they] felt [like], "What am I doing here? What is my place here?" For instance, much of the material that is used is Hebrew. Now, I know you'll tell me you can go to a swami and start talking Sanskrit without knowing what it is. But the Hebrew that is used here is very worshipful. It's used in religious rituals. It's used in prayer. It's not something like just saying, "Om."

Lex Hixon: What you're pointing out is really that there has to be a universalization of the Kabbalah that will not be so rooted in the speaking of Hebrew. In other words, if you go to India to traditional ashrams, as I know you have, you find—particularly if it's not in any way designed for Westerners—you have the same feeling: "What am I doing here?" And, in fact, Hinduism is very much like Judaism in the sense that it's a mother tradition that's indigenous to a holy land. It isn't a tradition that has reached out.

Perle Besserman: No, not at all. In fact, it hasn't reached out to Jews. So how can we ask Christians and Buddhists to practice it when Jews don't know it?

Lex Hixon: I think we can, but I think rather than talk on the abstract level, let's try to sketch out for people the meditative approach and system of Abulafia. His unacceptableness certainly doesn't stem from the fact that he wasn't thoroughly and completely Jewish and intensely involved in the tradition.

Perle Besserman: And he was probably as Orthodox as any very Orthodox person today.

Lex Hixon: As you pointed out in your book, all the mystics since Abulafia have made use of his techniques. *Tzeruf*, which we'll talk about, is the permutation of letters, a kind of letter meditation. Of course, this was already in the tradition to some extent, but he developed it in a very, very marvelous way. So, in a certain sense, although he has been excommunicated, he has been accepted by the tradition on one level.

Perle Besserman: I think his methods are absolutely used. He, as a personality has never been reinstated, but his techniques are indispensable to anybody who wants to practice Kabbalistic meditation. There [is] a woman that I know of in Jerusalem who's a North African teacher, who comes from Algiers, [who] very openly claims that she has incorporated many of Abulafia's techniques and puts them in a very secular context so that you don't know sometimes that you're practicing Kabbalistic meditations. Perhaps there are some Hasidim who are using the techniques that don't even know they are using them because they got it by way of the Ari [literally, "the lion," Isaac Luria], the 16th-century Kabbalist, who is perfectly acceptable. And actually there are manuscripts that show Abulafia's own hand offering techniques for letter mysticism that were used by the 16th-century Kabbalists in Safed. So I don't think that Abulafia was considered *non compos mentis* until, say, the 18th or 19th century.

Lex Hixon: All the more reason that this kind of prejudice can be reversed. Do most of his works exist in Hebrew now?

Perle Besserman: They are all in Hebrew. Very few are translated. The big problem is that when you want to start studying the texts for practice, you mostly have to interpret them yourself and you can get into trouble doing that. Abulafia warns you, in fact. In the texts themselves, he says to make sure not to meditate on thus and such or you'll cripple your right arm. I mean, he's that explicit about what you do to your body.

Lex Hixon: At the same time, we should point out that Abulafia himself claimed to be the first Kabbalist to write explicit works on the Kabbalah.

Perle Besserman: Yes, to reveal to the people exactly what others were doing in secret.

Lex Hixon: He wanted this to be available to everyone who had the sense of discipline. He had very stringent requirements for practice that you mention sometimes in the book, about the tests.

Perle Besserman: The tests are very similar to the Zen tests, if you remember people sitting outside of monasteries for six days in the cold. Well, he's not that stringent. [His are] mostly intellectual tests because you are using your brain and you're using texts.

Lex Hixon: But it's not like the concept of Transcendental Meditation or something like that, being available to everybody.

Perle Besserman: Oh, God, no.

Lex Hixon: There's a demand for a kind of intensity.

Perle Besserman: *Chutzpah.* He demands that you have lots of chutzpah.

Lex Hixon: Talking about that, you mentioned [Moses ben Jacob] Cordovero. Can you say a little bit about him and the kind of chutzpah that he had to bring the Ari's teachings back to life?

Perle Besserman: Cordovero already was in Safed in 16th-century Palestine.

Lex Hixon: When he was a young kid, is that where he did that?

Perle Besserman: You're thinking of Vitale, perhaps? Chaim Vitale, who was the disseminator of all the information?

Lex Hixon: Who had a circle of young companions?

Perle Besserman: Ah, you're thinking of Chaim Moshe Luzzatto. He is another one who was excommunicated.

Lex Hixon: Everyone I like was excommunicated.

Perle Besserman: Anyone who brought this to the surface was excommunicated.

Lex Hixon: Tell us about Luzzatto.

Perle Besserman: Luzzatto was a brilliant university student. He was Italian, very wealthy, an aristocratic young man who had a number of friends who were living in Padua at the time. Some of them were medical students; some of them were philosophy students. He became very taken with the works of the Ari two centuries before.

Lex Hixon: That's who I'm talking about.

Perle Besserman: What he started to do—he had one teacher who taught him the ABCs of Jewish mysticism. I don't think he taught him the practices. Luzzatto, like most people who start to learn Jewish mysticism, became really hungry for the practice. You can go to Gershom Scholem and sit there as I did, and have wonderful conversations in Jerusalem about Jewish mysticism without ever practicing it at all. So I can understand what happened to Luzzatto. He became very passionate about doing it. And when the teachers told him not to do it, which is exactly what you are told when you read it with a scholar, he went home and he started to practice it, at great danger to his life and limb. I mean, Kabbalah has always been known as a very dangerous practice for your mind—you become unstable and so on. I believe he wasn't married at the time. I don't think he was 40. I don't think he had any of the qualifications you're supposed to have to be a practicing Kabbalist.

Lex Hixon: But he gathered a circle of friends around him...

Perle Besserman: He started secretly to tell a few close friends. One friend, who was a medical student named Gordon, said, "I have to tell this to the world. How can you let this be secret? You're having all these wonderful visions. When you teach us, we begin to feel this warmth going through our bodies." And they had all these real physical sensations. So they gathered this little circle together in imitation of the Ari circle in Safed, and started to live the Kabbalah secretly in the middle of their ordinary lives. They then got married, and then finally their parents found out what they were doing, and they continued this thing, reading the Zohar all night, doing these meditations, using the Abulafian letter techniques, and so on.

Lex Hixon: But at the same time, on a very serious level, it wasn't like a kind of mere bohemian interest. I mean, these people were deeply sincere and had great spiritual longing.

Perle Besserman: You see, that's one of the advantages and disadvantages of the Kabbalah. You can't dip into it. You can't say, "Oh, I'll meditate on it for 20 minutes in the morning." You can't. It's a way of life.

Lex Hixon: If it's a totally devouring, consuming flame, I really couldn't recommend anyone to get into it. I don't see why one couldn't get into it at one's own pace.

Perle Besserman: That's what Luzzatto did. That's what Abulafia did.

Lex Hixon: People who are listening now, a lot of you have had some experience of spiritual practice and probably, in that sense, have had a head start over Luzzatto, who had sort of dredged it out of his own mind and perhaps made a lot of mistakes. Just a few basic concepts of spiritual practice can guide one in—for instance, maintaining a balance of mind in the midst of intensifying experiences. So I feel there's a cultural and spiritual setting now, in which sincere people can begin Kabbalistic circles. This is what our manifesto is. I would call right now for people to begin circles.

Perle Besserman: There are such circles, but I would tell you this: It's a lot like groping in the dark by yourself in the United States. If you make one trip to Jerusalem, almost every 10 blocks you will find somebody there who may not be an enlightened being in a robe, but you will [also] find somebody there who is open and willing to teach you and really knows what he is teaching.

I met somebody there this summer I never dreamt I could ever find, just a 37-year-old man who's just a man, like you, Lex— in fact, he looks like you. He's one of the most brilliant teachers of Kabbalah I've ever met. The problem is that you are stymied by cultural things, like you can't teach women. I had to go there and use all sorts of tricks and ruses to learn the Kabbalah.

Lex Hixon: This is the kind of thing that, in our present cultural setting, can also be avoided. If people like Luzzatto and women like you begin by taking a lead, it simply will bypass a lot of the traditional things. One of the exciting things about Abulafia is the fact that he taught Christians and secular people and Muslims.

Perle Besserman: And women.

Lex Hixon: It gives us further inspiration, particularly this letter meditation, [which] is accessible to people of all walks of life. Let's get into a little bit of the detail of it.

Perle Besserman: Okay, but you should emphasize that there's a preparation before you sit down.

Lex Hixon: The key access here is through language, as far as I can see. This is what makes it available to people of all cultures, all walks of life, because we all have this kind of intimate connection with language, and precisely with the components that make up language, which are letters. And not in a metaphysical sense.

These letters are reflected in various historical languages, for instance, like Hebrew or Sanskrit. Some of them are surrounded by an aura of sacredness simply because great mystics have practiced in them. Great mystics have visualized Sanskrit syllables on various lotus petals in the subtle body. Various great Jewish mystics have practiced the permutation of the Hebrew letters. So, in a certain sense, there is a kind of special quality to some languages, but all languages per se should share the same essence, which is kind of tapping into the whole structure of the mind and consciousness. I know a Tibetan lama, for instance, who very much recommends the meditation on the letter "A" as a kind of primal thing.

Perle Besserman: Sound.

Lex Hixon: Not as a sound, as a visualization of the letter.

Perle Besserman: Oh, the English letter "A."

Lex Hixon: No, this is precisely the point. He says you can use Tibetan, but you can also use English. And this is when I began to realize the cosmopolitan nature of this kind of meditation. It doesn't have to be confined to a particular sacred language because it is language itself that—again, not in its mundane sense, but in its mystical sense. Now, can you explain what letters meant to Abulafia?

Perle Besserman: What you brought up is a point that the 19th-century Hasidic master Rabbi Nachman made, who did teach all kinds of unlettered people, even illiterate people. And, as you know, the Hasidim tried to take it out of the province of scholarship and make it mysticism for the masses. So that Rebbe Nachman would tell people, "Go out into the field and call out in your own language. Forget about Hebrew if you don't know Hebrew. If you're a small *shtetl* dweller in Poland, speak in Polish."

I know somebody who takes people out into the fields, outside of Jerusalem, into the wilderness, and I think Herb Weiner talks about this in his book, *Nine and a Half Mystics.* The experience is to go out and start talking in whatever language comes to you naturally. Weiner describes the experience happening to him in English. He's an American rabbi and there he was with a bunch of Israeli rabbis shouting in Hebrew. He was shouting in English. But he had the same experience. Ultimately, he got the same connection that they were getting in Hebrew.

I don't think it has to do with the sense of language. I know it doesn't. In fact, *tzeruf* means a disorientation of the senses. So when you talk about verbal use of language to communicate things in terms of sense, they want you to get to nonsense, or beyond sense.

Lex Hixon: So, to contrast the Kabbalistic approach with the Hasidic approach...

Perle Besserman: The Kabbalistic approach is part of the Hasidic approach.

Lex Hixon: But what the practitioner of tzeruf does is to go to the essence of all this yelling and enthusiasm, which are the letters themselves in their innate power, and visualize them with various prescribed methods, and, in a sense, get to the essence of the same experience, but without a great deal of outer emotionalism.

Perle Besserman: Without too much ecstasy intruding at the beginning.

Lex Hixon: And when the ecstasy comes, it's a kind of inner secret ecstasy. Therefore, when most of us think of Jewish mysticism as a living tradition, we think of the Lubavitcher tradition, which is Hasidic in nature. And because of this emphasis on outer, they tend to emphasize also outer observance of all sorts of technical things that have built up in Jewish tradition. As you pointed out, not all of Jewish tradition shares this.

Perle Besserman: That's right. Hasidic mysticism is maybe one-10th of Jewish mysticism. And it's a late one. And it's a European interpretation. You have to remember that Jewish mysticism is an Eastern discipline, as is always pointed out to me when I go to Israel. It's an oriental discipline. It's Semitic, it's closer in many ways to Sufism than it is to what the Hasidim have made it.

Lex Hixon: At the same time, we're tremendously grateful to the Lubavitchers for at least maintaining some of this stuff, which would otherwise have been lost or relegated to books, and people would have no way of approaching it. But what I'm suggesting is that many Jews—let's begin with Jews, forgetting non-Jews for a moment—who are not strictly observant, feel, "I can't go the Hasidic route because of Lubavitchers, so I guess I'll never make it with Jewish mysticism." But ... this inner letter meditation doesn't stress outer observances. You're not calling outwardly to the divine with your outer voice. There's a kind of inwardness to it, which you can do as Luzzatto did, in secret, without anyone knowing it, going about your ordinary life.

Perle Besserman: I haven't teased apart the problem from the practice. That is, the observance that you see and that we all see as rigid, hard orthodoxy that doesn't permit people to be spontaneously mystical.

Lex Hixon: I refuse to say "rigid and hard."

Perle Besserman: Well, I have to say "rigid and hard."

Lex Hixon: I have Orthodox friends who are listening. They're not going to like me to say that. Let's say "specialized," Perle.

Perle Besserman: One very important quality is women can't do it. If you are traditionally Orthodox and a woman, you just don't do this. So that, to me, is rigid and hard.

Lex Hixon: Yeah, that's bad.

Perle Besserman: The important thing for me was to see that this doesn't exist in every circle. I had to go to Jerusalem into the home and office of one of the most renowned rabbis in the world to find that I could sit down and practice. And the funny part of the story is I had to go to see him. I was told to go see him all dressed up as an Orthodox woman. And I dressed in this costume as a very Orthodox woman. And after two and a half hours with him, he said, "Well, you take off that ridiculous costume and the next time come back as you really are." And I sat and studied with him in jeans and a polo shirt. And he's very Orthodox.

These Orthodox practices—let me put it this way: They were originally preparations. "Why did you do these commandments? To put you in the same state of mindfulness that a Zen Buddhist monk would be put in when he stops before eating?" Every gesture was supposed to put you in a state of single-pointed concentration, what the Jews call *Kavanah*, very focused intention on every act of life in the most ordinary context of daily living, right? Those things were preparations to mystical practice. What happened is those things became ends in themselves. So Luzzatto did practice things like being kosher or keeping the Shabbat, but to maintain this concentrated awareness, not just for its own sake, and once he reached the depths of Shabbat, he could really start to practice these letter techniques.

Lex Hixon: I think we have to understand there are different kinds of orthodoxy—for instance, the rabbi in Jerusalem who's strictly Orthodox, but who taught you when you were wearing jeans, and that kind of thing. It didn't take away from his orthodoxy. There are different styles of orthodoxy, and I personally feel that. Speaking in this lifetime as a non-Jew, I asked Shlomo Carlebach, "Why am I apparently in a non-Jewish body in this life?" He said, "That's all right, you were on Sinai. Don't worry about it." But, speaking as a non-Jew, I think that non-Jews and non-observant Jews should know that true orthodoxy is long forgotten [along with] tremendous respect for the tradition.

Perle Besserman: No, if you went into a real typical American synagogue and started to talk about longing for God, you'd be made [to feel] very uncomfortable. I had a big argument with a rabbi in Jerusalem, a very brilliant young rabbi. I'm writing a new book and I'm putting all these incidents in the new book. He said something about dinner with wine, why you can't drink wine with a Christian, and I became really wild at that. It really bothered me. I asked him to explain it to me and he gave me all these legalistic little ins and outs. Finally, I said to him, "What does that have to do with God, with knowing God?" And he said to me, "You want to know God? Become a Hindu."

Lex Hixon: Very wise rabbi!

Perle Besserman: So, in many synagogues, you can't walk in and talk about God.

Lex Hixon: You go to rabbis for wise advice. Well, anyway, I think it's a long process. It's not going to happen overnight, but I feel very, very strongly that this will be open.

Perle Besserman: It has to be. It's been predicted by Kabbalists that the secular people are going to bring the Kabbalah back.

Roshi Philip Kapleau
1979

Born in New Haven, Connecticut, in 1912, Philip Kapleau briefly studied law, then learned court reporting. He went to Germany as chief court reporter of the first Nuremberg Trial in 1945; in 1946, he reported the Tokyo War Crimes Trial in Japan. There, he discovered Zen Buddhism and began attending lectures by D.T. Suzuki. Later, back in New York, Kapleau renewed his acquaintance with Suzuki, who was teaching Zen at Columbia University, but, rejecting Zen's primarily intellectual treatment, he returned to Japan in 1953 to seek its deeper truth. Back in Japan, Kapleau used his court reporting skills to record interviews with Zen teachers, teachings, and even *dokusan*, traditional intimate meetings between teachers and students, for *The Three Pillars Of Zen*, published in 1965, the same year he was sanctioned as a Zen teacher. One of the first books to reveal the details of Zen practice, it has remained in print ever since.

In 1966, he returned to the United States and established the Rochester Zen Center, where he founded his own lineage and taught for 20 years. Today, Roshi Kapleau's descendants are teaching around the world; his many books on Zen include *Awakening to Zen* and *Zen: Merging of East and West* (originally titled *Zen: Dawn in the West*). He died at the Rochester Zen Center from Parkinson's disease complications in 2004.

Lex Hixon: There is an unusual sense of silence as I sit down to talk with Roshi Philip Kapleau here in the Rochester Zen Center. Do you suppose we can make a radio interview like this?

Roshi Philip Kapleau: You know, it's said, Lex, that silence is more appropriate to Zen than speech. Now, where would that leave us?

Lex Hixon: Why should speech be any less appropriate than silence? We hear that when someone goes to an interview with a Roshi in the formal setting of the *dokusan* room, it is the voice of the Dharma that is speaking there. It's not simply the conditioned, limited voice of an individual person.

Roshi Philip Kapleau: Of course, that is quite true. The Dharma—the truth, if you like— speaks through the Roshi when he is no longer self-consciously trying to do anything. He doesn't even know that he's using his tongue. This is why it is said in Zen, "Speak without using your tongue." That's what I'm doing right now. I'm speaking without my tongue.

Lex Hixon: That's what I thought! But you're very natural and relaxed about it. I don't feel any different than I would talking to an uncle or an old friend.

Roshi Philip Kapleau: Well, that's a great compliment that you're paying me. So we should be able to have a very nice interview—a speechless, speechful interview.

Lex Hixon: Maybe, to give a little bit of background, could you characterize in a few words a brushstroke painting of your life and your development?

Roshi Philip Kapleau: You're asking me to do a very hard thing, Lex. Nothing comes to me right now about my background. So you'll have to remind me about some of these things.

Lex Hixon: That's true speechless speech.

Roshi Philip Kapleau: What I'm interested in really is this moment, not my past and not my future. All that matters at this moment is just that you're talking to me and I'm talking to you.

Lex Hixon: In a traditional setting, if I was approaching a Zen teacher, I would never ask about his background, which would be totally inappropriate, but our culture has different mores, and it seems you want to bring Zen into this kind of framework. Is that so?

Roshi Philip Kapleau: Yes, that's absolutely so. Having experienced a great deal of the awe and the sense of mystique that Westerners feel in the presence of Eastern teachers, and knowing that, in many cases, this is nothing but an attitude that the seeker or the student creates for himself, I've tried to disabuse Westerners of any sense of mystique or awe. We all have Buddha nature so there's no need for you to feel any sense of awe or for me to feel any sense of superiority. We are both equal.

Lex Hixon: Do you think there are cultural and personal limitations to an enlightened person?

Roshi Philip Kapleau: This is a very intriguing question. My own feeling is that everyone, enlightened or not is to one degree or another hostage to their own culture. This is one of the great handicaps that I think every foreign teacher has, who comes to North America to teach. It's extremely difficult for them to let go of the cultural forms that they grew up with that they've practiced since they were children.

We American teachers are more fortunate—since we are born into this culture, we are able to move in it very freely. If we've been privileged to have had training in the Eastern cultures, I think that we are the ones who are better able to adapt these teachings. Foreign teachers have done a tremendous thing here, of course, and we're all indebted to them. But after the foreign teachers have helped us all that they can, then the burden will have to be on the Western teachers to carry on in a way that will fit our culture. We'll have to carry on their superb teachings. This is about all we can do.

Lex Hixon: When you read Philip Kapleau's most recent book, *Zen: Merging of East and West,* you will find him clearly stressing the fact that Zen is a religious practice. Roshi, how do you respond to people who try to make Zen into a secular therapy or a mind-opening experience? Is Zen effective that way, or does it need to be rooted fundamentally in a religious dimension of life and culture?

Roshi Philip Kapleau: I usually say, if you want to use Zen in this way, you can do it. You can use it as a therapy of one kind or another. But this is comparable to taking a tiny bit of the cream off the top of the bottle of milk. There's a good deal more to a bottle of milk than just the cream on top.

But someone did ask me in Majorca just recently, "Is Zen a religion?" I said, "It all depends on how you define religion." The word "religion" comes from the Latin word *religare,* which means to bind—to bind one, of course, to God. Zen doesn't teach us to be bound to anything. The teaching is to experience our innate freedom.

If one thinks of religion as an organized body of beliefs, dogmas, creeds, and a belief in vicarious atonement, then, certainly, Zen, by Western religious standards, is not a religion. On the other hand, if you think of religion as something that teaches a person to answer the fundamental questions that every human being has asked, like, "What is the meaning of my life? Why was I born? Why must I die?" then Zen definitely is a religion. So, it's all in how one looks upon religion.

One of our members actually wrote in and said that she joined the Center in order to have Zen, not to have religion. She wanted to take the Zen without the Buddhism.

You can do that. But you would be just skimming the cream off the milk. I think you're cheating yourself, really, because these traditions and in all of these practices, come out of a 2,500-year-long experience of working with the human mind. And when these masters tell us that these practices are vital to the whole process of bringing us to awakening, then we would do well not to disregard them. And besides, when you do the practices, it's a wonderful feeling. So you can't lose, really.

Lex Hixon: Actually, if you try to do Zen without the Buddhism, I doubt if you'll even get any cream; because in your book, *Zen: Merging of East and West*, you mention that many people have come to you from various human potential movements and various therapies and various contemporary styles of trainings, that draw very heavily on Zen. They've asked you to test the assumed enlightenment that they have achieved through their way, and from your standpoint, as someone who is trained and authorized to test enlightenment, you honestly could say that none of them had even had a small taste of genuine enlightenment.

Roshi Philip Kapleau: You are absolutely right. But you'd be surprised how tenaciously people resist anything that smacks to them of religion.

Lex Hixon: How does a young man who started an atheist club in school, as you did, explain the fact that you're now so open to the religious dimension?

Roshi Philip Kapleau: There was a time when I was auditing courses at the Columbia Union Theological Seminary with Dr. Niebuhr and Dr. Tillich. I remember Dr. Tillich saying, "The atheist is far closer to God than the man going to church maybe once or twice a month, or maybe even every week." If a person can say, "I hate God," with great passion, that person is actually much closer to God, because he can only deny God in the name of God, thereby affirming God. But of course, in Buddhism, we don't have any God. Many people say to me, "Now, you've said a lot of things, but I want to ask you one thing very frankly, do you believe in God?"

If one postulates a God, then one needs to experience that God. There is a reality beyond the senses and the intellect, and yet not apart from them, that is real, and Buddhism teaches that one must experience this reality for oneself.

Even to call it reality is giving it a name. Getting caught in concepts, and not experiencing the thing itself is precisely what Zen Buddhism is striving to avoid. But if one truly understands the meaning of "God," well, then there's no need to talk about God—the concept disappears.

Lex Hixon: Can a Roshi become angry with his students?

Roshi Philip Kapleau: He becomes angry, but his anger is like snow that falls on a wet pavement. It evaporates very quickly. One does, however, feel anger at so much of the injustice, the evil, and the stupidity that one sees in the world. But, of course, one knows that events have their own pace. Shakespeare says, "There's a destiny that shapes our ends, rough hew them as we will." This destiny, in Buddhism, we would call karma.

So you get angry yet you don't get angry. You don't get angry for your own self. There's a difference in the kind of anger, but it's a mistaken notion to think that masters simply have impassive faces, that they never show any emotion because they've gone beyond it. That is absolutely not Zen.

Lex Hixon: Is it joyous to be a Zen teacher? Or can a Zen teacher become depressed?

Roshi Philip Kapleau: There's certainly a great joy in working with people. It's not a euphoric joy. Speaking for myself, before getting into Zen, it was as though I was on a seesaw. You know, you have your highs, your euphoric highs, and you have your depressed lows.

Gradually, as one develops, you get closer and closer to the center of this seesaw. And so while one feels strong emotions about things, one doesn't exclude them. There aren't these violent swings. So there is joy, but it's a contained joy, it's not a wild, euphoric kind of thing. And there are times when I feel sad, certainly. But it's never despair or anything that throws one into a depression.

Lex Hixon: What do you think about Roshi Kapleau?

Roshi Philip Kapleau: I think that my teaching falls far short. There's a lot more that I can do, not only in terms of teaching, in terms of my own life. I'm constantly trying to simplify my own life to try to follow the teachings of the Buddha, to help people help themselves. I know that in the process I'm really helping myself. Many times, after some kind of counseling, people will thank me very much, and I'll say, "Don't thank me. I'm grateful to you, because you're giving me an opportunity to exercise my compassion."

I'm sharing with others what I am trying to do for myself here. I don't consider that I am giving the people anything because, as you know, in Buddhism, in Zen at any rate, one cannot really teach anybody anything. Everybody already has everything that they need. All that they need to do is to disabuse themselves of their mistaken notions, their wrong attitudes, so that their inborn purity and wisdom and compassion can function freely.

At my teacher Harada Roshi's funeral service, there was a piece of calligraphy which he'd done five years or so earlier. It said: "For 40 years, I've been selling water by the bank of a river. Ha ha ha!" That's all every Zen teacher is doing, really.

Lex Hixon: It's been an honor to speak with you, Roshi. As the author of the marvelous Zen classic, *The Three Pillars of Zen,* which is going to be coming out in a new edition this January, from Doubleday, would you allow yourself to be named one of our national treasures?

Roshi Philip Kapleau: No. I think, though, it would certainly be a good idea for our country to have people as national treasures. But not me.

As you know, Japan has a custom where certain people who have accomplished a great deal are designated national treasures and are given a stipend and honored in certain ceremonies. Often they are artists or craftspeople who enhance the dignity, the stature of the nation as well as its people. It always struck me as a very fine thing to do.

Lex Hixon: Please accept very informally from those of us who are listening in New York City the title of "National Treasure." And the stipend will simply be our gratitude.

Roshi Philip Kapleau: That's okay. That's enough. Let me say that it was a pleasure for me to talk with you, Lex, in this interview. I hope that you will come again and see us here in Rochester. In any case, I'm sure we'll meet again.

Huston Smith
January 6, 1980

Huston Smith literally wrote the book on world religions, in 1958, with the release of *The Religions of Man*. Born in 1919 in China and raised there, he later became a professor of philosophy and religion, teaching at M.I.T., Syracuse University, and University of California at Berkeley. He is the author of 14 books, and the Christian Science Monitor once called him "Religion's Rock Star." The Dalai Lama once wrote that Smith, who became his friend in 1964, knew the "real taste" of religion; Ken Wilber, Deepak Chopra, and Karen Armstrong have cited him as a major influence on their work; Bill Moyers, who, in 1996, produced a five-part PBS series featuring Smith, said Smith had not only studied the world's religions but "practiced what he had learned;" and Michael Murphy, co-founder of the Esalen Institute, has commented that, "Of the many presenters we've had over the past 50 years, only a handful 'glowed in the dark,' and Huston Smith was one of them." —*Dana Sawyer*

Lex Hixon: I want to begin just by reading a little brief selection from *Forgotten Truth: The Primordial Tradition* by Huston Smith, who's with us this morning. But this book is such a tightly woven one that one thing really can't be taken apart from the rest of it, so this is just to give you a little flavor of the writing here, which is one of great philosophical precision, but at the same time with a beautiful poetic side and a sense of there being a sage speaking through these words, as well as a scholar. So this is from *Forgotten Truth: The Primordial Tradition*:

"*History shows grotesque aberrations, as well as achievements. We do not have to be reminded of tyrannies of alter and throne. The rigidities of imperial legalisms or the closedness of respectable morays and the secretarian spirit. It is only in cosmic outlook that we see the past as superior to our selves, and qualified to be our teacher. That there have been in this world, and are today in lingering pockets, metaphysical doctrines that are complete along with the means for their realization, this is a notion that for moderns is fairly conceivable. But it has emerged as the thesis of this book. In this day of neophilia and reflective embrace of the new, when what's new has become the standard salutation, in this time, when clergy themselves have grown trendy in the worship of their God, who is not yet, in this age of flourishing futurists, when almost the only way to get attention is to claim to be privy to some new discovery, it gives us the most exceptional pleasure, the most piquant delight to announce that what in today's climate opinion may be the most novel, original and unexpected prediction imaginable. The wave of the future will be a return to the past.*"

And then Professor Smith quotes T.S. Eliot: "*There is only the fight to recover what has been lost and found and lost again and again.*" And the Svetasvatara Upanishad: "*I sing the songs of olden times with adoration. The needed return, a kind of homecoming is in outlook only. It is in worldview and sense of reality, and even here, phrases such as going back are imprecise. For the issue does not really concern time at all, it concerns truth. Truth of the kind that is timeless. If we have appealed to past ages, it is because we see them as having been bathed in such truth to a degree that we are not. In this respect, we would indeed be pleased to see life on earth recover a lost dimension, and are grateful for persons who are working to reknit the rich coherence of a fully human consciousness, which the cramped and aggressive rationality of modernity has bruised so badly.*"

Huston, how would you characterize modernity? What are the key presuppositions it holds? What are the important doctrines on which it depends?

270

Huston Smith: I think there has been, in our times, a noticeable loss of the dimension of transcendence. Another way to put that is an enlargement in our view of the material aspect of existence, not that that in any way is unimportant, but it has come to fill our field of vision. It's a disproportionate enlargement of the material side of life and, along with that, a greater thrust towards control. Those aspects of being that we can bring under control must somehow or other be confronted.

Lex Hixon: In your book you unerringly go to the worldview of science itself as—

Huston Smith: Can I correct that? Scientism.

Lex Hixon: Yes.

Huston Smith: I have nothing against science, but I have everything against scientism.

Lex Hixon: Which you explain in detail as a kind of misreading of science.

Huston Smith: Right.

Lex Hixon: But it's a subtle point, and many scientists would probably not see that clear distinction that you make. I mean, I think that many scientists do [make that distinction] almost unconsciously, accept the scientific criteria for what is real as being their leading criteria. And so, that would make them, in your definition, involved in scientism.

Huston Smith: Yes, but I'm uncomfortable about loading this on them. Again, this is a dualism, and I think it's just not right to paint scientists as white-coated bad guys. This is something that's characterized our own time. It's a part of the winds of doctrine that blow around us in the modern world, and the non-scientists, in some respects, are more vulnerable to these winds than the scientists because they're not close enough to it to see what many of the scientists are able to see, meaning they see through such pretentious claims.

Lex Hixon: The scientific worldview is something that has permeated all of our culture, and we find it in business.

Huston Smith: Sure.

Lex Hixon: Therefore, I agree with you, we can't single out the scientists personally.

Huston Smith: Right.

Lex Hixon: But the point remains that something of the fascination of the power of explanation of modern science, which comes from its focusing down into a very narrow focus, has captivated our age.

Huston Smith: Right.

Lex Hixon: And in your book, the very fact that you obviously have studied science, and the history and philosophy of science, and that you have a feeling for science, makes your criticism of *scientism* believable and acceptable. I don't find any animus in your book against science per se.

Huston Smith: I taught at MIT for 15 years and I never had any problem with the scientists there. In fact, I don't think it's too much to say that I love them. I would go to all the lectures, which they would give for the general public, and I valued being in their presence. It was the social scientists and my fellow humanists that I had a lot more problem with, because they seemed to be importing *scientistic* ways—that is, methods that are quite applicable in dealing with the material world—to treat human beings and the human spirit, and that's where the problem lies.

Lex Hixon: Judging from *The Forgotten Truth*, when you talk about science, you do so with a kind of sureness and familiarity that I can see that 15 years at MIT must have [given] you. There are a lot of people today who have some vague idea that science and spirituality should become unified or friendly to each other, but they don't seem to have a very deep understanding of science. I think that somehow you really have that understanding, but that enables you to criticize even more deeply, because there's still a kind of fascination; for instance, someone who takes Einstein's theories, let's say—

Huston Smith: Right.

Lex Hixon: And gets all excited about that, and says, "This has a great relation to spiritual life." But I don't see that it does. I think Einstein was a brilliant man who was talking about the surface of reality—or, you would say, the first plane of reality— in his scientific work, and that doesn't really penetrate at all into anything like a spiritual dimension. Although, as a human being, obviously, he lived in a very higher place.

Huston Smith: Right, and played the violin, and of course is widely quoted for his own testament to the mystical sense about the universe. But if you believe it then, why, it's only a warm fog, you might say. I do think we need some clarity in what the relation between science and the human spirit really is.

Lex Hixon: In your book, you turn to what you call the primordial tradition, not confining it just within the traditions of Christianity and Islam and Hinduism—although those traditions are part of the primordial tradition, as you see it. In other words, you say that it's the primordial tradition that we have to turn to for really deep understanding. And that science, no matter if it's superspace or antimatter, or any of these new scientific discoveries which are definitely breaking through some sort of limited veil, still doesn't seem to have anywhere near the power or the wisdom to guide us as this primordial tradition does.

Huston Smith: Powerless. They are symbols really. Seeing a symbol, I find contemporary developments in science the most powerful of anything around. But only as symbol. Now, what a symbol can do is to direct the mind by way of an analogy to a realm of existence that is higher than itself. If we use an image, it's a little bit as if we were walking on the floor of a quarry, and there may come a moment when one's eyes are just so aligned with a piece of quartz that it will pick up the rays of the sun and turn that piece of quartz on fire for a moment. However, with a next step, it becomes simply slag. That's what a symbol is: It can redirect our vision to something higher. So what science is coming up with is to repeat a powerful reflection of other domains of reality, but by itself it can in no way prove the existence of those other realms.

Lex Hixon: In your book, you say, "The goal, it cannot be stressed too often, is not religious experience, it is the religious life."

Huston Smith: Yeah.

Lex Hixon: So even if science or something else is able to catch on fire for a moment and spark some sort of deeper experience or insight, what we need is a way of living that nurtures this, and it seems to me that science doesn't provide that. Many scientists say things like, "Well, the laboratory, that's our chapel; and this is our communion, studying the molecular motions; and our chalice is the electron accelerator," and things like that. But I really doubt whether those things can really replace an actual cathedral, actual chalices, actual meditative practices, and actual religious symbols that come from this rich primordial tradition.

Huston Smith: There's the question that's raised often: Can science save us? When I've come upon that question, I've been tempted to answer, "Possibly it might save the scientists, but it won't save the rest of us." Meaning that they may have a kind of devotion to truth, science at its best, which can be purifying; and in [some] ways they're like monks, you know. Their laboratories are like their monasteries. Their dedication and willingness to sit down like a child before the fact—those are very human and spiritual qualities, but the fruits that come out of those laboratories cannot save the rest of us because it's in the dedication itself that their purifying effects are felt by the scientists. One cannot confer spiritual benefits in this way. Each person has to work them out himself.

Lex Hixon: You characterize the scientific way as the tendency of science to explain the *more* in terms of the *less*.

Huston Smith: Right.

Lex Hixon: That's not scientism, that's actually science. That's scientific method, for instance, in the realm of biology, to try and explain the appearance of intelligence from something that wasn't intelligent initially.

Huston Smith: Right.

Lex Hixon: Because if you claim that there was some intelligence in the first place, then, as you say in your book, you're begging the question. You're involved in circularity; you're not doing a scientific explanation.

Huston Smith: Yes. So that endeavor should explain the more in terms of the less, and I think we ought to push it as far as we can, and it's the business of science to do that. But [we should] not think that the best that can come up through that route is the best that we have by way of explanation.

Lex Hixon: I agree with you. I don't really have an animus against science, I don't think, or scientists. But I am a little concerned by the tendency—not only by scientists, but by our whole culture—to explain the more in terms of the less.

Huston Smith: Right.

Lex Hixon: For instance, Darwinian theory, the idea of natural selection—that the intelligence and brilliance and sensitivity of human beings came out of a chance process of natural selection—you point out in your book that even the scientists themselves are beginning to question this. It just leaves too much unexplained.

Huston Smith: Right.

Lex Hixon: And the biologists have to ignore too many divergent findings in order just to hold onto the general theory of natural selection.

Huston Smith: Right.

Lex Hixon: In your book, you make a very beautiful analysis, where you suggest that the evolution of species is something metaphysical, that it is not going from the less to the more, but that more was already there, that the nature of reality is intelligence, and that, as the planet began forming and cooling and environments were made possible for biological expression, that this intelligence, which is the nature of reality, began to spontaneously express as biological forms.

Huston Smith: Right.

Lex Hixon: But how many scientists do you think would feel comfortable with this point of view?

Huston Smith: Very few, because these cards, you might say, are not in their deck. We can put it quite simply by saying that Darwinian theory is not a very good theory in terms of how much of the data it is able to explain, but the point is, it's the only theory that is available to them, because if they try to account for the progression in terms of some intelligence already present within the nature of things, that is, as you say, to beg the question. So they methodologically are locked into this mode of explanation, and I think that's what we need to see.

Lex Hixon: And there's this amazing little point in your book where you go to a colleague who's involved in logic and symbolic logic and you ask your colleague, "Is there any way of clearly expressing this fallacy of begging the question?" And he sort of begs the question a little bit by saying, "Read this article, that article." And finally you say, "Listen, I don't have time to read these articles, I came to you directly. What if a student were to directly ask you, 'How do you express this fallacy of begging the question?'" And how did he reply?

Huston Smith: "I would say that no clear definition of begging the question exists."

Lex Hixon: Yes. It's fascinating that science is locked into explaining the more in terms of the less because [scientists] don't want to beg the question, but when you go back to the logical fallacy of begging the question, you find that there's no clear understanding of that in the first place. They're locked into something that is itself nothing solid.

Huston Smith: Right.

Lex Hixon: I want to read just a paragraph from *Revision Journal*, where scientists and spiritual practitioners can get together. This is a review of *Forgotten Truth* by the editor, Ken Wilbur:

"Forgotten Truth *is the single best introduction to religion ever written. It is the single best elucidation of esotericism available. It is the single best commentary on the transcendent university of religions. And it is the single best explanation of the perennial philosophy yet to appear.*"

This is pretty strong praise, but I have to say I would agree with that.

But I want to have people have a chance to meet Huston Smith more directly, and let him talk a little bit about his life and his development, because this is not an intellectual matter, this is not a matter of sheer scholarship or objectivity, it involves the whole life of a person.

Huston, could you tell a little bit about your life, your development, how you got involved in the study of religions, and some of the people that were important for you?

Huston Smith: Insofar as [lives] have beginnings, mine began in China. My parents were Methodist missionaries. When Edwin Reischauer was appointed ambassador to Japan, there was a press conference, and he was asked what was his connection with Japan. He answered in one word: umbilical. He, too, was born over there to missionary parents. My mother—though her parents were American, they were missionaries before her—was born in China, so the roots go back in that country.

I mention that because one never knows precisely what happens in this respect, but to have been born and raised, not necessarily specifically in China, but to generalize that, in a traditional culture, I think has its effect. One senses that there can be a different, what should we say, weather systems for the human spirit, I guess, and gives a certain perspective on one's own. My parents being missionaries, it was a devout home, Christian and positive. One of the advantages, perhaps, of such a life was that we went off to boarding school at age 12, so I missed all that period of adolescent rebellion. That just passed me by. I have the fondest and most positive feelings about my parents, and particularly their rootedness in their own tradition and dedication to the life that they lived.

That had its effect. Then, coming to this country, moving into religious studies, which was a natural outgrowth of my background, and then into philosophy, heading for a vocation—at first I thought the ministry, but then ideas jumped to the fore. I think in the Indian tradition that you are so well-versed in, Lex, I discovered I was the Jnani Yogi, that ideas, or to say, visions, really—one almost has to get visual element in it—visions of reality just really obsessed me, took me over, and I wanted to know the meaning of it all. That led to graduate school at the University of Chicago. The next moment that stands out in my memory was one night when I was in Berkeley for a year, working on writing my doctoral dissertation, and I was working on value theory and came upon the problem of pain.

I went to Wheeler Library and looked in the card catalog under "pain," and checked out four or five titles, and went back to my rooming house, and after dinner I sat down at my desk with these books before me. One of them had a title that looked more interesting than the others: *Pain, Sex and Time* by a man called Gerald Heard. I'd never heard of him, so I started with that one. By page two, I knew absolutely clearly that it had nothing whatsoever to do with my doctoral dissertation, and I kept on reading. I would say that was the most important single reading experience of my life. It's the only time that I've read the whole night through. When dawn was breaking and I finally put that book down, I had made two vows: One, I would not read another line that man had written until I had my degree in hand. I obviously was afraid that I might not go on. The other was that when I did have my degree, I would read everything he wrote, which I proceeded to do.

What happened that night was I found out something else about me: Namely, I'm a mystic, I must say immediately by temperament, not by attainment, because my actual mystical attainments are very low level indeed. But I nevertheless say that I am a mystic because as of that night, I have invariably resonated to what the mystics said—in the sense, it's something within me [that] rises to a firm yes. That is true.

That discovery led me to Aldous Huxley, who was a close friend of Gerald Heard. When I went to St. Louis, one of the two, Heard or Huxley, said, "Oh, you're going to St. Louis, there's a very good Swami there." *Swami*? I'm not sure I even knew what the word meant. But they were referring to a member of the Ramakrishna Order, and so, due to my esteem for those men, when I got to St. Louis, I looked him up in the telephone book and found his name. That was when Asian thought really broke over my consciousness, because even though I'd come from Asia, it was through a Christian background. The richness of the Indian perspective—for a decade, it just enveloped my life. It was like new vistas of reality opening at every turn, and I found it absolutely absorbing. Incidentally, it didn't feel like I was leaving my Christianity, because the truths just came through as being so much alike, and the differences as though they were simply differences of dialect.

Then, after 11 years, I went to MIT. I left St. Louis, and Zen Buddhism at that time was coming on the horizon. And I had the good fortune to have a Fulbright scholar who was himself a Zen Buddhist in Japan come to my university and teach a course with me. And through that, I became fascinated with the spirituality of East Asia, again, where my roots were. The rice and the tea and the chopsticks just all felt very much like home. That led to going to Japan, and my 40s were, in effect, my Zen Buddhist years, you might say. Daisetz Suzuki was very important in that whole period as well as Goto Zuigan Roshi.

One never knows what life is going to bring. I wouldn't have anticipated any of these stages. But in 1969/1970, I guess it was, while taking a student group around the world, we stopped in Iran—it was a very different Iran from today. Doors began to fly open and I was admitted into the inner sanctums, one might say, of Sufism, the mystical dimension of Islam. Now, that was very important because, up until then, even though I had already written *The Religions of Man,* the chapter on Islam was really hard for me to write. The others were not. The Quran had just been impenetrable. But by virtue of being introduced to the mystical dimension of that religion through the Sufis—the mystics, as the saying goes, all speak the same language—the skies opened over the Arab world. It's been an extraordinary odyssey. In one way, I feel a little sheepish about all these stages and transitions. It sounds a little bit like linear monogamy, one might say. And I don't at all recommend this kind of cafeteria-like approach, which it may sound like. But we all have our own destinies, and this has been mine.

Lex Hixon: I can't call it a cafeteria-like approach. It sounds like you've had some very good meals in different restaurants.

Huston Smith: That is absolutely true. The great, good fortune is these teachers, as you yourself know. That's what makes a difference. Not when you come upon the ideas, but when you come upon these ideas incarnate in lives, persons actually living them out. That's where the power is manifest.

Lex Hixon: In *The Forgotten Truth*, you mention the idea of progress as something which has obsessed the modern era, something to do with the whole scientific worldview. You suggest that there is no progress, that the primordial tradition doesn't hold out that sense of progress, but more a sense of the individual being able to fulfill more and more of the unbelievably rich human possibilities. They're so rich in the primordial tradition that one doesn't have to develop some idea of progress in order to seek satisfaction, because one can see so much tremendous possibility right here and now in the human being.

Huston Smith: I remember Baker Roshi, at San Francisco Zen Center, quoting his own teacher, that wonderful man Shunryu Suzuki, saying, "Everything you need you already have right now."

Lex Hixon: If we could only hear that.

Huston Smith: That's right.

Lex Hixon: That's pretty substantial training. I wouldn't call it cafeteria-style at all.

Huston Smith: Well, all right.

Lex Hixon: And then the 15 years that you spent at MIT and, you mentioned earlier, that you developed a real student's attitude—you went to a lot of the talks given by the advanced scientists. In a certain sense, you really spent more than a decade as a student of Western science. And with the best scientists. I think we have to count that in your spiritual development.

Huston Smith: Very important, yes.

Lex Hixon: That's why I think you can write a book like *The Forgotten Truth*, which does try to revise our whole idea of the priority of science, but you can do it authentically. I think that your voice is the best possible voice for the scientists themselves and for the people who sort of accept science as the first priority of the human being. Your voice might get through and make some sort of clarification.

Huston Smith: I don't know about that. I'm not, of course, a scientist, but I am a lover of science. Science itself—what it says and what it's finding out about this incredible, extraordinary nature of reality, even if we limit ourselves to the physical level of it—is just mind-boggling in the most exciting way that I can imagine. I remember Fred Hoyle himself saying as early as 1950 that no story that any fiction writer could have dreamed would have been a hundredth as fantastic or incredible as the plain truth. They're not plain, but the truths that science has discovered.

Lex Hixon: You really are talking like an initiate—this kind of enthusiasm means that you have sort of had an initiation into science.

Huston Smith: A company of the sciences.

Lex Hixon: I feel that you've had that company, and you've really absorbed something there. I agree with you: We have to have this principle of non-duality pervading our whole approach. We can't somehow cut out science, or leave science on the outside. But to a certain extent, I think that we have to, and I think this is the point you make in your book: that this primordial tradition has to be seen as lying at the basis of everything we do, including science. Whereas, right now, in the modern West, and modernity itself, there is an unconscious sense that the scientific enterprise is what is really lying at the basis of our culture.

Huston Smith: Then science becomes scientism, which is a kind of nothing-but *ism*, and that's the deadly thing. If we can avoid that, why, science as far as what it positively says, is all to the good.

Lex Hixon: You specifically say you're not oriented to the future, that you have everything now that you need. But is your life tending in any particular direction now as far as spiritual practice or adventure in consciousness?

Huston Smith: Well, one keeps a practice going. I think that's vital. But as at every previous stage, I never anticipated any turn in the road, and in one sense, there haven't been turns, it's just been a new lap. No, I don't foresee it. What seems clear is continuing effort to deepen the actual realization of the truths that the great traditions unite in proclaiming. That's the work that lies at hand.

Lex Hixon: In the epilogue to your book, there's a brief chapter on what you call the psychedelic evidence. Did you have any direct involvement with psychedelic experimentation?

Huston Smith: Rather major, I guess, in the sense that I've already mentioned Aldous Huxley, who made no pretense to be a guru at all, and yet I was at an impressionable age where I very much respected and looked up to him. It was through his book that the doors of perception [opened] wherein, as you recall, he came close to equating the psychedelic experience with mysticism. We have to remember that was in a very different day and a very different climate of opinion, but my interest was aroused there.
I had a part in bringing Huxley to MIT for a semester and he came to MIT at just the time that Leary came to Harvard, having ingested his, what, seven mushrooms on the side of a swimming pool in Cuernavaca. Of course, Leary looked up Huxley, and Huxley introduced me to Leary. So for two and a half or three years before that whole scene went bad, I was a part of the experimentations at Harvard with psychedelic substances. I was sort of in on the ground floor of that.

Lex Hixon: That's important because it means that whether or not psychedelics are ultimately seen as very important spiritually, they certainly were important culturally at a certain point in our society. I'm happy to know that you can also speak out of direct experience with that movement. I think of you as a young elder of our spiritual culture. I think many people listening now would be happy to know that you at least had that experience, too, and that you're able to report on a whole spectrum of different possibilities. But in the appendix to your book, when you talk about that, I felt a strange sense that you were falling prey to the very scientism that your book so eloquently speaks against.

Huston Smith: I'm glad to talk about that and really tease you out on that perception. There are a number of persons, as you might suspect, among them some spiritual guides that I immensely respect, who like the book but feel that it degrades it to have that appendix referring to psychedelics in it.

Lex Hixon: I wouldn't agree that just the reference to psychedelics degrades anything, but in that appendix, a lot of it is devoted to discussing Stanislav Grof's work and it just doesn't seem as well digested as the rest of the book.

Huston Smith: All right, let me try to say why I did that. A small point, just to lead into it: I did insist—you may not have noticed this—that it be put not only in an appendix, but in even smaller type, that's 10-point type rather than 12-point type, to indicate that this is less, on a different basis from the rest.

It's only Stanislav Grof's work that would have led me to mention the psychedelics. Because we must note now that he is reporting over 3,000 hours spent with subjects who are taking psychedelics in the course of therapeutic counseling and treatment. The interesting part [of that report] is it shows a progression to different kinds of experience, which look to me to be isometric—or isomorphic—with the levels of consciousness that the great traditions affirm. So it seems like a kind of psychological excavation of going deeper and deeper and deeper into the depths of a person until at the end, one touches base with this *shunyata* or Godhead or whatever you want to call it.

Lex Hixon: But scientists have developed the idea that by doing experiments, you disturb what you're experimenting on, so therefore, [with] the results of your experiment, you're not just getting a picture of what's there, but [you're also getting] a picture of your own instrumentation, your own way of penetrating.

I feel that with LSD that it's using a foreign, sort of disturbing instrument to bore in there. You could say that maybe the original *sauma* [drink] in the Vedas had psychotropic effects, but the point is that those substances which are sometimes ingested in various parts of the primordial tradition are totally infused or, you might say, alchemically changed by the fact that they're given in the primordial tradition.

Huston Smith: Absolutely.

Lex Hixon: Whereas with LSD, the 2,500 cases that Stanislav Grof is involved with were given [the drug] in some sort of clinical atmosphere, which was almost entirely bereft of the primordial tradition.

Huston Smith: Then what do you make of the fact that even in such sterile surroundings, nevertheless the perception surfaced?

Lex Hixon: I agree with you that the primordial tradition is true, that this is the nature and structure of the self. But, for instance, if you put someone in prison in Siberia with nothing but rats in their cell, and they're cold and they go through tremendous suffering, spiritual perceptions will also surface. But that doesn't mean this is a helpful way of looking into it. I would say that the primordial traditions themselves provide the way of exploring these things, and that exploring through LSD in a clinical atmosphere is a case of scientism. ... Do you feel I'm being too harsh?

Huston Smith: I think it might be useful to back up just a step or two. I'd like to give a little fuller statement on my own perception of the psychedelic. I had a total of, I don't know, eight or 10 experiences, I suppose, all of them 15 or so years ago, of which I would say three were important. But now I come to a puzzling thing. The utility of those experiences for me began by being great and went into a very sharp decline. So it was the first three in decreasing order of importance, after which they ceased to be important altogether to the extent that I cannot conceive any circumstances in which I'll ever take those substances again. Nor would I recommend that anybody else take them. And yet, when I'm to be true to my own experience, I have to say that those three experiences, to this day, I continue to credit metaphysical insight to. After all, William James is on my side in that, all right? So I don't think it's an issue of recommending whether persons take these, but in the case of Groff, I don't know that we'll ever again see a psychiatrist who will spend 3,000 hours with patients in the, you might say, secular [world]. He started in the Eastern Europe and Communist cultures, with their very Pavlovian views of human beings. If, even in that kind of setting, one comes to experience of this kind, it looks to me that it's part of the data, which is not totally devoid of metaphysical import.

Huston Smith with his biographer, Dana Sawyer

Stephen Gaskin
April 6, 1980

As a Korean War veteran-turned-Beatnik, Stephen Gaskin, born in 1935, attended San Francisco State College on a GI Bill scholarship, earning a Master's degree in 1964. He became an English professor, and, in 1967, started an informal philosophy seminar known as Monday Night Class, which drew a big following. Concerned that San Francisco was slipping into drug-induced decadence, he and 300 followers caravanned to Tennessee to found The Farm collective on 1,000 acres. In the 1970s, approximately 1,500 people lived there, keeping no liquor, guns, or chemical drugs; eating only vegetarian food; practicing meditation; and working for the collective. In 1976, he married Ina May Middleton, who [as Ina May Gaskin] wrote *Spiritual Midwifery* (1978) and, with her students, delivered 2,300 babies at The Farm. They had three children, and Gaskin had two children from other marriages. In 1980, Gaskin received a Right Livelihood Award from Sweden for founding the charity Plenty International, which rebuilt homes after earthquakes and ran an ambulance in the South Bronx. The Farm survived disease, hunger, serious debts, and Gaskin's yearlong incarceration for growing marijuana; today, with 175 members who pay rent and have jobs outside, The Farm runs a press and produces radiation detectors used by law enforcement. Gaskin once quipped, "We're high-tech hippies now!" Gaskin died at home in Summertown, Tennessee, on July 1, 2014, at age 79.

Lex Hixon: Stephen Gaskin is a hard person to introduce, but I want to try. I know personally that Stephen is an instrument for something very powerful and very beautiful. Now, if you look at his community, The Farm, on the surface, depending on your particular prejudices, you may think it's great or it's weird. But it was generated way back in almost another generation, you might say, when a whole bunch of folks just got in buses and left the West Coast and meandered through the country and finally ended up on a piece of good, fertile land in Tennessee. They settled down there and really started growing things. One of the main things they've been growing there are human beings.

There are so many things The Farm offers, I couldn't possibly touch all of them, but this one is very close to my heart. Any woman in this country, or in the world, who is pregnant and is considering abortion, can come to The Farm in Summertown, Tennessee, and have the child there. They will train her in natural childbirth and accept the baby into their family and raise it there. If the mother ever wants to take the baby, she'll have no trouble.

Stephen Gaskin: Within limits of the midwives' ability to do all that.

Lex Hixon: I'm unhappy that Ina May Gaskin, Stephen's wife, was not able to be here too, because I've interviewed them together before, and it's important to realize that one of the things The Farm is doing is reconstituting our whole culture's idea of the feminine energy in many, many ways. Ina May has written a book called *Spiritual Midwifery* that is a very important contribution to that ancient art, and comes out of her long experience delivering babies on The Farm. They have delivered 380 babies in natural childbirth with better statistics than hospitals have as far as problems [go].

Stephen Gaskin: Ina May's over helping deliver a Muslim baby right now. That's why she's not here. Yesterday, Ina May talked to the Muslim ladies at the mosque over in the Bronx. They're in kind of a good place, being midwives, because that gives them an excuse to tell the men, "We're doing our thing," and they say, "Okay, you get to do it." So she's working out with the ladies.

Lex Hixon: If anyone missed the Sixties or the Seventies, don't worry about it. The Farm is right in the center of the Eighties. It's actually the essence of the Eighties. The Farm has a hospital ship, and an organization called "Plenty," which is doing a tremendous amount of service, recycling funds where they're needed. There's nothing that's going to make The Farm stagnant. They have a project in the South Bronx, where Stephen is staying while he's here in New York. They even have a band called the Nuclear Regulatory Commission.

How did the whole drama begin, Stephen? You were just talking to some people out in San Francisco regularly, on Monday nights, right?

Stephen Gaskin: That was the night that the experimental college had a room open that I could borrow. I got to meet there for a couple of years, and got to get rolling before I had to leave that nice shelter, but it got to where you couldn't get to the middle of the campus anymore because they had so many cops in white helmets and long riot sticks all over the campus. We pretty much had to flee.

It was a good time, you know, but it's way back there. Right now, it just seems there's so much happening in the world out frontwards. That's why I wanted to talk about the Eighties. Folks try to hook me to the Sixties in a way, but if anything, I'm a child of the Forties, not even the Sixties. I was over 30 before they said you shouldn't trust anybody over 30.

Lex Hixon: Talk about the Eighties! That's what I want to talk about too. You say we're a long, long way from there, but where are we now?

Stephen Gaskin: The Farm has changed in a lot of ways. When we first left San Francisco, we were trying to distinguish ourselves from Charlie Manson, for instance, or anything in the group mind about hippies and longhairs. When we got to Tennessee, they called us hippies, and we couldn't afford to be called hippies right then. It would have been too hard on us. We said, "No, we ain't hippies, we're beatniks!" Then after we got done living there for a while, getting to be friends with those folks and defining ourselves, then we said we were hippies all along.

Defining ourselves made a different thing, because now we know who we are and what we're doing. Now it really seems like a time to reach out and get in touch with a lot of people and take charge of the business of running the world, you know, as the grownups of this generation.

These are the kinds of things The Farm is trying to do. The Farm is still designed in such a way that it's necessary for us to earn our own money and pay our own bills and make our own way. We've put together a lot of systems: a primary health care system, nutritional system, farming system, construction, electronics, book publishing company, and, among the other systems, just as one of the things we've been building all these 10 years is how to govern ourselves.

So we've consolidated ourselves in a lot of ways to be able to stay there, and we've taken on other projects and we've taken on the nukes—that's great fun. The band is the main intervener against the Sequoia reactor down in Chattanooga. A lot of what we're about now is meeting other tribes. We have pretty close relationships with some other tribes. For instance, we've been the radio operators on the Greenpeace boat for their last several campaigns. We've been arrested with them in Iceland and Newfoundland and England and Spain.

Lex Hixon: I want to re-identify what we're doing here over at WBAI in New York City. I've been doing this kind of program for 10 years over the station, trying to open up a space of truth, and growing more and more in it. I've been realizing that nothing about our concerns for justice and harmony and inner illumination should be excluded from the spiritual life, and that the spiritual life is not just for a few special mystics, or people who were called to sit quietly and repeat mantras, but every human being is called.

In a sense, this radio station is very much a community like The Farm. It's a community of people who, unfortunately, can't see each other, but there's a real closeness here. And we work on getting the money thing together too, everyone does. It's a matter of responsibility.

Now I want Stephen to talk about his spiritual teaching, because it's all very well to have this kind of commitment against nukes and all these other things, but if the whole thing isn't put on a very solid, practical, spiritual basis, where people are living lives of truth and love, then it just won't work. The Farm would have disappeared back in the Sixties, or it would have petered out in the Seventies. It certainly wouldn't still be here in the Eighties gaining power and wisdom. And Stephen has helped give it that spiritual basis. It's rooted in truth, and that's why it survives. How else could a bunch of pot-smoking hippies survive in the middle of the South? It's a miracle in itself.

Stephen Gaskin: I pick up a spiritual book a couple of times a year and crack it open and look in and check out the old Sanskrit or the old Japanese. And I think the teaching that we really came around to was that there are so many folks talking that it's just more fun *to do*. By just doing, you can get past all the stuff and get around to doing something and being able to be friends with people who are different than you are.

And we can't say that we are spiritual or in any way trying to follow a spiritual path if we're not reaching out as far as we can. We can't just make a small circle and say, "These are our people." We have to really try to include everybody. I feel well educated and, with a lot of benefits that came down to me through being a member of Western civilization, and when I see the route that my country takes and the actions that my country takes against other people in the world, I am ashamed. I am a patriot. I am ashamed to see my country stoop and do wrong things. Some people say I'm more political than I used to be, but I don't think anything about the whales and the nukes and the Indians is political. That's just stuff that's about right and wrong, and where we should be doing right. It's not political to recognize right and wrong.

I got into talking about creation and stuff the last few weeks on The Farm because they're going to make the schools start teaching special creation. I get cynical when I hear that stuff. They even have schools where people don't learn real biology, which means you can have a lot of people working in the nuke plants who don't know the danger they're in. You know, the thing that seems spiritual to me is just stuff like trying to get a little intellectual honesty back into our culture. I think too many people fall for simplistic solutions because the real solutions are so hard to think about. The real solutions are things like buckling down and getting it together day after day, decade after decade until you're old, and doing a good enough job on your children that they'll carry it on down the line. It's a longtime project.

Lex Hixon: Stephen Gaskin, for those of you who don't know anything about him, it would be basic to say that he's a spiritual leader of a community of about 800 people or so in Tennessee called The Farm. Stephen's Farm is sort of becoming an ordinary household American word. That's very much [due to] their approach to spiritual life. It should be kind of a household thing.

Stephen Gaskin: We consider ourselves householder *yogis*.

Lex Hixon: Stephen will be giving a Monday night class here, so come and hear this homegrown spiritual teacher. I don't know if you characterize yourself that way.

Stephen Gaskin: That's about the way I do it myself. The press in Tennessee always asks if I'm a teacher or a leader. I like to say, "If you lose your leader, you're lost. If you lose your teacher, you might learn something and be able to cook on." So "teacher" seems the right choice.

Lex Hixon: When we talk I always feel an immediate connection with Stephen because of our shared feelings toward Suzuki Roshi, the founder of the San Francisco Zen Center. Stephen has a very strong connection with him. I consider him to be an unconventional

Dharma successor on some level. Suzuki Roshi lived and radiated out in San Francisco for many years, and his book, *Zen Mind, Beginner's Mind,* has been so powerful for all of us.

Stephen Gaskin: I was in San Francisco and just coming in to spirit and all the wild happenings on Haight Street, and looking for teachers, and there were people in San Francisco who saw a different teacher every night, seven nights a week. It was really a hot scene at that time. I wandered around through that, and I suppose that a lot of people have looked back on the Sixties and become aware that one of the things that we had was such incredible third eyes that we could just look for fly specks at 100 miles, really, you know?

I was looking around at people then too, but when I walked up on Suzuki he was just all beautiful, out as far as I could see, humorous, intelligent, and kind and wise. There's another side of him, which I always like to bring up. That's the real old-fashioned tough Zen master, like in the stories, you know? He would say, "Life is like stepping onto a boat which is going to sail out to sea and sink." He was uncompromising at that level.

I do feel that there was something that passed between us. Even though I wasn't Japanese, Zen was the cleanest thing I ever hit; you know, Buddhist psychology and Zen is just like ice water in purity. There were some things I got from that, which changed my whole life. A piece of me is always Buddhist. There were people who were Suzuki Roshi's students, who ranged from the most hippie-beatnik-dope yogis to the most austere shaved-head, black-robed monks, who did it right down the line and chanted the Heart Sutra in Japanese, you know, from that whole spectrum.

Lex Hixon: I'm looking at your face right now, Stephen, and on the right-hand side I can see that far-out dope yogi, and on the other side, I see this shaven-headed, black-robed monk. Tell us what you said about what you can do with Suzuki Roshi's picture.

Stephen Gaskin: Oh, the picture of Suzuki on *Zen Mind, Beginner's Mind,* if you cover one side, and just look at one side of his face, on one side you'll see him look just as gentle and innocent like a new baby, and on the other side just as tough as a drill instructor. I think he was aware of that. Not only was he aware of that, but his master called him "Crooked Cucumber," and I believe that's what that reference means.

I was so in awe of him that every time I ever met him I could never assume that he remembered me from the last time because I felt so insignificant and he felt so incredibly heavy that I always started off by introducing myself to him, 'til it came to the point where he said, "When are you going to quit explaining to me who you are?"

Lex Hixon: At the beginning of Ina May's book, *Spiritual Midwifery*, there is a picture of Suzuki Roshi, and Stephen says that he likes to put a picture of Suzuki Roshi in front of just about everything he does, which says a lot to me about Stephen. If someone is in a position of teacher, that person always feels provisional about it and is always making some sort of gesture away from himself, and this is certainly a beautiful way to do it, but it doesn't entirely succeed because this picture of Suzuki Roshi looks like Stephen. He's got this zany little smile on his face and he's holding these little glasses up in front of his eyes.

Stephen Gaskin: That's an unpublished picture. Somebody gave me a copy, knowing how I loved Suzuki.

Lex Hixon: I think the humorous resemblance between Suzuki Roshi in this picture and Stephen himself might say something about a transmission which could have taken place. But I don't think transmissions take place in time. We think they do, but they're kind of always already there.

Stephen Gaskin: Yeah, the non-space/time-ness of those planes is really a thing.

Lex Hixon: As this picture documents, there's some dimension of the enlightened mind of Suzuki Roshi that was going to be guiding a farm of good, earthy, spiritual yogi householders in Tennessee. This is one of the mysteries of the way spiritual transmissions work.

Stephen Gaskin: Just before he died, I heard he was sick and going to die. We had a car that someone's father, who was an Air Force Colonel, had given us. It was one of those hot 450-cubic-inch Buick muscle cars. If you throw a picture on the dashboard, it reflects in the windshield. I had Suzuki's book lying on the dashboard and put his face reflecting on the windshield, so I was looking through his eyes as I was driving. We made an incredibly fast trip out to California and I almost scared the people at the Zen Center because I came off a 2,200-mile fast drive and in the door, still running. Baker Roshi was there, and I said, "I heard Suzuki's sick. It's okay if I don't see him if he's too sick, but I came to see him."

Baker Roshi took me right in to see him. As usual, here I am, running these 2,200 miles to see this dying saint whom I love with all my heart, and I come in and he starts telling me he's going to die. He's cool with it, but he's trying to put it on me gently so as to not blow me away with it too much. He's putting it on me tentatively, like, "Of course you realize these things happen."

One of the things that I came to show him was a photograph of the children on The Farm sitting Zazen. It's a beautiful picture of a whole bunch of little children. I gave that to him because I hadn't kept very good contact with him, and I wanted him to know there were about 400 or 500 people in Tennessee who loved him, who he may not have known about. It was a heavy time to see him. He was so strong, an amazing man, just so graceful in the face of death. It was really like a Zen master is supposed to be, according to the book.

I feel that I honor Suzuki as someone who's keeping alive a tradition that's 2,500 years old, and bringing it down and really demonstrating transmission of mind. I believe that when you meet up with a man like Suzuki, you're shaking the hand that shook the hand of Gautama Buddha. I honor that, and I honor the Hindu tradition, and the Christian tradition. But at the same time, I realize there's something happening right now, and that we should honor that thing that's happening right now. All those heavy traditions are something that exploded on a generation and became part of the "mind furniture" of mankind from then on, timelessly. And this tremendous spiritual revival that's happening in this country did not come from Buddhism, did not come from Christianity, did not come from Hinduism. It came from this culture right now. It came from this incredible hothouse of cultural pressures, ranging from poverty to affluence.

It used to be that when people were starving in Timbuktu, that was the end of the world, and what could you do about it? And now that dude in Timbuktu's got a transistor radio and he knows who won the World Series and he also knows that you're over here not starving.

This cultural pressure is hothousing something that's happening. That's why I feel that there's an obligation on all our part to look at what is with new eyes, with children's fresh new eyes and see what's going on and don't forget that it's really dynamite happenings now. Just dynamite. So that's why I got to be able to be down home with all my friends.

Back to the old archetypes and roots and stuff: I feel like that thing that happened 12 years ago was such a mind-blower to everyone across the board. Even down in Tennessee, they still say, "The flower child was something else. A flower child wasn't dangerous, you know, like some of them folks." They wanted to know if it was real like it said in the papers. They wanted to know if there really was such a thing as a flower child.

Lex Hixon: And there they are with 800 of the post-flower children, "flower grownups," living on The Farm right next door to them.

Stephen Gaskin: I've got some friends down in Tennessee who are unemployed young men who like to drink and fight on Saturday night, and when I go to talk to those guys, I drink whiskey with them. I don't drink whiskey with anyone else because it makes me sick. I drink whiskey with them and it *doesn't* seem to make me sick. I drink it with them because the atmosphere is so charged with the amount of tension that ordinary people like that have to live under, a little whiskey seems like an all right thing. I burn a little bush with them or something, you know, and they are comfortable with me. They don't think I'm any of this stuff you've been saying I am.

Lex Hixon: I'm comfortable with you, too.

Stephen Gaskin: But if you blow my cover that bad, those guys ain't going to be comfortable.

Lex Hixon: That's true. I feel very comfortable, and I thank you for drinking whatever I'm drinking, with me.

Ida May and Stephen Gaskin at The Farm

John Daido Loori
April 17, 1980

Born to a Catholic family in Jersey City, New Jersey, in 1931, John Daido Loori forged a birth certificate when he was 16 years old so that he could join the U.S. Navy, and served on an aircraft carrier from 1947 to 1952. Afterward, he attended Rutgers University and the Polytechnic Institute of Brooklyn, and then worked as a chemist for 17 years. Already an accomplished photographer, Daido began studying with the famous photographer Minor White in 1971 until the end of White's life. From White, he learned the concept of "mindful photography," which led him toward Zen practice and influenced his own later teaching. Daido's serious study of Zen began in 1974 with Soen Nakagawa Roshi and Eido Shimano in New York and continued in Los Angeles with Taizan Maezumi Roshi, who made him a priest in 1983 and gave him Dharma Transmission in 1986. After acquiring a large Catholic monastery in 1980 on 230 acres of land in Mt. Tremper, New York, Daido and Maezumi Roshi established Zen Mountain Monastery, and Daido founded the Mountains and Rivers Order. Eventually, he became the monastery's abbot and led weekend workshops in the arts, environmentalism, and social action, during which participants were required to follow a strict Zen schedule and rules.

He wrote many books on Zen, some including his own photographs, and created Dharma Communications to publish the Buddhist quarterly, *The Mountain Record*. Daido died at Mt. Tremper in 2009 from lung cancer. Zen Mountain Monastery and Fire Lotus Temple in Brooklyn, New York, continue to operate under the leadership of his successors.

Lex Hixon: "*The moment built up slowly. Yesterday [while] waking from a nap on a ledge, the Lobos surf was speaking English. What other language do I understand? The green and brown pastures of kelp in the surf feeding gulls, the seals, the fish, the millions of one- and two-celled things living in and out of time. Not each can have a soul. An economy of souls, a reuse of souls, akin to the metamorphoses of all organic matter. Reincarnation. The surf chanted with the voices of drowned thousands. Reincarnation. Could I disbelieve?*

Last evening [photographer Edward] Weston talked about his peppers and shells. Yes, he knew about the plus in them. So many see only a sex. "I made them for their beauty," he says. Something else crept in. If sex, [it's] regenerative sex. Food to nourish souls. This morning at Lobos I started out by saying to myself, "What will I be given today?" I had a long session photographing surf. Watching the swirling water by small eye movements gives the eye a part of a second of still images. And the water is seen frozen in fractions, not in motion. It's like seeing a camera, seeing as a camera for one-25th of a second. Watching moving water was and always is mesmeric. Heightened suggestibility. But who gives the suggestions?

I followed the shores of a familiar beach, the one we call Weston Beach, and was pleased to observe a mounting excitement. Old faces were as if new. Never had the rocks and tide pools seemed so alive and glowing. The path my feet took was lined with images. Whole gardens of pictures. With exposures I picked bouquets, each more vivid than the previous, and finally a gathering of gemlike flames in the low tide. Beautiful of light. Beautiful, I chanted. It is beautiful. I thought I'd forgotten how to use my camera. So I counted each step of the process aloud. Shutter speed. Aperture. Cock the shutter. Though I feared to lose the sense of beauty, no loss occurred. The sense of rapport was strong beyond belief. I made two identical exposures just to be sure.

Glancing out from under the focusing cloth, a strangeness. Was the sky darkening? The light was going. The vision itself was flowing away. As I looked, a few million years swept back, covering vision with today. There must have been a long pause. A thought broke through: I don't know the words anymore. What must animate my pictures from now on I want no name for. In need, and even if not knowing how, I will call on it. It is not be foreign to the city, nor to anyone. It is everywhere under the sun. For vision. For magic. When Edward opened the door, one glance told him a wish had been granted. His smile was an affirmation. His handshake a toast to the invisible Point Lobos, a connection to the invisible Stieglitz."

Those were the words of Minor White, a great American photographer. And we have with us in the studio one of the students and one of the bearers of the transmission of Minor White, John Loori, who is a dedicated Zen student and practitioner and a dedicated photographer, and it's pretty hard to separate those two in his case. Zen and photography are intimately linked in his life. John, maybe you should give, like, some sort of historical perspective of, you know, when Minor White ended the passage from his journal, *The Invisible Stieglitz*. Maybe you should start there, with Alfred Stieglitz, and tell people how photography has unfolded in this country since then and what's happening to it today.

John Daido Loori: Minor considered Alfred Stieglitz as one of the first photographers to tie in with the sacred traditions of the other arts. Photography is a relatively modern art and it has no sacred tradition to speak of, in the sense that painting does. But the work of Stieglitz began to go beyond the surface possibilities of photography and to get involved in the spirit of the relationship between the photographer and the subject. That tradition was also a big part of Edward Weston's work and Minor White's work, in fact [Minor's] whole life was dedicated to photography as a way of inner growth, as a spiritual practice. So that's what he was referring to there, kind of the patriarchs of photography, which has a very, very short [history], it's probably the most modern of the modern arts.

Lex Hixon: What's happened to it since then? We were talking about that earlier, we're almost in the third generation of photographers now, since Stieglitz.

John Daido Loori: A few weeks ago, I attended a conference with the Society of Photographic Education, and I had been out of that for a couple of years while I was away in Los Angeles practicing at the Zen Center there. And this was my first opportunity to go to one of their meetings in about three years. And it was amazing. I was really amazed at the total absence of the personal, spiritual aspects of art in all the talks that I attended there. So much of the photography had to do with photography, photographs themselves, photographs about photography.

It really pointed out a thing that's happened, in my eyes. Primitive art grew out of the religious experiences of the artist, in fact, that's what the art was all about, to try to communicate that. And down through the years of our history, art has always been associated with the sacred. But in our modern world, particularly the last 10 or 20 years, it's gradually begun to vanish, not only in photography but in all the art forms. Critics rarely talk about it. Artists rarely direct themselves to it. I sat with some friends and we looked at many, many [photographs] of students that were there showing portfolios, and it was incredible. Here and there, there'd be one or two students who still had that connection.

Now when I'm talking about the connection, it's the kind of sense that many of our artists have had, like when you listen to Bach, you know that something was going on there, that this man was communicating something beyond the obvious. That sense of spirit—so much of that was lacking in the work that we saw.

Lex Hixon: I know that [when] we talked earlier, you clarified to me that in your teaching of photography as a meditative art, you try and get away from verbal assessments of someone's work and you try to show people how to relate nonverbally to the quality of what you called "spirit in art," and precisely in photography. But since we have a verbal medium, or at least a partially verbal medium that we're working with now—radio—what is it about Stieglitz's work, what is it about Minor White's work, and what was it about Minor White as a living human being as you knew him and studied with him, which gave you this link? Maybe some people would be put off by calling it spirit. What is it that gives you a sense that this work is grounded in what we would call the wholeness of body, mind, and spirit?

John Daido Loori: Of course the simplest and most direct way is to just simply experience one of Minor's photographs. It's all right there. But in that piece that you read, he mentioned several things that have to do with that way of working that opens up the possibilities for other things to happen. For example, the way he describes his walking down the beach, it was obvious that it wasn't deliberate, that he had no preconceived ideas of what he was going to photograph, that he was following an intuitive sense, waiting to discover that which appeared before him.

There was also an obvious reverence, an attitude of reverence, for all things, particularly for the process itself and the subject. And then there was that sense of having forgotten the self, when he lost track of time. Suddenly there was not enough light to photograph. He realized that the day was completely gone. Where was he? Where was Minor White when that was happening? That's what Dogen Zenji was talking about when he talked about seeing forms with a whole body and mind. Hearing sounds with a whole body and mind. One understands them intimately. So there's no separation between the subject and the photographer.

Lex Hixon: So maybe the spirit that you speak about is one of unification with the universe. You mentioned one of the problems with a lot of modern photography that you saw, was that it was self-conscious in the sense, that it was photographs about photography, which indicated that there really hadn't been any union with the universe. But there's a kind of heightened awareness, maybe, of even the separateness of photography as a practice from the flow of nature itself.

John Daido Loori: The spirit is there. It's always there, it permeates everything and everywhere. It's what we call "Buddha nature." And just like you can't see that at all, you can't experience that at all if you're turned and constantly involved in this delusion that ourselves and everything else are separate, that everything inside our skin, us, and everything outside is other. So long as that illusion persists, there's no way to see things for what they are—we're constantly evaluating and analyzing and comparing and judging. But when all of that falls away and there is no self, when there are no ideas, no opinions, no judgment, there's only the thing itself. That's a whole different reality than the dualistic way of separating ourselves from it.

Lex Hixon: I've had a chance of watching our guest this morning, John Loori, on one of his photographic haunts, and I wish I'd had a chance to see him more, but it looked a little like maybe a cat looks when walking though a garden—up on things, down on things, underneath things.

And at one point, I turned around and he was photographing his own reflection in some sort of large window with plants in the way and he was holding up both hands and taking the photograph without looking through the lens of the camera. And this, to me, is symbolic of a kind of merging with things.

And there was, I might say, great joy and delight in John Loori's way. In fact, he called some of his friends to look at the beautiful image that was there. It wasn't the kind of quietistic, very somber, separated thing; there was a lot of joy and naturalness in this photographic play. But there was a sense that the camera was just one small element in the whole process, and that the whole process was life itself. Maybe, John, you'll tell the story about the modern Zen Roshi, Soen Nakagawa Roshi, and this might give us a hint as to what Zen art [is], the kind of healing and illumining process it can have in people's lives. And this is obviously why you teach it. Do you think that would give people a way in?

John Daido Loori: Yeah, of course.

Lex Hixon: And then we can return to Minor White's words, too.

John Daido Loori: Of course the relationship between Zen and the arts has a long, long history. In fact, it goes back to before Zen came to Japan, when it was still in China. Chinese Zen was very, very much influenced by the Taoist paintings of the time, the Song Dynasty. And so there were schools of calligraphy and brush painting and poetry that were very closely related to the practice of Zen.

When Zen came to the shores of Japan a whole new thing happened there. The impact was incredible. Seventeenth-century Japan was touched in every aspect of life by Zen and the arts in a way that went beyond the walls of the monastery. And, in fact, all of these arts originated in the monasteries, like the founder of the tea school was for many, many years a Zen priest and learned, actually, about tea in the monastery. And it became a very popular art of 17th-century Japan. There are many, many Zen masters, like Hakuin Ekaku Zenji, a very famous Zen master and founder of the modern Zen art system. He used painting as a way of teaching the Dharma, and haiku poets and calligraphers and even in the arts of war there were many Dharma teachers involved, [teaching] aikido and archery and so on.

In the modern 20th-century monasteries, the tradition of the poet priest or painter priest has still continued to a very large extent, particularly in Japan. Zen has happened here in America, and a lot of Zen practitioners are also artists, and it becomes very obvious when you see their art, the influence of the practice of Zen on the art. And also, the teaching of the Dharma through the arts continues.

The example that you were talking about had to do with Soen Nakagawa Roshi. There's a story about him in the book *Sun Buddha, Moon Buddha*. It seems that Soen Roshi was [approached] by the parents of a young woman in Japan who had been studying ballet and had dedicated her life to that, and at one point in her life, an unfortunate accident left her paralyzed from the waist down, which caused her great remorse. Her parents tried doctors around the world—they were fairly wealthy people and were able to do that—but no one could do anything for her, and she became more and more despondent, and no one seemed to be able to help her.

One day they asked Soen Roshi if he would come and talk with their daughter. And he said he would, but of course he knew nothing of psychology or modern medicine, so there was nothing he could really do. But if it pleased them, he would come. And he did. And in the process of talking with her he reached into this little bamboo basket that he always carried with him and took out a sheet of rice paper and a brush and a little dish that's used to make the ink and slowly began to make ink, rubbing the stick back and forth on the surface of the dish. That in itself is a marvelous thing to watch because the process itself is meditative. It takes about 20 minutes to get the ink to the right consistency and the right depth of color. And then he proceeded to paint a small Jizo bodhisattva, and showed it to her and asked her if she could do that. She knew nothing of painting, but took the brush and painted a reasonable approximation of Soen Roshi's bodhisattva, and he encouraged her and was very pleased with the result, and asked her if she would do a few more and he would come back the following week.

And she did. He came back and she had 10 more then, and he was very pleased with the progress, and he asked her to start numbering them and to try to do 30 or 40 during the next month, and he would come back. And he did, and she had 30 or 40. Next month, he asked for 100, and the following month 200, and the next month 500, and he asked her to keep counting and numbering each one, sign each one of them, include a poem on each one of them. And within six or eight months, she had forgotten all about her despondency, was very, very much involved in the painting and the whole sense of the brush and the paper and the particularly exciting way Soen Roshi has of explaining these things. And her whole life began to change.

A couple of years ago I was at a monastery here and saw the two millionth Jizo bodhisattva that this woman, [who is] now in her 70s and recognized as one of Japan's finest artists, has completed. This is, to me, the Dharma working for the arts. This was Soen Roshi teaching meditation without telling her that she had to sit cross-legged and keep count her breath, for example. The very act of painting was a realization of herself.

Lex Hixon: So many people are drawn to the tradition of Taoism, which John Loori has said was really at the basis of of Zen arts, and maybe his own teaching of photography would be a way of practicing Taoism in a modern setting. Because, as John just said, it's not the question of sitting cross-legged and doing the traditional form of meditation, although John does that, and most people who study with him find that very inspiring and very helpful to their photography. But the real essence of the practice is moving around in the universe with a camera as part of one's own being. You can say that it's so beautiful to grind the ink, the 20 minutes of grinding ink, but there's no reason why the technical requirements of photography can't take on the same meditative value, would you think, John?

John Daido Loori: Oh, sure. Definitely.

Lex Hixon: Although it may not sound as romantic to us to choose a right film and put it in a camera, as grinding ink, presumably we can take it in the same spirit.

Daido John Loori: Sure. In the darkroom, for example. There are many, many different kinds of darkrooms—some are just another crazy house of sloppiness and a lot of activity and things spilling all over the place—but it's possible to conduct oneself in the darkroom, for example, the same way that the tea masters conduct themselves in making tea. It's the same thing—handling of liquids and dishes and movements. But there's a certain reverence, a certain attitude toward each of the steps of the process.

And dealing with a camera is no different than dealing with the sword, the way the sword master did, or releasing the shutter, like releasing the arrow for the archer. So there are a lot of techniques and camerawork that we practice over and over and over again, so that there's a place for that spontaneity to arise from. It comes out of a discipline, using the thing. In fact, the whole business of Zen photography really begins when a student has mastered the media in the sense of the traditional way of dealing with it and still finds big gaps, still finds big questions, starts asking the questions: "What's this all about? What am I doing? What's my photography about? Who am I? What is self-expression?" When those questions begin to arise, then the business of Zen photography begins.

Lex Hixon: Some of us maybe are not literally paralyzed the way that young girl was in the story, but have been paralyzed in some sense, have to give up our aspiration to dance [when] as younger people we had the sense that we would dance in this universe. And some unfortunate accident has happened to us as far as our socialization and acculturation, so that we feel the we can no longer dance and we feel kind of despondent and there's this paralysis. Maybe the practicing of Zen arts and photography is one of the most accessible ways to lift that despondency—and it's wonderful to think that.

Our guest this morning, John Loori, has moved to New York City and is here, available for the teaching of this art. And it seems to me that professional photographers who don't regard their darkroom work as a Zen tea ceremony yet, as well as people who are complete beginners in the art, would benefit from some contact with John. John, you've been giving seminars all over the country, but you had a particularly interesting experience a while ago up in New England someplace, where you gave a seven-day Zen and photography seminar. Can you talk about that? What went on? And the response? It was essentially to professional photographers?

John Daido Loori: It was primarily to students whose whole lives were wrapped around photography. And in fact, many of the questions of sacredness and the spiritual aspects of photography were there, but they were kind of under the surface. They were concerned at that point about making good photographs, so-called good photographs, and being accepted critically and that sort of thing. And of all the workshops I've given over the years, that was the first one that I gave overtly as a Zen priest and used the form that's used in Zen training, rather than putting the whole thing in the perspective of psychology and so on. And the response was incredible. The students couldn't get enough of it.

This is a community in which, normally, people would go to bed at four o'clock in the morning after partying part of the night, and here we were asking them to get up at four o'clock in the morning and begin Zazen at four-thirty. And we followed a rigorous training schedule that's used in a Zen monastery, the Zen Training Center. And the results were incredible, not only in the photography that happened during the seven days, or in the fact that a meditation group started in that community and continues two years later—it's still going strong—but in the impact that it had on their lives, just the relationships between people. There were several couples that were separated prior to the workshop that ended up getting back together and communicating.

Lex Hixon: Unification, unification.

John Daido Loori: It was like real coming together. Photography's just another way of expressing Zen. It can be done in everyday life. Whether we're talking about typing or washing the dishes or making photographs or growing a garden, raising kids, doing our work, it ultimately boils down to the everyday life situation. It needs to do that. That's what the whole thing is about, our daily existence.

Lex Hixon: Can you remind me of the Japanese word for photography, which I think is a significant one?

John Daido Loori: Yeah, the word is *shashin*. And that translates as *sha*, mirror or reflection, and *shin* is truth or reality. It's very much the way that we use photographs in these workshops, incidentally, because everything we do is a mirror of ourselves, and particularly a photograph. So when you're looking at a photograph that you made, what you're looking at is a mirror of some aspect of yourself—and really seeing that photograph and really understanding what's going on helps you understand the self. And as we continue to examine the self that's being expressed in our self-expression, what we're doing is coming to grips with basically what Zen practice is all about.

Lex Hixon: And that mirror of reality—suppose one's photographing a rock. Suppose we're photographing a rock, the reality is not a rock, but the reality is the whole thing that you and the rock are a part of.

John Daido Loori: Exactly. And the camera and the photograph.

Lex Hixon: And the appreciator of the art, looking at the photograph, is also as much of the whole thing as the rock would be or the camera. So it's this sense of a unified universe that is accessible through the sacred tradition of Zen and this art of Zen photography.

John, [you are] showing us the mystery of the body, because the body is the most ultimate camera, you might say, the mechanical camera that we've developed is just a symbol for the body-mind. And it's a helpful external symbol, but it's just that, and ultimately, one can begin going around taking photographs without film. Presumably a real, living Zen photographer goes around all the time unified with the universe in the way of the Zen photographer. Most people think of photography so much as separating oneself from the world, so they think how terrible it must be to be going around, taking photographs in your mind all the time. Doesn't that make you self-conscious, or doesn't that separate you? But from your understanding, John, of photography, you're going around being the universe all the time, which is quite different from taking snapshots of it.

John Daido Loori: The wonderful thing about photography is it really makes the moment's aliveness very, very clear. I remember one day sorting out some photographs that I was getting ready to exhibit, and the room was filled with them. There were, like, 60 or 70 photographs around the edge of the room, and it represented a couple of years of work. And I looked at them and I realized that if each one was one-60th of a second exposure, that the whole thing represented one second in time. And there it was, two years of work.

In Zen, it's important to be able to realize or see that each action, each moment, from moment to moment, is the first moment and the last moment. With that kind of an attitude, nothing becomes redundant, nothing becomes boring, nothing becomes old; it's always new and it's always exciting. And if you go out with a camera that way, you find what Minor White was finding: bouquets of images around him all the time. And it doesn't have to be with a camera. Now, when we put the camera aside, the bouquets are still there. But in order to see them, we have to let go of ourselves as a separate and distinct entity from everything else. We have to forget the self, in the words of Dogen Zenji.

Lex Hixon: This kind of healing experience is going to be happening this Sunday when John Loori will be giving a one-day seminar in the practice of Zen photography at Wave Hill in the Bronx. Wave Hill is a beautiful, old estate that has been given to the city that everyone from Mark Twain and Toscanini and others have at one time or another lived in. And it has beautiful grounds, and the spring is just budding out there.

But if you can't make it then, there are going to be a series of these, there are going to be three of these seminars given at Wave Hill. The next one John will give in a month or so, and then, the last one of the series, later this spring, will be [given with] Peter Matthiessen, who some of you know as the author of *The Snow Leopard* and *Far Tortuga*, and many, many fine novels. Both John Loori and Peter Matthiessen are members of this new Zen Community of New York, which has sprung up in the Riverdale section of the Bronx, around a very remarkable man, Sensei Bernie Glassman, who has been on this program long before, and who's a New York kid from Brooklyn who went into mathematics and the aerospace industry, and finally ended up in Japan studying Zen, and came back and is now a qualified Zen teacher.

John has got some publications. *Of The Way of Everyday Life* is one of his recent publications, in which a text, an important text from the Zen tradition, is translated by Maezumi Roshi and is accompanied by some very vibrant photographs by John Loori. John, is there any direction you want to go in right now?

John Daido Loori: I'd like to mention that the workshop at Wave Hill is not primarily directed to photographers, but it should be of interest to artists or art students or people that just appreciate art. I think they'll find that what we'll be dealing with is an exciting new way of seeing and relating to not only art but to our environment. The series is called "Art, Aesthetics, and Ecology." And Peter Matthiessen is also very well known as a naturalist. In fact, he's working on a book right now on the American Indians, and he's living with the Indians. And so much of the relationship of the community environment to the culture is part of what he's discovering.

Lex Hixon: And Peter is an activist in Native American rights and in the field of ecology, so this is another interesting connection that we can make in this country. I don't know whether any of the traditional Zen artists were also social activists, but this is a mix that we can bring to this country.

John Daido Loori: That's right, it's really interesting what's happening to Zen as it takes root in the West. Sensei Glassman is one exciting example of it, with his particularly unique way of teaching Zen in its Western sense so that it's really relevant to us and what we do here in this country.

The title of the first meeting of the workshop, which is this Sunday, is "The Aesthetics of No Aesthetic." It has to do basically with the Zen aesthetic and the art of seeing—in the Zen sense of the word "seeing." That is, perception with the unconditioned eye. So much of our perception is based on our conditioning, so much so that we sometimes see things that are not even there. So it's a process that deals with coming in contact with some of the conditioning that affects our way of doing things. And as in Zen, the practice is letting go of ideas and opinions and whatever comes up, until finally there's just the thing itself. So we'll be dealing with that, and the process of the creative audience, and how it applies to this particular kind of thing.

In the following workshop, we'll use that, actually, with some of the art on the premises and with people's own portfolios. And the third one, the one that Peter will join us for, that one's called "Birds, Beasts, Blossoms, and Bugs." We're going to take this whole aesthetic and way of seeing and relating to art and apply it to our own environment. We're going to use the flora and fauna of the Wave Hill setting to take it a step further.

Lex Hixon: So there could emerge a kind of Zen ecology, which might make a major contribution to our whole idea of the ecology movement.

John Daido Loori: Oh, it sure does.

Lex Hixon: Because it's all very well to love the earth abstractly, and of course everyone would agree that we shouldn't dump poisonous materials into the earth. But that doesn't mean that people who are committed to ecology in that sense have yet come to unify with the earth to the degree that a Zen artist can.

John Daido Loori: That's exactly what we're talking about in this workshop, going beyond that separation between us and others, so that the things that are around us are, in fact, nothing other than ourselves.

Lex Hixon: And the many years that Peter Matthiessen has been practicing Zen certainly haven't taken any edge off his social commitment and his social activism. We might also mention, in this context, [the poet] Gary Snyder, who people know a lot about. One mustn't feel that Zen practice and this unifying with the universe somehow turns you into a bland sort of blah non-activist person.

John Daido Loori: Right! I was interested before when you were describing a photograph, you were talking about it being vibrant and that sort of thing. So many people, when they think of Zen and photography, begin to think of misty landscapes and that sort of thing, that that's what tranquility and Zen is all about. But it's not. It goes so far beyond that. Nothing is outside of it. It has no edges. So that which is exciting, that which is sad, that which is joyous, is all part of it. That's the everyday life part of it.

Lex Hixon: But I have to ask you this question, which I've asked Bernie Glassman himself on the air. How is this distinguished from a sort of old-fashioned, existentialist view of the universe, where you sort of take everything as it comes? Even in your own case, you don't just practice photography, you yourself have practiced years of sitting in Zazen and meditation. In fact, after you studied with Minor White and you knew in your bones what kind of photography you wanted to do, the first thing you did was to get really in touch with the Zen practice. So can you elucidate this point? I mean, it's not just an attitude to art; it seems that it's a moving, living, sacred tradition that has a lot of impact.

John Daido Loori: Yeah, it's not an attitude even. Zazen is the key—the sitting meditation is the key. Because, until that happens, it's just a bunch of ideas, more words and more concepts. I mean, that's really all that's happening here. We're talking about it and not doing it. When it becomes our own personal realization; when it arises out of ourselves, not of some idea, not of some opinion; where, in fact, there's not even an awareness of what's happening, where there's not knowing, it's just happening, it's just seeing, it's just walking, it's just eating, with no reflection, no conceptualization—that's what we're talking about.

Lex Hixon: But to get there—

John Daido Loori: Zazen.

Lex Hixon: Zazen, which is, as the Zen Community of New York and any genuine Zen community practices it, not just a simple thing, like, all right, let's sit around quietly. It involves a whole way of life and some traditional practices that come from India, China, Japan, all the way through the whole Buddhist heritage.

But I think, as you pointed out earlier, people are more willing to accept Zen now. I mean, this community of photographers that you went to didn't object to getting up in the morning at four o'clock to do Zazen, when ordinarily they would have been going to bed after a party. I mean, there seems to be a new receptivity in the culture of trying the sacred tradition as long as it's not presented as something dogmatic.

John Daido Loori: I think in general there's a real receptivity among artists because they're so much in touch with just the very process of doing art. There's a kind of working *samadhi* that develops when you're really involved in it. Minor White used to say, "At least once in every artist's life, he walks on water." And it's that once-walking-on-water that kind of opens the crack in the door.

But talking about forgetting the self and Zazen, Dogen Zenji said that to study the Buddha is to study the self, and to study the self is to forget the self. Dogen Zenji goes on to say to forget the self you let body and mind fall away, and so on. As far as Sensei Bernie Glassman is concerned, to forget the self is Zazen—in the very process of Zazen, that's what's happening, the letting go of the self, and the letting go of everything that comes up.

Lex Hixon: Earlier, John said that what we are doing here is just words and ideas, but maybe not entirely. Both John and I are people who try to practice a daily meditation and daily quiet sitting, so therefore even our words and ideas may have a little bit of that presence in them; otherwise, I really wouldn't want to do a program like this and sit around and ask people to listen for an hour to words and ideas. It seems to me that what the Eighties needs is for words and ideas to be infused with personal practice. And so some of you may, I'm sure, find in listening to John Loori, that there's something calming and inspiring just about the way he says everything. His life has been permeated by this sitting meditation, and so it's ceased to be just something he does when he sits; it's something he does when he lights a cigarette as he's about to do. The Zen tradition is very liberal, it's not a moralistic tradition.

John Daido Loori: It's not a moralistic tradition, but there is a morality that grows out of it exactly the same way that the everydayness grows out of the sitting meditation. I mean, the Bodhisattva ideal is an ideal, it's something you can talk about, it's something that you can form precepts around. But out of the meditation itself, realization arises; out of the meditation itself actualization arises. And it's that that has the impact, that's transformative.

Lex Hixon: I think that there has been a tremendous impact of Zen practice on the arts in America. We think of John Cage as someone who's had a longtime love affair with Zen. We mentioned Gary Snyder before, one of our great poets, who's had a longtime Zen practice. Peter Matthiessen, who is a member of the Zen Community of New York, is probably emerging as one of our great novelists. And he owes this Zen practice for the kind of total integration. If you read his book, *The Snow Leopard*, you'll see so many vivid haiku and Zen photographs. It's just overwhelming. And he's used his technical knowledge as a naturalist, and he's integrated it with his Zen seeing, and what comes out is something very vivid and special.

And John Daido Loori, who we're speaking with this morning, is one of our major emerging artists and photographers. He represents the Zen tradition. So, forgive me for leaving out lots and lots of names. W.S. Merwin is one that comes to mind. He's a Pulitzer Prize-winning poet who has been studying Zen for years. And who else can you think of?

John Daido Loori: William Merwin and Anthony Newman both are going to be doing programs at Wave Hill in conjunction with the Zen Community of New York, and Anthony Newman may even move to the community here in New York and live and practice with us. But they've both been practicing a long time.

Lex Hixon: For those who don't know Anthony Newman, can you just mention who he is?

John Daido Loori: He's a classical harpsichordist who's known well to anyone that's involved with classical music.

Lex Hixon: And he's supposed to be one of the best interpreters of Bach around now. Well, this is the kind of thing that's flowering, and this estate that belongs to the city up in the Riverdale section of the Bronx, Wave Hill, is becoming a focus for a lot of this.

We want to end the program with some of the words of Minor White. This time, John Loori, a student of Minor White, will be reading these words, and they are a kind of beautiful, clear statement of what Zen and the Zen arts are all about.

John Daido Loori: *"As if I could give anything. Take not images. Be. Give not. Be. Make not. Be. Know not. Be image. Count inhalations. Count exhalations. Count nothing. Be breath."*

John Daido Loori teaches a class at Zen Mountain Monastery

316

Rabbi Aryeh Kaplan
June 6, 1980

Born in 1934 and raised in the Bronx, New York, Aryeh Kaplan was an Orthodox rabbi, writer, and physicist. He completed his rabbinical training in Jerusalem and was ordained there in 1956 by Rabbi Yehuda Finkle, one of Israel's foremost rabbinic authorities. He then went on to earn a B.S. degree with high honors at the University of Louisiana and an M.S. in physics at the University of Maryland. After completing a fellowship from the National Science Foundation, he changed career direction by taking a full-time position as a rabbi in Mason City, Iowa, in 1965. From then until the end of his life, he held positions as rabbi for congregations in many states across the country, ending up in Brooklyn, New York. Rabbi Kaplan wrote more than 50 books, including many on Kabbalah and meditation, but is best known for *The Living Torah,* a scholarly translation of the Torah with an extensive index. His writings displayed a wide knowledge of Jewish thought from basic introductory material to scholarly Kabbalah and Hasidut. Rabbi Kaplan married Tobie Goldstein in 1961, and they had nine children together before he died suddenly in 1983 at the age of 48 from a heart attack.

Lex Hixon: This morning we're going to be talking about the Kabbalah, or Jewish mysticism, in Rabbi Aryeh Kaplan's book *Meditation and the Bible.* He has written many books; some of you may be familiar with a widely circulated book called *The Handbook of Jewish Thought*.

When I read his book, *Meditation and the Bible*, although I've been studying and practicing meditation for quite a few years, I learned some very interesting new information. He quotes a great deal from the sources of Jewish mystical tradition, which are newly translated from Hebrew.

Aryeh, let's talk about some of the themes in the book. Where do you want to start?

Rabbi Aryeh Kaplan: The main subject of the book is Jewish meditation in general. One of the reasons I wrote the book was because so many people have no idea that Jewish meditation even exists. That is why the book is not so much my writing, but to a large degree, I'm citing ancient and not-so-ancient sources that discuss Jewish meditation to show the history.

Lex Hixon: You mention that you got interested in Kabbalah when you were writing *The Handbook of Jewish Thought*.

Rabbi Aryeh Kaplan: I consider *The Handbook* the most important thing I've ever done. I wrote most of it about 12 years ago. While I was writing it, I gradually realized that Jewish philosophy almost comes to an abrupt end in the 14th and 15th centuries. And from there on, almost all of Jewish philosophy and Jewish thought and theology is dominated by Kabbalah.

Lex Hixon: For non-Jews listening, would you say Kabbalah is the way of referring to Jewish mysticism in general?

Rabbi Aryeh Kaplan: Kabbalah literally means, "Accept it." Taking or acceptance. It really means tradition, with a capital T.

Lex Hixon: Rabbi Kaplan reminded me that he's not just a Kabbalist, he's Orthodox as well, and in the rich soil of orthodoxy is where these beautiful Kabbalist flowers grow. The Kabbalah doesn't grow in thin air.

Aryeh, you told me earlier that you'd been meditating ever since you were a boy, but not realizing it.

Rabbi Aryeh Kaplan: Let me just elaborate on that. As anybody who's familiar with the Jewish community knows, the Orthodox Jew prays three times a day, and the central part of that prayer is a prayer known as the Amidah [or Standing Prayer]. If one says that prayer correctly, with intense concentration, one gently pushes away all outside thoughts and is drawn close to the Divine.

We never thought of this as meditation. When people come to me and say, "I'm a religious Jew, I pray every day. How should I meditate?" Now, I say, "Make your daily prayer into a meditation." There are other meditations a person could do, but the major meditation that a Jew does can be part of the service. And this whole methodology was part of the Baal Shem Tov's teachings in Hasidism. Although many other schools of Jewish meditation had existed, what the Baal Shem Tov did was to make the normal prayer service the integral part of Jewish meditation.

I might add that in Kabbalah, one of the important teachings is that every act that a person does throughout the day can and does become a meditation; that every act that a person does throughout the day can create a unification.

Lex Hixon: I like the idea of unifying oneself with God, because it's a more intimate expression. It shows that the essence of the mystical path in all the traditions, which is forgetting oneself in the Divine, is also functioning in Jewish mysticism. There's a point in the I/Thou relationship where one forgets that there's any separation at all between the I and the Thou.

Rabbi Aryeh Kaplan: There is nothing but Thee.

Lex Hixon: Nothing but Thee. The fact remains that if you had never gotten into Kabbalah, and your awareness hadn't been sensitized by reading and studying with these great masters of Kabbalah, you might never have recognized Jewish practice as meditation.

Rabbi Aryeh Kaplan: I would have been meditating, but not applying the word to it.

Lex Hixon: So Kabbalah is available in the world today. It's not a lost tradition.

Rabbi Aryeh Kaplan: By no means.

Lex Hixon: Jews, who karmically have more direct access to their tradition, but also, non-Jews who are drawn [to it], should know that Kabbalah is a real, living tradition, and we can have access to it. And in fact, Rabbi Aryeh Kaplan, teaches classes in Brooklyn.

Rabbi Aryeh Kaplan: Kabbalah is a very powerful source, if one actually studies the Bible very carefully, one can find the root of all of Kabbalistic tradition right there in the Bible itself.

Lex Hixon: Let's talk about the Hebrew word for meditation that you've focused on. Can you explain the inner meanings of that word and why translators and even Hebrew scholars have overlooked the fact that it really means "meditation"?

Rabbi Aryeh Kaplan: Yes, the word for meditation is *Hitbodedut*, which literally means "self-isolation." If you look in most translations, even important meditative texts, they just translate it as "isolation." You don't get any idea that they're talking about meditation.

The first clue I found was in a text by Maimonides' son, where he speaks about isolation. And he says there are two types of self-isolation—there's external isolation and internal isolation. And using that same word, he says external isolation is going into caves and forests and deserts to be alone with the Divine. Internal isolation, he describes as isolating one's mind from all thought and from all sensation. So Hitbodedut means isolation, but isolation more in the meditative sense than the physical sense—secluding yourself from this world as a way to open yourself to the spiritual world.

Lex Hixon: You write as some length about Ezekiel's vision in the Bible. This is a rare instance in which a prophet spoke about the method of experiencing [meditation] and then described the form of the experience. Can you illustrate what you've said about meditation in terms of Ezekiel's vision?

Rabbi Aryeh Kaplan: According to the Talmud, Ezekiel's experience was experienced by every prophet before him. He was among the last prophets, and he was the only one to explain it.

As it begins, he sees a stormy wind coming from the north and a dark cloud flashing fire. The Zohar explains that these were the different mental states that he was experiencing. When you first start meditating, you feel all the storminess within yourself: All the conflicts, all the problems come to the surface. This is the stormy wind. Then, everything goes blank, and you're in Ezekiel's dark and deep cloud. You feel that there's no place to go, that you're lost. Next, you start seeing a light, but you can't stand it. It's like a fire. If you're not prepared, it will burn you. Then you see the glow, out of the dark.

Lex Hixon: And then, out of that light in Ezekiel's vision, comes the silent voice...

Rabbi Aryeh Kaplan: *Hashmal.* It's a very mystical word, Hashmal, that Ezekiel speaks about, which is translated as "everything." In modern Hebrew, it became the word for electricity, even though it has absolutely no relationship at all to electricity. Hashmal—in the Talmud, it is described as the "speaking silence." One gains a total inner silence, one is able to really listen, and only then one can hear. What people usually ignore in Ezekiel's vision is the very end. The whole vision is a meditation in preparation for hearing the Word.

Listening is probably the most important element in Judaism. In fact, the creed of Judaism begins, "Hear O Israel." We're told that we have to listen, we have to open up our minds and our hearts to hear the truth.

Lex Hixon: Can you share with us one of Rabbi Nachman's actual techniques that people can use in their daily life?

Rabbi Aryeh Kaplan: Rabbi Nachman of Breslov lived around the end of the 18th, beginning of the 19th century. He was a great-grandson of the Baal Shem Tov, who was the founder of the Hasidic movement. He felt that Jewish meditation should be open to anybody. Rabbi Nachman said that if you want to meditate, go out someplace where nobody's going to bother you, a field or a quiet street. Or in a room by yourself under your covers at night, or sitting perhaps in the house of study, looking at a book so nobody will disturb you. Then just talk to God. Talk to the Divine in your own words, quietly, deeply, with longing and yearning for unification. Express your own words to God. Do this, he says, for an hour every day.

This method doesn't require any training. It doesn't require any great knowledge. Just your own words. His students started doing this. Once, one of his students came to him and said, "But Rebbe, Rebbe, I don't have any words. I sit, and nothing comes. What do I do then?"

Rabbi Nachman said, "Take the words, 'Lord of the Universe,' and just say it over and over and over again."

It is told that years later a Hasid came to Rabbi Nachman and said, "In my city, we have a great genius who knows a thousand pages of the Talmud by heart. Can you imagine that?" Rabbi Nachman said, "That's very impressive. But I have a little Hasid who can say the same prayer a thousand times. I consider him to be just as great."

Any person can sit down in a quiet place and just start: "O God, help me. Bring me close to you. I want you. I want to experience you. I want to feel the sweetness and infinite joy of being close to you." Everybody has his own words for this. Rabbi Nachman says that the smallest child, the simplest person could make use of this method, and so can the greatest scholar and the most spiritually advanced person.

Lex Hixon: It's a beautiful unification of all the different levels, and I think that it would be so important if people realized that meditation is something that can be done by the simplest, most childlike person, and the most advanced person. They will see that their soul is the same.

Rabbi Aryeh Kaplan: There's a whole literature on Kabbalistic meditation. You really needed a very, very skilled master; otherwise, it would be very easy to go astray. In his method, Rabbi Nachman felt that anybody who would begin this method would automatically go on the straight path, and could advance without any outside help.

Lex Hixon: Could you give us one more approach to meditation?

Rabbi Aryeh Kaplan: When we talked about the speaking silence, I mentioned the importance of listening. Every Jew knows the creed of the Jew is Shema Yisrael: "Hear, O Israel, the Lord is our God, the Lord is one." Deuteronomy 6:4.

How often do we really think and contemplate what these six words mean? The message there is that God is one, that there's a basic unity to all creation. But first you have to listen, Israel. Listening correctly is essentially a meditative exercise.

Then we say *Hashem Eloheinu*: "The Lord is our God." When we say "our God," it means that we have access to Him, although you're speaking about a unity beyond anything that the human mind can grasp. The first Lubavitcher Rebbe puts it very nicely when he writes that just like the hand cannot grasp a thought, so the mind cannot grasp the Divine. Our God is not abstract. We have access to Him. But first, you have to listen. You have to learn to open your mind, open every cell in your brain, so that this message of unity can enter.

Perhaps the best meditation of all, and one of the most effective that I've used has been to say the Shema itself these six words. Let us just think the words right now: *Shema*, listen; *Yisrael*, Israel; *Hashem*, the Lord; *Eloheinu*, our God; *Hashem*, the Lord; *Ehud*, is One.

Lex Hixon: Can you use that as a mantra? Would that be something to repeat with each breath?

Rabbi Aryeh Kaplan: No, don't repeat. Just say it once, very, very slowly and very, very deeply. Let's try it. I'll be saying Hashem instead of the divine name. But I think the general mood will come across.

Let's prepare ourselves. Actually, the morning service, as introduction to the Shema, starts out by taking us up to the cosmic world, to the world of the stars and the planets. Then the service takes us up even higher to the world of angels. And in the prayer service, we speak about how the angels sing praise; "Holy, holy, holy, is the Lord of Hosts. The whole world is filled with His glory." And we go yet higher. "Blessed is the glory of God from His place." And even higher and higher and higher, until we come to *Havas Elom*, the Universe of Love. And we enter into this universe of love and unification. And finally, when we have reached that level, we're ready to listen. And at that point, we say the Shema: *Shema Yisrael Hashem Eloheinu Hashem Ehud.*

In the Torah, the very next word is translated as "You will love." If you really listen, the love comes of its own.

Lex Hixon: Aryeh, thank you for your scholarship and for your many books, and thank you very much for coming and helping create a *Shabbas* mood. It's been a joy.

Rabbi Aryeh Kaplan: It's my pleasure being here.

Allen Ginsberg
January 2, 1981

Allen Ginsberg was born in Newark, New Jersey, in 1929, and grew up in nearby Paterson. His father was a poet and schoolteacher. His mother's mental illness and communist upbringing became recurring subjects in Ginsberg's own poetry. Ginsberg befriended Beat writers William S. Burroughs and Jack Kerouac while studying at Columbia University, and poet Gary Snyder while living in San Francisco in the 1950s. His first poem, "Howl," published in 1956, was controversial. Obscenity charges brought against his book *Howl and Other Poems* were dismissed in court, but the attention brought him recognition as a new voice in American poetry. A lifelong nonviolent, anti-war, anti-nuclear power, pro-gay rights, and anti-censorship activist, Ginsberg became a practicing Buddhist after meeting Trungpa Rinpoche, and helped him found the Naropa Institute and its Jack Kerouac School of Disembodied Poets in Boulder, Colorado. He lived with his partner, fellow poet Peter Orlovsky, in New York's East Village, where he died in 1997. He remains one of America's most important poets.

Lex Hixon: We're always addressing the theme of religion and the evolution of understanding here. I see contemplative practice as the most revolutionary act one can engage in, because it automatically connects with the efforts of the whole culture to purify and restructure itself.

But today we are going to talk about some serious contemporary revolutionaries. One of them, Allen Ginsberg, is here. Allen, you were a major participant in a radical [theatrical exorcism], the levitation of the Pentagon [in 1967], weren't you?

Allen Ginsberg: I helped work on some of the ideas, but that was Gary Snyder's idea, as far as I know. I was in Venice at the time, sitting next to Ezra Pound one day and talking with him about it. I wrote a little poem about it at the time, but I was far distant. Gary and Keith Lampe and a lot of poets worked on that.

But the levitation of the Pentagon was a pretty successful gesture—it did not leave the ground, of course. So was John Lennon's song, "(Happy Xmas) War Is Over" and Phil Ochs's song, "The War Is Over," and my own poem, "Wichita Vortex Sutra," in which I said, "I here declare the end of the war!" It's simply setting up a counter-image to the powerful imagery hypnosis projected by the government. Somebody up in the government says, "There's a war, you gotta go to it," just because Congress gets together and says so. It's just a lot of words. So the poet or the musician or the artist can set up a counter force field of his own will, or of his own intelligence, or his own perception, and formulate a statement that reaches into the common unconscious of the nation. Because our daily consciousness is drowned out by media consciousness, or by advertising consciousness, the artists can set up a different set of platforms, so that a war doesn't seem so inevitable. You puncture the hot air, basically.

But I don't know if that's going to do any good, actually. I was just looking over some old newspaper clippings. The *New York Times*, April 4, 1977: "Groups Favoring Strong Defense Making Gains in Public Acceptance." This is a story describing the formation of the National Strategy Information Center, and the Committee on Present Danger, which are two pro-military groups who seem to propose heavier and heavier police state and military-industrial concentration in America. Edward Teller, Maxwell Taylor, and all sorts of weird professors and ex-generals, AFL-CIO [president]

Lane Kirkland, and Norman Podhoretz of *Commentary* magazine support it. Those guys are really organized, with a lot of money, from industry. It's like a plutocracy that can supply them with enough money to get them computers and offices, and millions of dollar's worth of stuff.

And also, here in the *Times* on Wednesday, December 17, 1980: "The American Security Council, a conservative defense-oriented group released a television film today, called 'Attack on Americas.' It describes guerrilla warfare in Central America as a threat to the United States. The documentary, with a $1.5-million budget, will be shown on local television stations across the country; a special 16-millimeter version [was] prepared for special showings at church groups." It says, "The organization was begun in Chicago in '55 and has since moved its headquarters to an 850-acre estate in Virginia."

How can anybody fight that kind of stuff? It's such a monolithic accumulation of money....

Lex Hixon: You resist it with the kind of resistance that the Tao has, that bends but doesn't break and isn't monolithic.

Allen Ginsberg: I'm just astounded by the enormity of the computerized organization. For one thing, I was astounded that anyone would have that much interest in getting everything so organized to push their opinion. I get more and more doubtful of my opinion every day, and more and more dubious about my own motives. The idea of Norman Podhoretz organizing armies on a television program just to push their dopey ideas on everybody is just a great piece of egocentric chutzpah, for one thing.

But they do seem almost unbeatable—they did elect a president, and now those Moonies have taken over the hotel next door to WBAI. I just passed by, going to the station. I looked in and there are all those people organized like a beehive. So anybody who wants to just relax and not get organized into a monolithic force really doesn't have much of a chance, because the very nature of just relaxing and enjoying life and taking it easy and pursuing your mind and living a healthy human life seems quite the opposite of this aggressive, inter-organized push to insist on militarization.

Lex Hixon: I think pointing in the direction of uniting "with an ordinary mind" is eschewing the hyper-technical organization and power that capitalism and Marxism have by putting tremendous faith in the power and the rightness of the ordinary mind. From the Buddhist perspective, are we justified in having faith in the ordinary mind, Allen?

Allen Ginsberg: Well, what ordinary mind means in Buddhist terminology is non-panicked mind. Or panicked mind maybe, but at least aware of its panic, and not trying to get out of it by shooting John Lennon, or bombing Russia, or bombing America. Ordinary mind is sort of a catchphrase in Buddhism for avoiding extremes of hysteria or fantasy.

One thing I've been thinking recently, partly because of the experience of going to Eastern countries, is that communism and Marxism don't seem to have any answer. The plutocracy in America, or Nicaragua, or El Salvador, and the plutocratic concentration, like in this Committee of Present Danger, of power heads propagandizing, with armed police enforcing their ideas—don't have an answer either.

I think one problem with the Sixties and Seventies political left in America was that their reference points, like Che Guevera and Mao Tse Tung, dissolved as reliable models or inspiration and the middle class intuitively sensed that. And that's probably why the right wing is on the ascendancy today, because the left really didn't have a positive program, but had a symbolic mystical program depending on the cult of personality, which doesn't make it.

Lex Hixon: But I think people will find that the reference points for the right have no foundation, either.

Allen Ginsberg: Well, definitely not.

Lex Hixon: Possibly that's the effect of ordinary mind, maybe the revolutionary power of it is that all your reference points dissolve.

Allen Ginsberg: When all the reference points have dissolved, then you've got a pretty good chance of trying to think out what's the actual situation. By reference points, I mean the symbolic and sentimental ones. I must say that was something I was guilty of myself for the last 30 years, since my mother was an old Communist. I had a somewhat sentimentalized hope that Communism would work out.

I would say socialism has worked out pretty well in Austria, and maybe in the Scandinavian countries. Austria is neutral, pretty well relaxed. But the Communist idea, I just don't think it's going to work.

Something I've been thinking about after John Lennon's death is how innocent and how good he seemed to be. He accumulated a huge karma of reputation, fame, and money and he tried to deal with it in a very even way: demystifying himself, being a Democrat, walking around in Central Park, signing autographs for autograph hounds, not closing himself off from the world. He worked in politics and became disillusioned, so he registered that publicly and worked it out that way.

He made the great statement: "I don't think I can save the world on a stage." But he was still willing to work. So you could say he espoused a kind of individualistic anarchist openness, a vulnerability like Christ, like the lamb. The traditional vulnerable lamb. But then, when someone shows that vulnerability—either the Communists or the capitalists or the nuts or the power heads—anyone who wants power will rush in and grab it, or kill him, or shoot him. You know, the lamb has no protection.

Lex Hixon: But does the lamb need protection?

Allen Ginsberg: [Yes], I mean, unless you say the function of the lamb is to be crucified over and over, which it may be.

Lex Hixon: Isn't that precisely the function?

Allen Ginsberg: Well, it seems to be the function of the Christian lamb, but I don't know about that. I don't want to get crucified. I don't like the idea.

Lex Hixon: But you've had no police protecting you.

Allen Ginsberg: Well, I'm not that famous. But I assure you, I'm beginning to worry about it. You know, like, wow, what if I say something really truthful, clear, penetrant, so that the light shines out of me? *BAM!*

Lex Hixon: Allen Ginsberg, you've been doing that for a long time!

Allen Ginsberg: I haven't been that clear. The light attracts the darkness. Lennon's sanity attracted worship or inquisitiveness on the part of the insane. The interesting thing is if you get really good, as perhaps Allende was in Chile, open, vulnerable, then you have no protection.

How does vulnerability and innocence protect itself from the inexorable pressure of egocentric power concentration? Do you have to organize against them, apparently?

The gestures we've been making for many years maybe tipped the balance of the Vietnam War, but basically have not cured or even approached the root problem of the concentration of greed, wealth, power, consumerism, and the need for oil in America. Reagan got in by a small majority of voters. Not even a majority. A quarter of the possible voters voted Reagan in. No mandate, no landslide at all. Only a quarter of the possible voters.

I do feel more liberated from older fantasies, more interested in an ordinary mind solution rather than one in which I turn out to be an apocalyptic hero, or anybody else does. How do you find a sensible solution?

Lex Hixon: How about this, Allen: How do you maintain a just society with the chronically distorted human ego in charge of it? There's no other way than to have the egos in charge of it. Can you have illumined sages in charge of your government and in charge of your industry?

Allen Ginsberg: There was that proposition by Plato, the philosopher king. What about the idea of a philosopher king? Is that so repulsive to the democratic American practice? One thing I've been digging lately is we don't have a democratic American practice at all. That's a big myth manipulated by left and right. The development and use of nuclear weapons, the largest single political decision of the century in America, a supposedly democratic land, was actually taken by a small group of plutocrats, or scientists.

Lex Hixon: So I see that possibly what you're suggesting is if you involve a wide range of people in a decision, that you come closer to egolessness.

Allen Ginsberg: We're trying to clear the cobwebs out of our heads, as Burroughs cleared them out of my head, that at present we do not have a functioning democracy in America at all, because the biggest decisions are made by a small group of people, and in secret, and confusing the public purposely.

So, once people realize we're not living in a democracy to begin with, we're living in a place where there are a lot of supermarkets, where everybody has something to eat, but we're not living in a free democracy where there's discussion and decision on the part of the populace—then we might be able to decide what kind of system do we want.

Lex Hixon: I feel that what you're saying clears out cobwebs. I feel that we shouldn't have sweetness and light at the expense of a critical analysis of the flaws—not only of the capitalist system, but the Marxist system, the ego system.

Allen Ginsberg: And the anarchist system. And the religious flower-power system.

None of them seems to have provided a *modus operandi* system for an overpopulated world.

Lex Hixon: And when these reference points dissolve, then there's a possibility of discovering ordinary mind. There's a possibility of tremendous power being generated from the people. Just like you do fission or fusion with an ordinary atom and you create tremendous power.

Allen Ginsberg: There was an idea that a real democracy would be more or less in line with what you were suggesting, which is that individuals would change their own cells. That is, the cell of the social body is the individual, and that the individual is cleaning up his own act, beginning where he is, which is his own body and his own mind and his own speech. He could then maybe cumulatively have an effect on the whole scene.

But on the other hand, you've got to realize it's not likely that a majority of people will clean up their act. In fact, it gets dirtier and dirtier and more and more violent. It may be a large enough minority to help, but it doesn't quite cultivate the conditions that you idealize as democracy. Still, the most reliable idea is that people have got to clean themselves up, and then they can have some effective relationship with the rest of the world that's a little less aggressive and disruptive.

Lex Hixon: And I think that saints and sages in various cultures have come to this kind of hypercritical analysis of the human situation.

Allen Ginsberg: Now, assuming you have maybe five million people in the United States of America "cleaned up," what do they do? How do they organize? Do they organize? Do they just do their thing where they are and spread that cleanup sensation around? In their office? In their garbage dump? In their poetry school? Or on the radio?

Lex Hixon: They do magic and counter-magic and counter-counter magic.

Allen Ginsberg: But that's still not integrated.

Lex Hixon: I'm not so sure, Allen. I'm not so sure.

Allen Ginsberg: Well, they're safe, certainly.

Lex Hixon: I'm not even sure it's safe. You said yourself that one would have thought that Lennon was safe, if anyone was safe.

Allen Ginsberg: That was a shock that Lennon is not safe from volcanos, he's not safe from tornados and rude winds from the cosmos. He's not safe from the rude wind of paranoia or the confusion of an individual autograph hound. He's not safe from natural accident. It's really interesting, because it's like Christ's situation. Maybe I'm overdramatizing the purity, but he was a good guy, basically.

Lex Hixon: I feel the same way, but I feel that there's something that Christ demonstrated, and other great visionaries that have been sacrificed like that. They've demonstrated something very powerful that has infused human beings deeply for centuries and centuries afterward. I don't know if John Lennon's energy will be that extensive, but it certainly has infused millions of people in this present moment.

Allen Ginsberg: The words and music of Lennon's songs as well as his performances of them are permanently around. Even if the electric plug gets pulled, there are still the tunes and the words in people's heads. John Lennon stood victorious in the sense that everybody realized the impact of his death. As soon as he perished, they realized that they had lost something intrinsically good and pure. I thought immediately, "My God, that guy probably laid more physical joy on the entire world than the whole pack of politicians—every one of them laid some fear trip. But Lennon actually physically gave some real lamb-like joy."

Lex Hixon: And so do you, Allen Ginsberg. We're really grateful for you.

Father Daniel Berrigan
July 1981

Peace activist and writer Father Daniel Berrigan was born in 1921 in Minnesota, and raised in Syracuse, New York. In 1939, he entered the Jesuit Order, and was ordained in 1952. He and his brother Philip, also then a priest, founded the Catholic Peace Fellowship, which denounced the Vietnam War as immoral, and participated in the historic Civil Rights march at Selma, Alabama. In 1968, Father Berrigan and eight accomplices, known as the "Catonsville Nine," raided the Catonsville, Maryland, draft-board office, and burned hundreds of files. In 1980, he founded Plowshares, an anti-nuclear arms group whose first act was raiding a missile manufacturing plant in King-of-Prussia, Pennsylvania, and hammering on missile cones. Often arrested for his protests, Father Berrigan spent almost seven years in prison. He has taught at Le Moyne College, Cornell University, and Fordham University, and has reflected on his career in 35 books of essays and poetry. He died in New York City on April 30, 2016.

Lex Hixon: Father Daniel Berrigan and seven of his dear friends [committed] a very radical, spiritual, artistic, political act by breaking into a General Electric [GE] plant in King-of-Prussia, Pennsylvania, and damaging some weapons being produced there. In a week or so, they will go on trial in Pennsylvania for doing that. Father Berrigan is going to tell us the saga of that action.

Daniel Berrigan: Well, "saga" is a very nice word; I don't know whether we deserve such a word. We looked upon what we did as a modest attempt in a bad time to cry out from the heart of the world about life, about death as a social enterprise, and about a religious tradition. Part of the hopelessness the world feels about the nuclear impasse is this technological lockstep that has the technocrats saying, "Nothing can be done or should be done, and don't embarrass us with ethics. Don't embarrass us with the fate of the children either. Let's make war our business and let's be serious about it."

We wanted to introduce the idea that it's possible to start over by identifying what could be *undone*. We wanted to show that we were not hopelessly tangled in that skein of murder that started at the Hiroshima bombing. Any religious tradition worth its salt will have to be able to say that to the kings and satraps and shahs and juntas: "People can start over. What has been done badly can be undone well."

We were thinking also, how ironic, that in all the hundreds and hundreds of international talks about disarmament since Hiroshima, not a single weapon has been destroyed. The weapons stockpile that has been mounting and mounting and mounting is a crime against the future, a crime against the cosmos. So we thought it was significant that we did disarm, we did destroy two manifestly atrocious first-strike weapons, and they will not be dropped on children. That's a pretty good accomplishment. I'd be willing to die having said I had done that. We eight people, wandering into that plant, did what no one had ever done since the first bomb was put together. So, without making a big deal about it, I think that was quite a morning: September 9, 1980.

Over a period of months, we had tried to decide what could be done if something was to be done. We had been at the Pentagon and the White House and the Congress for years, trying to yell and scream about the genocidal madness that was underway, but nobody had ever invaded one of these plants. They went on churning out their doomsday machinery day after day and year after year. So we thought, "Well, maybe it would awaken people, and stir the imagination, if we could destroy one of these weapons."

The Mark 12A missile, as Daniel Ellsberg has said, is one of the two or three clearest indications of first-strike willingness on the part of the United States. This weapon makes no sense as a deterrent. It means to hit the hard installations of the enemy before they can discharge their weaponry. What that comes down to is simply this: that on some morning, when some general, or group of them, has been personally piqued or provoked—or when they have been prodded from the State Department or from the multinational corporate world or from the White House—[they] will simply push a button, under the mad pretext that we can be winners on the last day of creation.

We know that this whole structure is out of [the] control of anything like a sensible authority when you have [Alexander] Haig passing from the armed forces to the chairmanship of United Technologies, which is currently concocting the Trident submarine, and then back to the State Department. We know that anything like the separation of powers is a pure fiction, and that the worlds of the big buck and the big bang are one.

Daniel Ellsberg called us after our action and said if he had the opportunity of choosing any one weapon of the U.S. arsenal to destroy, he would have chosen the Mark 12A. So that reassured us.

First of all, on that day, the plant was surprisingly accessible. The guards were unarmed and seemed fairly indifferent to anything like high-level security. Well, we did—against all chances—get into that plant. We thought that perhaps we had a 30 percent chance of reaching one of those weapons. We had no interior maps. We knew that the re-entry cones were stored there in a highly secret area, but whether or not we could ever get to them seemed to us a very slim chance. Well, within three minutes of entering the plant, we were there with the weapons right in front of us. We couldn't help but believe we had been led there by a very unusual providence. We were carrying small hammers and bottles of our own blood, and we had two plans. If we reached the weapon we would destroy whatever we could. They're made of a ceramic which is heat-resistant since they have to reenter the atmosphere and withstand that heat, so they're extraordinarily brittle and they can be easily broken. We destroyed two of the nuclear reentry cones and one interior metal sheath, which evidently lines the cone. As a bonus to our day, we found all sorts of secret documents spread carelessly about on planning tables, and were able to pour our blood all over them and rip them up before we were surrounded by the usual authorities, and at that point we lay down the hammers and bottles, formed a circle and prayed until we were carted away.

Our group includes very interesting people. I would like to mention each of them. Molly Rush is a mother of six from Pittsburgh. She had been working out of a center called the Thomas Merton Center in Pittsburgh for about six years, and had been arrested several times at corporate headquarters around the Pittsburgh area. She came to our action after long months of preparation in her own family for this quite risky business. It is really most moving.

Anne Montgomery is a sister, teaching in New York, here in East Harlem. She has taught among the poor for many years, and brings to us the tradition and discipline of her order, and, of course, has drawn her order into this whole serious business of peacemaking.

Then we have a graduate of Yale Divinity School who has been working for many years in New Haven at a peace center. We have a lawyer and the father of three children, who has been doing great work, since we were all arrested, with prisoners at the county jail there in King-of-Prussia. My brother Phillip, [who was] a Catholic priest, is now married and the father of two. Elmer Moss was a professor of history for many years, and is an outstanding musician. Carl Cabot [is] a priest who comes to our group after many years of working among the wretched of the earth in northeastern Brazil. And then [there's] myself, who most recently has been working with the dying here in New York City, and writing, and talking around the country on the whole question of nuclear arms, and getting arrested periodically, too.

So we feel that the community of eight people who assembled for that action can speak to various backgrounds and vocations, and we're very grateful for one another.

The texts that we meditated on in the days immediately preceding our action were from the Prophet Isaiah and the great promise that the swords will be beaten into plowshares. We took our name, the Plowshares 8, from that text. It's a very interesting text because it speaks about force. The original says the weapons are "beaten, broken, and refashioned." Those texts came out of a period of extraordinary violence and turmoil and, I think, point clearly to the fact that peace is not just conferred. People have to beat a peaceful existence out of the implements, the horrors, the mentality that makes war. There is simply no way that we are going to be able to turn this business of nuclear extinction as a political and social method around, except by some kind of crazy adherence to this word. But politicians are not going to confer plowshares and a peaceable community. The people are going to decide whether or not the people and their children are going to survive.

Lex Hixon: Father Berrigan, you're still a member of the Jesuit Order in good standing. What do your Jesuit superiors feel about your action, and how far can they support you in this? How does it relate to the Church?

Daniel Berrigan: Well, Lex, since, let's say, '68 in Catonsville, [Maryland], when we destroyed the draft files, there's been an enormous change in the Order. I suppose it might be reflective of the changes in the Catholic Church in this country, but right now there's a good solid support for what we did. I remember when we were sitting in the pokey right after this action at King-of-Prussia, my superior came down from New York to say thank you. And after I got out on bail, he organized a New York group of Jesuits to spend an evening with me because he said it was the question for all of us.

Lex Hixon: So, in the course of a little bit more than 10 years between your action in Catonsville and now in the Jesuit Order, and in a lot of places, there has been an actual awakening to the vital relevance of the actions that you're taking. What are the prospects for the trial? You won't plead "not guilty," will you?

Daniel Berrigan: Yes, we'll plead not guilty because that's the way you get a trial and that's the public forum where you have a chance to make the arguments for why you did what you did. We're going to be tried in an extraordinarily fascist atmosphere down there. I've thought of it many times as a kind of "Mississippi north." I've been before a lot of courts in my checkered career, but I've never seen anything quite like that place. We're going to have to try to get ethical people and weapons experts and international law experts heard in the courtroom, but with a small chance that they will be.

Lex Hixon: Yes, I remember that the precedent was set in the trials during the Vietnam War, where the judges wouldn't entertain moral arguments as admissible.

Daniel Berrigan: Well, see, it isn't merely that they won't admit a moral argument or, let's say, even an international law argument. They won't even admit expert testimony on what was going on in that plant. The economy is so tightly dovetailed with the courts and the jails down there that you're really facing GE [General Electric] in the courtroom. And, of course, if the main income of a given area is genocidal weapons, the spiritual pollution in the public structure is really terrifying.

Lex Hixon: Do you have good lawyers representing you?

Daniel Berrigan: Ramsey Clark is helping out, and then there are two very fine local lawyers down there, but we're going to defend ourselves.

Lex Hixon: Is there any chance of that being televised?

Daniel Berrigan: The question has come up and, of course, the judge practically dropped his shoes with the laces tied when he heard that, because the last thing that those people want is any sort of public witness to their own contempt for the law. We're going to press the point, but I think the only people they are going to listen to are the media.

Lex Hixon: So you're going to be tried by a jury of local people in the King-of-Prussia courthouse?

Daniel Berrigan: Yes, and that, again, is going to be very interesting because the numbers of eligible adults who are connected directly or indirectly with GE is just overwhelming. I think we'd do best at present to sort of look on this thing as an example of the worst case and start from there.

Lex Hixon: Are you encouraging people to come?

Daniel Berrigan: We have sent out a lot of information on the action and the trial and are very happy if people can come, even for one day. I think it would be an enormously powerful education for them, as well as very heartening for us. We're also going to have public sessions every night during the trial down there in which the experts are going to be speaking to the public as they were denied that opportunity during the day, and the Plowshares defendants will be there, too.

Lex Hixon: Some people may know Daniel Berrigan mostly as one of our fine, contemporary poets. He's so involved in this action that he didn't even bring any of his recent poetry along. Can you talk a little bit about how your artistic life and your spiritual life and your political life have come together in the intimate way they have?

Daniel Berrigan: I'll try. I think the history of our own lifetime since the Civil Rights movement will show us that the test of the humanity of a political or social movement is the art that it produces. That immediately brings up the question: What is our vision of a human being and a human community? And then what symbols are available to us in order to dramatize the way we want to live, to awaken us to new ways of being human?

For many, many years, we've been drawing deeply on the primordial symbols, which have always been able to refresh and restore and verify human life at its source. We have poured our blood numerous times—blood, of course, being a symbol of life itself—and we've dug graves, which I think is, again, a very powerful idea, especially when the graves are empty, since that demonstrates the idea of life over death. We have planted trees right in the courtyard of the Pentagon. We have spread ashes and enacted the Last Day that will reduce the whole world to a moonscape. We have tried to find and energize the resources for a new start over these years. And, of course, poetry, street drama, dance, song must be part of our work. I don't think that there can be any step taken in the direction of social action without the arts playing a very powerful role.

My brother Philip's latest book, *Of Beastly Symbols and Images*, has been published on the West Coast. It is his record of life in community and outreach and public responsibility in the last 10 years.

Lex Hixon: Do you live in New York City?

Daniel Berrigan: I live in a Jesuit community here in Manhattan.

Lex Hixon: What about your recent writings? What can we look for?

Daniel Berrigan: Well, my last book just came out a couple of months ago here in New York. It is the stories of the dying people that I worked with in the last three years here in the cancer hospital. I got very attached to people and we worked through their last days together, and I just tell their stories.

J. Krishnamurti
March 31, 1982

Jiddu Krishnamurti was born in the village of Madanapalle in the south of British India in 1895. As a young boy, he was identified by theosophists Charles Webster Leadbeater and Annie Besant as the Theosophical Society's expected World Teacher. They directed Krishnamurti's education. They first took Krishnamurti with them to Europe in 1911, when the Order of the Star was formed to support his work. Following the death of his brother in 1922, Krishnamurti began to find his own voice. In 1929, he dissolved the Order of the Star, returning all the money that had been raised for him, and became an independent teacher. For the next 50 or more years, based at home in Ojai, California, he lectured around the world, reminding people constantly that we are human beings first, not a nationality, caste, religion, or any other divisive identity. Krishnamurti also cautioned his followers to care for the environment. His books include *The First and Last Freedom, The Only Revolution, The Book of Life,* and many more. Krishnamurti purposely left behind only a large archive of talks and writings, but no successors to continue his work after his death in 1986.

Lex Hixon: J. Krishnamurti was the first representative of deeper truth that I can remember reading. He has touched many generations all over the world, so I am very grateful that I have a chance to talk with him today, face to face.

I thought the best way to proceed would be to give the listeners some sense of the direct process of investigation he describes, which has helped to clarify so many people's minds. I've seen this process unfold during the last three days of seminars I have attended with Krishnaji. It is a careful and rigorous step-by-step approach to truth. Krishnaji is always slowing people down, because we Westerners want to jump immediately to the conclusion instead of examining things gradually. But he also reminded us constantly to observe the reality that the words point to with a sense of urgency.

Maybe I'll just begin by asking about how you describe this process of the inquiry itself. What does it mean to inquire in this way, Krishna-ji?

J. Krishnamurti: Sir, there are many problems all over the world. There are problems of starvation, problems of war and violence, and a general degeneration of human beings everywhere. I think we ought to inquire into this very complex situation, which is becoming more and more dangerous. There's the threat of nuclear war, which I doubt will ever take place. I hope it won't, but there is a threat.

Lex Hixon: You've pointed out that these complex problems, which appear to be outside of us, really are reflections of internal problems in our thinking process.

J. Krishnamurti: You can't have social order if there is no order within each one of us. Through our violence, enviousness, and greed we have created this society. We are the ones who have to change it, not the politicians, not the engineers. As human beings, we have to bring about order in ourselves. The world is the mirror in which we see ourselves.

Lex Hixon: So first we need to see things as they are?

J. Krishnamurti: As they are! Not distorted by prejudice, by opinion, by conclusions, by ideas. Just see things as they are. We see how Russia and America are going on building their armies and how every nationalistic country is doing the same. That's a fact. See it as it is. Why are human beings doing this? Because it is the easiest way to escape from what is. We don't know how to face what is. We don't actually understand what is. We always have this idea of what is and what should be. So this tendency to escape from actuality is at the root of this problem.

Lex Hixon: Why does this tendency to escape arise?

J. Krishnamurti: We don't know how to solve this problem. We are so conditioned to accept things as they are, to accept things like war, like violence, greed, and anger. We say that this is the most natural instinct of man.

Lex Hixon: How are we to get back in tune with the awareness, which simply observes things as they are.

J. Krishnamurti: Sir, that means looking at ourselves in the mirror of society. All the human beings throughout the world with their grandparents have created this society. This society is the expression of each one of us. That's a fact. Now, do we say, "This is the fact, so unless I change fundamentally, I cannot possibly stop war or change society"? No, we don't want to say that. We don't want to change fundamentally.

Lex Hixon: Then simply by seeing that clearly, will this fundamental change you're talking about arise spontaneously?

J. Krishnamurti: No, sir. Spontaneity can only exist when one is free. But we are not free. We are born and we live in prisons of our own making. And when we become aware that we are living in our own conditioning, then real trouble begins. We don't want to face it because it means unconditioning the mind from all our traditions, our nationalism, and religious beliefs, which are all our inventions. So, if you are concerned with the tragedy of this world; the misery, confusions, sorrow of these human beings, then you are involved in resolving it. You are responsible for all that you do. When there is the ending of suffering, there is love. That love is just there like the perfume of a flower. It is there! You see, we have always this idea that we must cultivate something. You can't cultivate love! Love is there when selfishness is not.

Lex Hixon: Is there any way that the limited self can bring about this state of affairs.

J. Krishnamurti: No, sir, because whatever that limited self does will always be limited.

Lex Hixon: So you're proposing that there is a complicated state of limitation in the external and the internal world. And then there is this state of love, which is not limited. It seems you're proposing two universes floating side by side.

J. Krishnamurti: No, sir. No. First of all, sir, what is happening in the world is created by each human being. And it's like a tide, going out and coming in. We have created the world and the world then shapes us. It's a constant movement, interrelating with the world and oneself. The world with its wars, brutality, anger, jealousy, and suffering, is not different from me. In my limited action, I create this horror. That's a fact.

So if you don't want to accept things as they are, as most people do, you begin to inquire into the whole process to find out why human beings have become brutal, violent, and nationalistic. Why have they become like this? After a million years. What's wrong? They are not changed, basically. The primitive man was jealous, anxious, frightened, and still, we are just like that! So, I believe one begins to inquire: Why? Why have human beings who are educated and living in an affluent society created a society where the rich people are getting richer and the poor people are becoming poorer, all over the world. Why? What's wrong?

Each one of us in this country must feel responsible for what is happening in Afghanistan and Beirut, what's happening in all the places where there is hunger and starvation. We are responsible because we have made separate America, Russia, and India. Do you follow why there is this terrible conflict?

Lex Hixon: Let's assume that someone is capable of feeling the reality of responsibility for the world. Does a particular action or insight follow?

J. Krishnamurti: Sir, you can't assume such a tremendous reality.

Lex Hixon: But I can assume that you feel this responsibility, or else you wouldn't be able to talk about it.

J. Krishnamurti: I'm not a hypocrite, I hope. I wouldn't talk about any of these things if I really didn't live it.

Lex Hixon: Exactly. So, at least we can assume in one case that someone has this full sense of responsibility. The question remains: Does some sort of action issue from it?

J. Krishnamurti: Of course an action must issue from it. That is, if I'm married and have children, my responsibility is to those children. How I educate them. The education will condition them so they can stand in their own vital strength, and not be driven in a particular direction. If I love them, I don't want them to kill or be killed.

Lex Hixon: But if you've taken responsibility for the entire human race, then it would seem that a different order of action has to come into being.

J. Krishnamurti: You are what you are. And if you realize that what you are has created all this ugliness, you start where you are.

Is it possible for one human being to radically transform himself? That is the responsibility.

Lex Hixon: So is that the essential action?

J. Krishnamurti: That's a tremendous action which involves my relationships. If I am married, it could be the relationship with my wife. That's a relationship where there may be fear or anxiety, and from that place, we can begin to see how as a self-centered human being, we act. We are talking of becoming absolutely selfless. That is my responsibility, because otherwise I can't bring about a change in myself or in the world.

Lex Hixon: But the problem remains that we are a fully-conditioned self, so there's no way to make that self into something selfless.

J. Krishnamurti: Of course not.

Lex Hixon: There appears to be an impasse.

J. Krishnamurti: No, sir. Impasse exists only when we don't observe the whole movement of the self. Right? What is the self? What is it craving? What is it doing in the world? Suppose I am self-centered: What are my actions? My actions will all be self-centered actions that keep me separate. Therefore, I am separate from you. I am separate and against everybody, including my wife, including my children, because I'm self-centered.

I may talk about love and responsibility, but as long as I am self-centered, I must act in that narrow, limited way. Now, is it possible, living in this world, not to be self-centered? Which means, do I realize the consequences and observe the activities of self-centeredness?

Lex Hixon: Who is it that is making this pure observation? It is certainly not the conditioned self.

J. Krishnamurti: The conditioned self cannot be purely aware because it's conditioned awareness. So, I inquire, "Why am I conditioned? What are the factors that condition me?"

Lex Hixon: So the conditioned mind looks at itself.

J. Krishnamurti: We are doing it now. Aren't you making it too difficult?

Lex Hixon: Well, you've been thinking about it for so many more years than I have. I hope someday to be as simple and direct as you are about it.

J. Krishnamurti: It is so simple. If I am conditioned as an Arab, right? And you, Lex are conditioned as a Jew, then because of that conditioning, we are at each others' throats. But we are really both just human beings. It's so clear.

Lex Hixon: But the difficulty is how to do it. How do we just be the human being and stop being the Arab or the Jew?

J. Krishnamurti: Don't be an Arab or a Jew. Let's be human beings, which means, don't be self-centered.

Lex Hixon: Can that be done as an act of will?

J. Krishnamurti: No.

Lex Hixon: So, the question of this over-serious interviewer remains: How do we make that transition to simply being a human being?

J. Krishnamurti: Sir, follow the inquiry: What is one of the causes of war? Go into it slowly. What is one of the causes? It's nationalism, right? Russia and America are made separate by nationalism—that means conflict, right? Economic, social conflict—ultimately war. Logically, it is so. So I won't be a nationalist. I'm finished with it because my intention is that I don't want to kill anybody because of my flag or my country. It's obvious. It doesn't need will. I am finished with nationalism.

Lex Hixon: But, as you pointed out, the conditioning process is so complex. It goes much beyond nationalism.

J. Krishnamurti: I begin with what I can observe. Logically. I can see the consequence of nationalism or competition. They are destroying people. Right?

Lex Hixon: And the human being can simply say, "I am not going to engage in nationalism or competition anymore"?

J. Krishnamurti: It is simple. If you don't want to compete, you end it. You don't want it.

Lex Hixon: You say that we can drop the desire to compete, but the question is, "Can we drop the whole thing?"

J. Krishnamurti: Wrong, sir! We say we can drop, but we don't do it!

Lex Hixon: But we are capable of doing it.

J. Krishnamurti: If you want to do anything, you can do it. But that means we have to learn what this conditioning is, you have to really observe the conditioning. You're not looking at it as you would look at a precious jewel. Look at it! Don't run away from it. Don't try to escape from it, or transcend it or suppress it. As you look at it, you see all the play of light, the beauty, the colors, it reveals more and more. But as you keep looking at it, finally it loses its glitter.

Lex Hixon: It is direct and simple, the way you express it, but I worry that maybe it's something only you can do. Being in the presence of someone like yourself who has dropped the entire conditioned realm—it helps one see the possibility.

J. Krishnamurti: It can be done. If one human being has done it, the others can do it.

Lex Hixon: The very fact that you say it is a transmission of energy. The core of it seems to be: "I don't want to be selfish. I don't want to be self-centered." That seems to be the core.

J. Krishnamurti: You can't just say, "I don't want to be selfish." It means nothing. First you must say, "What is the nature of the self? What is the structure of it?" Then begin to inquire, what is selfishness in [your] relationship to another, and observe in that relationship how [you] behave, how [you're] always thinking subtly behind all the words, of [your] own fulfillment, [your] own desires, so there is no relationship, like two railway lines that never meet.

Lex Hixon: So the essence of getting to the problem is that vast inquiry into the self.

J. Krishnamurti: You know, the Greeks had the saying, "Know thyself." Hindus have put the same thing in different words. And I say, "Look, I'm going to find out. What is the self? Can I know it?" You can begin to unfold like an onion, peel after peel, and at the end of it, there is nothing left.

Lex Hixon: And then there's love.

J. Krishnamurti: Later! You can't say that you have done it.

Lex Hixon: Well, you've done it. If you hadn't done it, then this conversation would be meaningless. If I was talking to someone who just speculated about this possibility, it would be a waste of time to talk about it.

J. Krishnamurti: Of course. Naturally. But that requires, sir, a great deal of inquiry, observation, deep honesty. Real honesty. Don't say anything that you don't mean. Don't say or think one thing and do quite the opposite.

Lex Hixon: Many people feel that there must be some sort of practice; some sort of method they can apply to this situation to eradicate this sort of selfishness.

J. Krishnamurti: We talked about it the other day, when we had the seminar. When you have a system, obviously, you practice. You follow it. And that makes the mind more dull.

Lex Hixon: So the practice is simply the action of observing and inquiring?

J. Krishnamurti: It all depends [on] if one is profoundly honest. We are such hypocrites. Right? We have got so many masks we put on. We are never free of them. Never without a single mask. To have no mask at all is really freedom.

Lex Hixon: I think that is certainly the essence of the matter. Thank you, thank you, Krishna-ji.

Krishnamurti as a young man

Rick Fields
March 14, 1982

A historian of Buddhism in the West and a poet and journalist, Rick Fields was born in Queens, in New York City, in 1942. He attended Harvard as a track star, but left before completing his degree. Back in New York City, he encountered Zen and met Allen Ginsberg and other Beat poets before moving to California, where he studied at the Zen Centers in San Francisco and Los Angeles. In the early 1970s, he became interested in Tibetan Buddhism, and in 1973 became a student of Chogyam Trungpa Rinpoche. His first work as a journalist was for the *Whole Earth Catalog* in 1969. Later, he was the editor of both *Yoga Journal* and *Vajradhatu Sun*, which became *Shambhala Sun*, and a contributing editor of *Tricycle* and *New Age Journal*. Fields also taught at Naropa Institute's Jack Kerouac School of Disembodied Poetics. His books include *How the Swans Came to the Lake: A Narrative History of Buddhism in America* (1991), and *Instructions to the Cook: A Zen Master's Lessons in Living a Life That Matters*, written with Bernie Glassman (1996). His last book, *Fuck You, Cancer and Other Poems* (1997) dealt with his experience with lung cancer. He died at home in Fairfax, California, in 1999. He was 57.

Lex Hixon: My dear Dharma brother Rick Fields is here in the studio with me. He's written a book called *How the Swans Came to the Lake: A Narrative History of Buddhism in America,* published by Shambhala in 1981. It's a magnificent book, and we are going to be talking about it today. It's not just about how Buddhism came to America and how it evolved here, but it's also the story of the early contacts that Westerners had with Buddhism before it came to the West.

How long did you work on this book, Rick?

Rick Fields: Oh, about five years.

Lex Hixon: Five years to trace the history and put it into a harmonious form that's a joy to read. It's successful, not just as a thorough piece of history, but it actually gives the feeling of what the life of the Dharma is like. You make some remarkable connections.

Can you tell us briefly how Rick Fields came to Buddhism, or how Buddhism came to Rick Fields?

Rick Fields: Probably in much the way it happened to a lot of other people. It was just a matter of coming across the teaching of meditation at the time when the whole inner world was opening up during the Sixties. More precisely, I think that Buddhism attracted me because it is so straightforward and down to earth. I first began reading the Buddhist texts when I was working in a hospital in Detroit as an orderly, and saw somebody die for the first time. I'd been reading a collection by Edward Conze that talked about the body as being perishable, so it kind of struck home for me.

Shortly after that, I was living in Mexico and reading *The Surangama Sutra,* about attaining enlightenment through the senses. So I picked hearing as the sense to meditate on. We used to sit on a hill and meditate while listening to the bells and the wind. When I came back to America, I wanted to look deeper into the practice of meditation. Somehow I came across a Zen Buddhist teacher here in New York, Reverend Nakajima, who had a small Soto Zendo on the Upper West Side of Manhattan. It was very lowkey. He was the one who introduced me to the practice of [sitting] Zazen. I had been raised as an atheist, so when he said that Buddhism was nontheistic, it made sense as a spiritual way that I could relate to.

Lex Hixon: And where did you go after learning to do Zazen with Reverend Nakajima?

Rick Fields: I went out to California, where I found Shunryu Suzuki Roshi at the San Francisco Zen Center, and I spent some time at Tassajara and learned more about how to sit. Eventually, I met Chogyam Trungpa Rinpoche when he first came to this country.

I think, for me, it was the teaching that cuts away illusion and the simplicity of the sitting meditation that was most attractive. I liked the no-frills approach.

Lex Hixon: Rick is continuing his practice with Trungpa Rinpoche, but also he's done some intensive sitting with Maezumi Roshi in the Zendo in Los Angeles. So he practices some Buddhist universality, which is reflected in his book.

I would say that this is one of the first of many books in the field of religion and spirituality that will be written by people who are practitioners. It does definitely give a different flavor.

If some of you are wondering who Suzuki Roshi is, and where Tassajara is, there is a whole world that will open up for you if you read this book.

I happened to read the advance galleys to the book on the way to India when I made a Buddhist pilgrimage this fall. I knew that Thoreau and Emerson were part of Buddhist history in the West, but I hadn't heard of people like Sir William Jones, an amazing Englishman who went to India ostensibly because of business, but ended up having a tremendous karmic connection to the spirituality and the culture, and did incredible pioneering work. And you reintroduced people like Colonel Olcott, the theosophist, who did tremendous work to try to unify Buddhists from different Asian countries for the very first time.

Rick Fields: One of the interesting things that arose when I was doing the research was how much influence Westerners had on Buddhist history, and vice versa. The history didn't just start in the Fifties and Sixties, but has roots going way, way back, to the Parliament of the World's Religions in 1893, and, as you said, Thoreau and Emerson. This coming together of the East and West is something that has been going on for a very, very long time. It's more of a dynamic process, rather than a pop explosion.

Lex Hixon: In the book, you talk about how Emerson was actually more drawn to the Vedanta of Hinduism, whereas Thoreau seems to have had the spirit of a Buddhist practitioner. Thoreau is really a core example of the searching quality in American spirituality. I'm a great admirer of his. We even gave one of our daughters Thoreau as a middle name.

Rick Fields: That's great. I always thought of him as an American Taoist. Thoreau was a natural contemplative, and he talked about going down to the rock bottom of existence, which is more of a Buddhist way of expressing something. I don't think he would necessarily call himself a Buddhist, but he certainly inspired me to look at our own culture as having that common contemplative meditative experience.

Lex Hixon: Thoreau essentially did that very thing that you were inspired by the sutra to do in Mexico. And it just surfaced naturally in him. But we don't know how much he may have studied.

Rick Fields: Actually he studied quite a bit. In those days, an educated person read English, but also Greek and French and German. So the Transcendentalists were reading all the latest translations from Europe as they were coming out. Sir William Jones, who we mentioned earlier, was like their D.T. Suzuki. He was somebody that they read very, very closely. They were reprinting these texts in *The Dial* magazine that Emerson, and later Thoreau, published. They called them "ethnical scriptures." The first Buddhist Sutra ever published in America was published in *The Dial* magazine. It was the Lotus Sutra, translated from the French by Thoreau himself.

Lex Hixon: We are not dealing here simply with teachings and sutras, but essentially with the great power that awakens inside people's minds spontaneously. There is little or nothing that could be considered conversion or proselytizing, wouldn't you say, Rick?

Rick Fields: No, not much. Traditionally, you do have to ask three times for teachings. It's spontaneous, but there is a practice of meditation that is a very individual path. It's your own mind that you're sitting down with.

Lex Hixon: I think your book is a classic. I don't know if anyone else will spend five years of their life writing anything like it. Even if they did, they wouldn't have the flair you have for bringing all this alive, and for weaving and interweaving the Asian and American aspects in such a harmonious way. Do you have any other reflections about what you wanted to do in this book?

Rick Fields: When I was looking for a way to begin the book, there was a sentence that turned out not to be in the book, but it came to me as a sudden flash, which was "Any book about Buddhism begins with Gautama." So the book begins with the story of the Buddha. This is the central truth or the central experience that all the various forms of Buddhism have in common, which is reflected in the practice of sitting meditation and mindfulness. I wanted to bring it all together. Buddhism began in India and went to all these different countries all over the world, China, Japan, Tibet, Southeast Asia, and developed along very specific lines in those countries, matching the cultural genius of each place.

The interesting thing is that in America, the Buddhism from all these places is coming together. It's as if Buddhism is coming home to this country, as if America is the India of this time, in a very interesting way. It was that journey that I wanted to show and trace.

Lex Hixon: I know that people in the Zen Community of New York in the Bronx have all been reading the book. It's not only educating people who as yet know very little about Buddhism, but also Buddhist practitioners who might be in a certain stream, and they are only vaguely aware of some of the other streams, and might not know very much about the roots of Buddhism in America. The book is having an effect of bringing American Buddhists together and letting them know about each other. Not that it will ever be any sort of monolithic religion.

Rick Fields: An important thing about Buddhism is that it is passed from person to person in what's called a lineage. One person teaches another person, and so on, right from the time of the Buddha up to the present. So it's very personal, and I think that gives it strength and vitality. At the same time, it makes it somewhat difficult because you're dealing with human beings, you're not dealing with an abstract idea.

Lex Hixon: I really feel grateful to you for writing this book. When I read it on the plane going to India, returning to the land of Shakyamuni to visit the place where he was enlightened and gave his teaching, I felt that I was in an immense circular drama.

Rick Fields: Buddhism has always been a way of looking at the world that is almost like that of refugee. It's traveled naturally, perhaps more than most religions, from one place to another. From the very beginning, the Buddha saw it not as part of any particular culture. I think it was the first world religion to have that message of universality. It was not about any cultural setting or any belief or dogma, but it was about directly looking at the nature of mind.

Lex Hixon: And we don't know what the next generation of Buddhism will bring in America. As you say in your book, the students of the great Zen Masters who came in the '30s and '40s to this country, and the earlier students of the ones who came to the Parliament of the World's Religions in 1893, could barely even sit for meditation.

Rick Fields: Five minutes was considered a long period of meditation. As a matter of fact, there are stories of some ladies fainting after five minutes of meditation. It's hard to say why now people can go into a Zen Center and sit for the first time for 40 minutes.

Lex Hixon: Now, some of the Tibetan lamas' students are doing *ngöndro* practice, which involves, among other things, 100,000 prostrations. No one can look past the stage where they are, so we don't know which direction Buddhism is going to go in the next generation, or the future. Maybe it will reveal itself as the practice of seeing into the nature of mind, but not necessarily bound up with culture and traditional practices. That's where I think Zen may be the door into the future of Buddhism in this country.

Rick Fields: I think that's happening already. The practice of Buddhism is not really limited to any particular practice or to living any particular lifestyle.

Lex Hixon: Thank you so much, Rick, for researching and writing this important book, and for coming to talk with us about it. You found some wonderful unique material, like this gem that I'm going to ask you to read to end the program. It features D.T. Suzuki, who made critically important contributions to our culture, particularly the series of lectures he gave at Columbia University in the Fifties and his many writings and translations that opened up Mahayana Buddhism to Americans.

Here's the vignette, with D.T. Suzuki and some intense contemporary embodiments of Americana, that suggests what a great joy he was.

Rick Fields: It's [pages 223 to 224] from the chapter, "The Fifties: Beat and Square" [and is reproduced here including Jack Kerouac's unedited idiosyncratic writing style].

The day *The Dharma Bums* was published, Kerouac, Ginsberg and Peter Orlovsky were on their way to an elegant penthouse party in honor of Kerouac's new novel, when Kerouac stepped into a phone booth and called up D. T. Suzuki. Kerouac said he'd like to stop by for a visit. Suzuki asked when he wanted to come by. "RIGHT NOW!" Kerouac yelled into the receiver, and Suzuki said, "O.K." Kerouac, Ginsberg and Orlovsky all trooped over to the brownstone on West Ninety-fourth that Suzuki shared with the Okamuras.

"I rang Mr. Suzuki's door, and he did not answer," Kerouac wrote *in a reminiscence published in the* Berkeley Bussei, *the magazine of the Berkeley Young Buddhists Association, in 1960. —suddenly I decided to ring it three times, firmly and slowly, and then he came—he was a small man, coming slowly through an old house with paneled wood walls and many books—he had long eyelashes, as everyone knows, which put me in the mind of a saying in the Sutras that the Dharma, like a bush, is slow to take root, but once it has taken root it grows huge and firm and can't be hauled up from the ground except by a golden giant whose name is not Tathagatha— anyway. Doctor Suzuki made us some green tea, very thick and soupy—he had precisely what idea of what place I should sit, and where my two other friends should sit, the chairs already arranged—he himself sat behind a table and looked at us silently, nodding—I said in a loud voice (because he had told us he was a little deaf) "Why did Bodhidharma come from the West?"—He made no reply—He said, "You three young men sit here quietly & write haiku while I go make some green tea—He brought us the green tea in cracked old soup bowls of some sort—He told us not to forget about the tea—when we left, he pushed us out the door but once we were out on the sidewalk he began giggling at us and pointing his finger and saying, "Don't forget the tea!"—I said "I would like to spend the rest of my life with you"—He held up his finger and said*

"Sometime."

Rick Fields in his later years

Acknowledgments

Boundless gratitude always to all of our precious wisdom teachers!

Of course we are also most grateful to Lex for conducting these interviews, and to Paul Gorman for envisioning the "In the Spirit" program. Paul Cohen of Monkfish Book Publishing Company saw the possibility for a book and fortunately pursued the idea for 12 years. He and Susan Piperato organized the book into an extremely accessible form. Susan's editing skills were instrumental in shaping the book. She also tracked down the interviewees' photos, negotiated permission to use them, and fact-checked their biographies.

Alison Rich did almost all of the transcribing. She had worked with Lex in the '70s and was completely familiar with the material. My family was involved for the entire project: Alexandra transcribed and helped with publicity, India read and gave advice from her own experience as a writer, Shanti worked for days with me identifying and marking the places in the final galley that needed to be fixed, and Shanti and Dylan encouraged me and gave feedback along the way.

The original analogue tapes were restored and digitized by Bob Kindler in his recording studio in Hawaii. He continues as the director of the SRV (Sarada, Ramakrishna,Vivekananda) Association that he and Lex co-founded in 1993. Max Stoupnikov created the final digital archive of the programs, and he and Karali Pitzele created the website LexHixon.com. Jennifer Greenfield managed the portion of publicity that was done in partnership with Tricycle magazine and its founding editor, Helen Tworkov, as well as directed the book launch celebration in New York City.

Photography Credits

Page xii: Photograph courtesy of Peter Cunningham

Page xxv: Painting of Sri Ramakrishna by Stuart Brandt, 1970; photograph by Alison H. Rich, courtesy of Sheila Hixon

Page xxvi Photograph reproduced by permission of Ramakrishna-Vivekananda Center of New York

Page 8: Photograph of Alan Watts, early 1970s, courtesy of CSU Archives/Everett Collection

Page 16: Photograph of Brother David Steindl-Rast, courtesy of A Network for Grateful Living

Page 24: Photograph of Guru Bawa Muhaiyaddeen, courtesy of America.Pink

Pages 31 and 42: Photographs courtesy of Robert Thurman

Page 43: Photograph of Swami Muktananda © 2007 SYDA Foundation

Page 54: Photograph of Swami Muktananda © 2006 SYDA Foundation

Page 55: Photograph of Swami Satchidananda, courtesy of Integral Yoga Institute

Page 63: Photograph courtesy of Integral Yoga Institute

Page 64: Photograph of Tarthang Tulku, courtesy of Odiyan Retreat Center

Page 73: Photograph of Zalman Schacter-Shalomi, courtesy of the Zalman M. Schacter-Shalomi Collection of the Jewish Renewal Archives at the University of Colorado

Pages 90 and 101: Photographs of Mother Serena and of Mother Serena standing before the altar in her home on the Upper West Side of Manhattan in the 1970s, courtesy of Society Rosicruciana in America

Page 102: Photograph of Mary Bailey provided by Lucis Trust

Pages 109 and 116: Photographs of Joseph Goldstein, and of him with Burmese meditation master Mahasi Sayadaw and three other Western teachers, courtesy of Insight Meditation Society

Page 117: Photograph of David Dellinger, courtesy of Alchetron.com

Page 128: Photographs of Eileen Caddy and Peter Caddy, courtesy of Findhorn Eco-Village

Pages 152 and 158: Photographs of David Spangler, courtesy of the subject

Pages 159 and 168: Photographs of Mother Teresa by Zvonimir Atletic

Page 169, 176: Photographs of Ram Dass copyright Rameshwar Das 1975

Page 177: Photograph of HH Dudjom Rinpoche in New York City in the 1970s, courtesy of Dungse Shenphen Dawa Norbu Rinpoche's archives

Authors' Biographies
Lex Hixon

Born on Christmas Day, 1941, in Los Angeles, Lex Hixon grew up in what he described as "the cultural openness and wild sacred energy of Southern California." His parents raised him and his two younger brothers in an environment of freedom, with a deep reverence for the natural world that was nurtured during the summers they spent at a family fishing camp in Northern Wisconsin. At 13, Lex left Pasadena for a Connecticut boarding school, an experience he credited with giving him the recognition that he was a poet, a philosopher, a musician, and a seeker.

Lex went on to major in philosophy at Yale University. His honors paper on Søren Kierkegaard opened new dimensions of spiritual thought for him. He also read Alan Watts and J. Krishnamurti and studied comparative religion.

At age 19, Lex became a Christian under the guidance of his Yale roommate's father, Rev. Vine Deloria Sr., a Lakota Sioux elder and Episcopal minister in South Dakota. They maintained a lively correspondence about their spiritual lives until Rev. Deloria's death. The Christianity that Lex embraced included both the indigenous Native American vision quest and the existential Christianity of Kierkegaard.

After graduating from Yale, Lex moved to Hawaii to teach, but relocated to New York City following the end of his first marriage and the birth of his daughter, Alexandra. He married Sheila King in 1965 on Maui, and they returned to New York to live in Greenwich Village, where Lex began working on a master's degree in philosophy at The New School for Social Research. Soon after arriving in New York, the Hixons met Swami Nikhilananda, who became their first serious spiritual teacher.

Lex transferred to Columbia University to complete his Ph.D. in religion. During his 10 years in graduate school, the Hixons had three children: Dylan, India, and Shanti. From 1971 to 1983, while studying the Advaita Vedanta tradition with Swami Nikhilananda, Lex began hosting the weekly radio program "In the Spirit." He completed his Master's degree on Ramana Maharshi and in 1976 defended his dissertation on the Gaudapada Karika and was awarded his Ph.D.

Meanwhile, Lex taught an evening class at the New School for Social Research in 1975. His lectures became his first book, *Coming Home: The Experience of Enlightenment in Sacred Traditions*, published in 1978 by Doubleday. An overview of sacred traditions with an experiential bent and a generous spirit of universality, the book has been widely recognized as a classic in its field.

In 1979, Lex founded *Free Spirit* magazine, a free directory of spiritual teachings and events in the New York area inspired by the contacts he made on the radio. He distributed the magazine using the family's Volkswagen Microbus. The magazine still exists today as *New York Spirit*.

The Hixons' practice of Buddhism began at the Zen Studies Society in Manhattan in the late 1960s, and eventually included Tibetan Vajrayana Buddhism. In 1981, they visited the Tibetan exile town of Dharamsala and several Himalayan monasteries and pilgrimaged to Bodhgaya and Sarnath. Lex wrote about studying and meditating in the Prajna Paramita tradition in his book *Mother of the Buddhas,* published in 1993 by Quest Books.

Lex accepted formal responsibility as Sheikh Nur-al-Jerrahi in the Khalwati-Jerrahi Order of Sufism in 1980, and made the traditional pilgrimage to Mecca and Medina with his Turkish teacher, Sheikh Muzaffer Ozak. Guiding several Sufi communities gave Lex a new understanding of cultural interaction and spiritual growth. The books that came out of this experience are *Heart of the Koran*, published in 1988 by Quest Books, and *Atom from the Sun of Knowledge*, published by Pir Press in 1993. Lex called these books "an informal peace initiative."

In 1983, the Hixons entered a three-year study of the mystical theology of the Eastern Orthodox Church at St. Vladimir's

Seminary in Crestwood, New York. They sacramentally joined the Church under the spiritual guidance of the great theologian Father Alexander Schmemann, whose Chrismation of them was one of his last formal acts.

The Hixons also traveled to Spruce Island in Kodiak, Alaska, for the feast day of St. Herman, who had lived and worked with the Aleut community. Lex began writing a book about his 12-year study of Eastern Orthodox Christianity, which was to include his travels to the ancient Greek Orthodox monastic community at Mt. Athos, but it was never finished.

Lex's 30-year involvement with the Divine Mother tradition of Bengal culminated in 1993 with a family trip to India. There, he introduced the book *Mother of the Universe*, English versions of poems written to the goddess Kali by a 16th-century Bengali mystic poet, and his own book, *The Great Swan: Meetings with Ramakrishna,* published in 1992 by Shambala, in which he imagined being among the disciples of Sri Ramakrishna.

In 1992, Lex contributed an essay, "Joint Citizenship in Parallel Sacred Worlds," exploring the problems and responsibilities of participation in multiple sacred traditions, to the anthology *The Way Ahead: Entering the New Millennium*, which included writings from Prince Philip of England, the Dalai Lama, and writer and Czechoslovakian President Vaclav Havel.

Lex died on All Saints Day, November 1, 1995. When he had become ill earlier that year, he was preparing to go to Japan to be installed as a teacher in the White Plum Asanga of the Soto School of Zen Buddhism. Instead, he worked to finish a book about the koan study he had completed as part of his teaching qualification. The book, *Living Buddha Zen,* was published in 1995 by Larson Publications. At Lex's memorial service, held at the Cathedral of St. John the Divine in New York, his teacher, Bernie Glassman, performed a Transmission Ceremony recognizing Lex—or Jikai, his Dharma name—as a successor and a teacher in the Soto lineage.

SHEILA HIXON

Sheila King Hixon was born in Chicago in 1940 and grew up north of the city and on the Hawaiian Island of Maui. She graduated from Smith College in 1962 and traveled around the world, returning to Honolulu. While working there, she reencountered her childhood friend Lex Hixon. In 1964, after moving with Lex to New York City, she began studying art at the New School. Later, the couple settled with their children in Riverdale, New York. A full-time mother, Sheila shared Lex's spiritual studies and practices, traveled with him, held spiritual events at their home, and hosted long-term guests from various spiritual traditions. In 2007, after studying with Bernie Glassman for 12 years, she received Dharma Transmission as Jinen Angyo Sensei. She serves on the board of directors of two family philanthropic foundations, based in New York and Hawaii, and still lives in Riverdale. She has a stepdaughter, a son, two daughters, and eight grandchildren.

Lex and Sheila Hixon with their children,
Dylan, India, and Shanti, in 1970